behind THE clutter

praise.

"*Behind the Clutter* is a thought-provoking and attitude-shifting book. It is more than a book; it is a way of living life in a more enriching way, leaving you thinking about the truth, love, meaning, and purpose behind your actions—and stuff!"

Debra Jay, nationally recognized bestselling author of *Love First* and *It Takes a Family*

"I love *Behind the Clutter*! I am always on the go and don't have a lot of free time, so this book made me look deep into my soul and understand why I saved the things I saved and helped me let go of "stuff" that was just taking up space in my closet and my life."

Amanda Leesburg, media strategist and expert

behind
THE clutter

TRUTH. LOVE. MEANING. PURPOSE.

june SARUWATARI

NEW YORK

behind THE clutter
TRUTH. LOVE. MEANING. PURPOSE.

Published in New York, New York, by Morgan James Publishing. Morgan James and The Entrepreneurial Publisher are trademarks of Morgan James, LLC. www.MorganJamesPublishing.com

The Morgan James Speakers Group can bring authors to your live event. For more information or to book an event visit The Morgan James Speakers Group at www.TheMorganJamesSpeakersGroup.com.

A **free** eBook edition is available with the purchase of this print book.

ISBN 978-1-61448-616-9 paperback
ISBN 978-1-61448-617-6 eBook
ISBN 978-1-61448-618-3 hardcover
ISBN 978-1-63047-444-7 audio
Library of Congress Control Number: 2014914618

CLEARLY PRINT YOUR NAME ABOVE IN UPPER CASE

Instructions to claim your free eBook edition:
1. Download the BitLit app for Android or iOS
2. Write your name in **UPPER CASE** on the line
3. Use the BitLit app to submit a photo
4. Download your eBook to any device

Cover Design by:
Rachel Lopez
www.r2cdesign.com

Interior Design by:
Bonnie Bushman
bonnie@caboodlegraphics.com

In an effort to support local communities and raise awareness and funds, Morgan James Publishing donates a percentage of all book sales for the life of each book to Habitat for Humanity Peninsula and Greater Williamsburg.

Get involved today, visit
www.MorganJamesBuilds.com

Habitat for Humanity
Peninsula and Greater Williamsburg
Building Partner

Dearest Mom and Dad,

Thank you for giving me the right stuff to begin with:
for teaching me that
happiness, love, and generosity,
being a good person and having a loving heart,
are the most important things,
and it isn't about the stuff.
Thank you for giving me the best stuff of all:
your unconditional love, support, and faith,
and
space for me to be all that I am,
for accepting me and my stuff,
which made me feel like
I could be, do, and have any stuff in life.

contents.

preface.

Thank you so much for choosing to go on this journey with me. I am truly and deeply honored that you are here reading this book.

First of all, I would love to manage your expectations from the beginning so you don't misunderstand what kind of book this is. This book is not your traditional "how-to" book on organizing, simplifying, and decluttering—rather it is quite non-linear and non-traditional in that the book itself is not actually organized, simplified, or decluttered at all—in the traditional sense. It is not about the ins and outs of simplifying and decluttering your physical spaces, nor is it a collection of instructions and guidelines about actual systems to implement on your journey toward decluttering your homes and offices. Instead, this book delves into what I believe is *behind* the clutter—the layers of mental, spiritual, and emotional stuff that tend to manifest in the form of physical clutter in our lives.

Ideally, the book will take you on a unique journey as you look at your own stuff, both internal and external, through a new lens. To best prepare for this journey, I would love for you to let go of any preconceived notions of how you are going to declutter, organize, and simplify your stuff, and not to search for the "how to." I invite you to simply absorb what I am presenting to you and go on the ride with me. And enjoy it!

the process. *for your miraculous transformation.*

Based on my experience with myself and my clients, I have found that transformation doesn't tend to happen in some methodical A-B-C way, but in a zigzag way that may not even make sense to your logical brain. If you trust me as your tour guide and do the exercises as they are presented, you will release the spontaneous free flow of intel hidden in the private recesses of your subconscious—your *TruthLoveMeaningPurpose*™—which will finally allow that "transformation" you so crave. You cannot force the change to come, but you can encourage it by gently accepting who you truly are, the stuff you are truly made of, and honoring your unique soul. From this fresh perspective about your life and your stuff, the "how-to" will organically arise. Suddenly, you may be compelled to let go of chunks rather than bits. Suddenly, your stuff will look different. Suddenly, you will allow yourself to be at one with your stuff so that it will tell you the real story and power of your stuff. Then, suddenly, one day you will start throwing away boxes of your stuff, having realized why you were holding on in the first place. When you understand the "why" behind your stuff, you will finally gain control of your life!

So think of this journey as a treasure hunt. You'll peel away the layers beneath your stuff, shine a light on the *internal* stuff lurking in the darkness, examine it with a fine-toothed comb, and decide whether you're supposed to keep it or let it go. I truly believe this path is the way to a long-lasting change in your relationship to your external stuff. Once you make the internal shifts, the external will shift to match what is going on internally. And you will see the amazing tapestry of your own life as a unique work of art. You will see the masterpiece you already are. You really won't need the "how to" from me—you'll know what to do next, and you'll be able to do it with love!

the map. *to your special treasures.*

Here's a brief map of our journey. First, the Stuff Test will give you a glimpse into both the inside stuff you are made of—and the outside stuff you may accumulate. To me, it's a continuum—both funny and profound. Again, once we finally deal with the stuff going on inside, the stuff on the outside will radically shift. The Introduction will give you a glimpse into why I believe what internally lies beneath the clutter is actually the most important stuff.

Part One, The Foundation, describes what I believe to be the core infrastructure beneath your stuff, space, being, and doing. In Me & My Stuff, you'll come to understand why I am the way I am, and why I have empathy for you on this journey of decluttering, as I am not at all neat or organized by nature. Then we will talk about You & Your Stuff, because the journey is really all about you, and nobody like you will ever be born here on this earth! Then, I will introduce to you four special words in a unique combination that form the criteria for all my decisions in life—TruthLoveMeaningPurpose. To me, this filter is all you will ever need to make the best choices for you and your stuff, whether it's simplifying, decluttering, or organizing your stuff, time, spaces, kids' stuff and schedules, homes, offices, relationships, jobs, or businesses! I believe you can use TruthLoveMeaningPurpose as the foundation for everything—especially to curate and create a life you love, love, love!

Really, with those concepts and exercises, you can get started on transforming your life.

However, from there we move on to Part Two, The Journey itself, where I get more specific (and vulnerable). Here I share my own personal life stories, thoughts, views, and insights related to my own quest to becoming simplified, as well as the experiences and insights I've gained in my work with others during my decades as a coach and professional organizer. I'll also share the thought processes and mindsets that have been valuable tools in helping me become clutter free, curating stuff I love, and creating a life I love. Think of this section as a treasure hunt, where you are seeking clues to your journey to help you get organized, simplified, and decluttered on all levels, whether it's money, love, people, or time. My hope is that you will recognize yourself and your own experience in my stories, and that the Exercises at the end of each chapter will help you shift your perspective about your stuff, your different forms of clutter, your thought processes, and your life.

how to use this book. *for your unique journey.*

You can begin by reading the book from beginning to end, and then freely use it thereafter as a reference throughout your own quest to become simplified and create a life you love. You can flip to any page for a message for the day, a powerful reminder that will activate something deep within, to create those long-lasting changes you desire.

Or you can read it, highlight it, write in it, and use it as a workbook or journal of sorts, taking your time to work through each section at your own pace and in your own order. If you do the exercises as I encourage you to, you'll finish this book with a list of your own insights, thoughts, and ideas about how to declutter, simplify, organize, and curate your own unique life.

Or you can read one chapter a day and ruminate upon it. Let the words seep into your consciousness and stir up something inside of you. By the end of the book, enough should be stirred up inside of you—mentally, spiritually, and emotionally—for you to finally take action in many different areas of your life.

Remember: the journey behind your stuff is not a straight and narrow path. Getting to the truth requires fearless meandering, sightseeing, self-examining, and self-reflecting. In my own personal experience and in my work with many clients over the years, I have found that this heart-centered approach and the spontaneous path, where we let go of what we think "should" happen, brings maximum and long-lasting deep results from the inside out.

Also, with tremendous respect for each and every one of you, I am letting you know that I have chosen to refer to the Higher Power as God, but this name could be Buddha, Allah, Vishnu, or many others. I honor the God within each one of us. I honor Jesus Christ and the religion of Christianity. I honor Jehovah and the religion of Judaism. I honor Buddha and the religion of Buddhism. I honor Allah and the religion of Islam.

This book is about *you* and the God I believe that resides within each of you, even if you believe in all Gods, one God, or no God at all. For me, because I did grow up Christian, the word *God* has a special meaning for me and resonates with me. And while I have evolved and grown into a deeper understanding of God through different teachings, I have come to accept that God lives within each one of us. God lives within us as an intuition or an inner knowing. God lives within us as love, compassion, and passion. I do not look at this God as someone who punishes me or watches my acts with a stern hand, but as an all-loving God who loves me for just being me, and as I have come to learn, a God who loves me for just living my TruthLoveMeaningPurpose. So I choose to use God to refer to this Source Energy, all-encompassing Wisdom, Infinite Intelligence, and Higher Self within me.

Thank you for opening yourself to a new way of seeing God in your own life and how the stuff of your life can be full of God-energy—and thank you for choosing not to allow that word to stop you from seeing the message beyond the stuff and its deeper meaning.

Living your life full of your own TruthLoveMeaningPurpose is God in action for you. Living and honoring TruthLoveMeaningPurpose in all you do and are is utilizing all of God's gifts to you, and it is your gift to God and the world. Living your life with TruthLoveMeaningPurpose is honoring God with your stuff and your life. It is the ultimate dedication of your life to your God.

May you move forward in these teachings with an open heart and mind.

stuff test.

- Are you unhappy, frustrated, overwhelmed, disappointed, angry, and depressed in life?
- Are you unhappy with your stuff?
- Do you hate your stuff?
- Do you feel out of control with your stuff?
- Do you feel you have too much stuff?
- Do you feel stuffed up?
- Do you feel your spaces are stuffy?
- Do you feel your mind is stuffed up with all these ideas and you're not doing anything about those ideas or taking action?
- Do you wish you had better stuff?
- Do you want to go shopping and buy more stuff?
- Do you just want to get a handle on your life and stuff?
- Do you want to simplify your stuff?
- Do you think you have way too much stuff?
- Do you want to let go of old stuff from the past but don't know how?
- Are you afraid to let go of your stuff because you think you will not have the money to replace that stuff?
- Are you afraid of people finding out about you and your stuff?
- Are you afraid of people finding out about the real stuff you are made of?
- Are you tired of having to organize your stuff?
- Are you frustrated with the fact that no matter how many times you organize your stuff, the stuff still keeps getting messed up?

- Are you just tired of being on this roller-coaster ride with your stuff, and instead want to lead a life where you are just so happy with your life and your stuff?
- Do you, once and for all, want to get a grip and get control over your life and your stuff?

If you answered yes to any of these questions above, you are not alone.

It is no coincidence that you are reading this book. If you are truly ready to get help with your stuff on a deep level, then you have come to the right place. I have all the faith in the world that, at the very least, your perspective about your stuff will shift, opening the doorway to change, and at the very most, you will let go of all the stuff that's bringing you down and then fill up your life with only the stuff you love!

I will challenge you to get to the truth behind your stuff, and encourage you to take action so you can lead a life where you are supremely happy with your stuff and love all the stuff of your life.

INTRODUCTION.

the journey behind the clutter. *the most important stuff.*

It's exciting for me to hear about people's journeys—what they learn along the way and how they learn it. What triggers the lessons? What catapults a person into doing something radically different? What was that defining moment? What was that one thing that put them over the top where they said, "I gotta change. I gotta do something different."

One definition of insanity is doing the same thing over and over again and expecting different results. Do you truly want different results? Then do something differently. Just one thing—and suddenly, you're on a different path. Don't underestimate the significance of doing just one small thing differently. It could have long-lasting and significant consequences, possibly changing the course of your entire life. Make one choice, take action on that choice, and it will begin to have a domino effect on everything else.

My mission is to help you see the beautiful masterpiece you already are. Your life is a work of art. So what kind of art are you creating? Do you need all this stuff? The stuff should not make you feel whole or complete, or define you. The stuff should merely be an extension of the magnificence of who you are and your amazing, unique life.

My intention is to demystify the decluttering process for you, to simplify it so that anyone can understand what it takes to lead a life of simplicity, clarity, *truth, love, meaning, and purpose.* I want you to ask yourself the right questions to get you to the answers you already have within. I want you to transform how you do things and how you see your life and your stuff. I want you to realize that stuff has energy and a life of its own, and like you, the stuff wants to be useful, serve a purpose, have meaning, and be loved. We can't take anything with us when we die. We come into this world in this lifetime with nothing more than deep-seated desires planted in our hearts. We don't come out of our mother's womb attached to stuff—only the umbilical cord that gives us breath and life. Breath is the only thing we come into this world with. And our last breath transports us to the next realm.

Do you feel suffocated by your stuff? Is it clogging up your life with confusion? Do you feel like you're slogging through mud every day? Do you want more energy?

Life energy has to do with what we bring into our environment, and what we surround ourselves with. We live in a physical universe, so of course, our physical environment will have a profound effect on our lives. But underneath this physical stuff are our mental, emotional, and spiritual layers of stuff. When you are surrounded by so much stuff, you feel bogged down mentally, spiritually, and emotionally. You can't budge. The stuff is holding you back from being all that you can be. It's holding you hostage. The stuff then is no longer serving you. You've become a servant to it. The stuff dictates to you how you should live your life. The stuff is no longer a tool to help you lead a better life—it's a burden controlling you and your actions.

When you crave a bigger space, why? Do you feel that bigger is better? And when you get more space, do you just fill it back up with more stuff, and then you run out space yet again? Do you really need all that space? Truthfully, do you really need all the stuff that's going to fill up that new big space?

The journey you're about to embark upon will make you conscious of the fact that everything you have in your life is there for a purpose. To teach you something. To help. To serve. To love.

When you're conscious of the purpose of every object, you won't cast aside that matchbook carelessly, stashing it away in some junk drawer where it'll sit for years, never being used to light a fire. You won't cast aside that bookmark you received from someone that you intend to use "one day." You will begin honoring that bookmark and the purpose it serves. You will put that bookmark with your other bookmarks so they can help you remember your place in your book and enjoy the journey of reading. If you don't want to spend the energy creating a comfortable home for the bookmark, give it to someone else who will use it for what it was intended. Give away what you don't want to someone who will honor it, respect it, cherish it, love it, and most importantly, give it life.

You give life to something by using it fully and deeply.

So why *do* you cast things aside? Because you're *un*conscious. Because you don't realize that the choices and decisions you make lead to the actions you take or don't take, and that, in reality, "creating" your life is a moment to moment endeavor with huge consequences. You don't realize that all your stuff, inside and out, is connected, and that it all matters.

Or perhaps you do realize it, but it's much easier to not deal with the feelings that come with the stuff, and you keep shoving it somewhere, hoping it really won't matter or no one will notice or care. You bury it deep somewhere so you never have to confront the truth.

But if you know that all your stuff is connected and it matters, how can you just buy more stuff and bring it into your life, when you have all that other stuff like it at home? C'mon, wake up and start dealing with it! Don't pretend to be in a coma with your stuff and act as if it's not there. Don't ignore your buried feelings and your stuff. Deal with it, and let it go once and for all if you are not truly using it fully and deeply. Give it to somebody who will consciously use that item and shower it with love.

There is no such thing as an unimportant item. Every item in your life is important and is there for a reason, to teach you something. There is no such thing as meaningless stuff. Otherwise, why have it? Why keep it? Why move it about? Let it go.

Why do you find it difficult to let go?

Fear. Do you fear that you might need it someday? That you won't have the money to replace it? Do you fear seeing empty spaces? Do they make you feel alone and empty? If you think of your stuff as friends and companions on the journey, why not have company that you love along for the ride?

Why keep things in your life that make you feel yucky? You know when you truly love something. If I ask you if you love this thing or that person, and you hesitate—that means you don't love it. When you love something, every fiber of your being oozes with passion. Your eyes light up, your heart beats a little bit faster, and you can't help but smile just because . . . oooh, it just feels so good inside. It feels right. You don't question it. You just know deep inside. Perhaps you can't quite define why, but you just know.

That's how I want you to feel about your stuff. I want you to become discerning with your stuff so the stuff that doesn't belong in your life will scream to you, "Let go of me! I don't belong."

Perhaps it did belong at one time. Perhaps one year ago, you were interested in the life of Sylvia Plath, and now you're fascinated with the works of e.e. cummings. Then, let go of those books that you purchased on Sylvia, and let e.e. reside in your home. Give those books away to someone else who will honor Sylvia's journey and who will go on the ride with her. Your ride with Sylvia is done. It was thrilling while it lasted, and now it's on to something else. Let go of the stuff that reflected your passions of yesterday, and create space for the fresh and new passions of today.

Live in the now. That means only keeping stuff in your life that reflects your present. That means honoring your truth, love, meaning, and purpose *now*—moment to moment.

So the simplifying, decluttering, and organizing process is a lifelong journey, not just something you do just once and that's it. You may have been organized a few years ago, but if you didn't remain vigilant on your journey, you may have gradually accumulated certain things and became disorganized again. You fell asleep at the wheel and allowed things into your vehicles, home, and being. You kept packing stuff in rather than taking the time and energy to process, to reflect, and to let go.

Does this item really belong now? Is this truthfully me now? Does this have meaning for me now? Do I love it still now?

Most of all, love the journey that you're on. Don't judge yourself. Don't be hard on yourself because you no longer love something that you spent your hard-earned cash on. It served you well for a season. You loved it for some time. You didn't waste it or dishonor it. The truth is that you fully loved it and squeezed the life out of it in each moment you used it. Even if it was a gift that wasn't really "you," and you haven't used it at all, you still fully squeezed the life out of it in the moment you received it—with gratitude—as an expression of love from the giver. There's no need to lament or overanalyze. Just let the truth be. The truth is: You don't love it anymore, it doesn't serve a purpose anymore, it doesn't have as much meaning anymore, and it's not really *you* anymore.

We sometimes hold on to things way past their usefulness for sentimental reasons. I remember this dress I used to wear when I was in college—that was the time when my boyfriend lied to me, and I broke up with him. The dress is a reminder for me to never again ignore my gut when it tells me that someone may not be telling me the truth. I remember this Madonna tape with my favorite song on it, "Borderline," which reminded me to stay strong despite the pain I was in.

I remember when my new boyfriend gave me this ring, and suddenly, I wasn't single anymore, I was engaged, and then—I lost the diamond in some hospital room while visiting my friend who was having a hysterectomy. Everyone around me was more upset than I was about the loss of the ring, and then I started to feel guilty, that I should have been lamenting more, but it taught me to stay grounded in my own perspective about stuff and not be too attached to anything.

Looking at this expired driver's license, I remember when I changed my name when I got married, and it felt strange taking on my husband's name, and then, I changed it back to my maiden name, and then, I felt guilty that I didn't take on his name, and then, I eventually got over it, but it's fun to see my name in print as an example of what could have been. Do I need all these things to remind me of all the lessons I've learned, the mistakes I've made, the pain I've endured? Do I fear that I'll forget the lessons and make some dumb mistakes again?

Looking at a tiara on the shelf, I remember when I was crowned homecoming queen, and I was queen for a day. Do I fear that I'll never be a queen again, and am I living in the glory of my past accomplishments? Looking at a pyramid-shaped crystal trophy, I am reminded of when I was voted "Team Player." Do I secretly fear that I'm really a selfish person, and looking at that reminds me that at one point in my life, I was noble and really was a team player? Or am I just overanalyzing, and do I keep these things because they bring me joy?

Looking at this velour robe that my mom stayed up all night to make for me makes me feel loved, special. The bathrobe is now tattered and torn. Do I need that bathrobe to remind me of how much my mother loves me? Would I dishonor all the effort and energy she poured into that item by letting it go? If I let it go, would that mean I'm being disrespectful and, in essence, not appreciating her love?

Going through boxes of photos, I remember having so much fun skiing with my college friends every winter break. I remember the people I used to ski with, but I can't remember all their names. The photos remind me that I did ski at one point in my life, that I was quite good actually, that I was adventurous and daring enough to ski down the diamond slopes, and that I may someday ski again. Do I really need all those photos to remind me of those times when I was a happy-go-lucky risk taker? If it's something I need to remember, won't my memory jog me into remembering it when I need to remember it? Do I need all those photos to remember those people, or will their memories and the special times we shared together live on in my heart forever?

So you begin to realize that the stuff has a life all its own, with its own stories, memories, feelings, and triggers that connect the past to the present. Sometimes they are tentacles to our past that keep us living in the past. We realize we don't want to let go of those times when we felt loved, safe, and secure. We don't want to let go of what the stuff represents. They are symbols for the way it used to be, of my youth and my sense of adventure. Are my youth and sense of adventure gone? Will holding on to those photos help me retain that feeling of being so young and alive? Will holding on to that dress remind me never to make that stupid mistake again? So does that mean that I don't have trust in myself, the present, and my future? Does that mean I'm living my life with fear, and not faith? Perhaps.

These are some of the issues you might begin to deal with if you let your stuff tell you the story, if you go beyond the superficial meaning of why you have it, and if you're willing to delve deeper beyond appearances to see what truly lies beneath the clutter.

The digging is what thrills me—it's like an archaeological dig into your own consciousness for the reasons why you exist, and your perceptions and feelings about life itself. All contained in your stuff.

I've seen it all. Buried underneath the stuff are dreams waiting to be manifested, talents waiting to be unveiled, passions waiting to be explored. Buried underneath the stuff are issues of anger, resentment, shame, and addiction, waiting to be healed. Buried underneath the stuff is the amazingly unique, one-of-a-kind, and once-in-a-lifetime work of art called *your life*, and the beautifully raw, authentic, brilliant masterpiece called *you*.

Buried underneath the stuff is TruthLoveMeaningPurpose.

PART ONE.
THE FOUNDATION.

ME
&
MY STUFF.

behind my stuff. *yes, i have lots of stuff!*

So what about me and my stuff? Who am I to be able to have such strong opinions about stuff? Why should you listen to me and read this book?

There are so many wonderful and brilliant books on decluttering, so many experts who have devised systems that make it easy for any layperson simply to pick up the book and get started on organizing. Does the world need another book on organizing, decluttering, and simplifying? That is exactly what I think every time I go into a bookstore and see the numerous books on self-improvement and self-mastery! It can be quite overwhelming, and I seriously just want to go home and take a nap. I conclude, let them read the other books.

But in my years of teaching, and even while writing the book and confronting my fears of whether I had enough worthy information to share with you all, I have gotten so many messages from the Universe and God nudging me to move forward sharing my "unique spin" on stuff. So here I am.

When I first started writing, I asked God to work through me to release the clutter in my mind and heart—the doubts of asking "who am I?" and not accepting my own greatness in presenting my perspective to you, and my fears of what you would really think about me if I revealed how I truly felt about stuff—my stuff, others' stuff, world stuff.

And then I remembered what I always tell myself before speaking—to release the pressure of trying to be good, aka ego: "June, focus on being a blessing to at least one person to relieve the pressure of having to please everyone." Suddenly, my fingers couldn't stop typing. It was as though God was whispering in my ear, "Yes, child, you have much to share. Go ahead and just continue writing." It's almost as if the words couldn't wait to be on the page and be shared with you, so I continued writing one word, one story, one chapter at a time.

Yes, yes, yes! I can't wait to share with you how deep this stuff goes, and the miracles I have witnessed in my life and others' lives, just by dealing with the stuff.

So what's the clutter behind why it has taken me so long to write this book?

I officially started this book more than ten years ago in 2001, writing in between clients and lectures—writing, writing, writing. I would write every time I gave another lecture, and more stuff would reveal itself to me. In 2005, I had more than 200 pages, had organized the book, thought I was nearly complete, was doing final edits, had started a newsletter, and was on a roll with my life's work—when suddenly, other stuff happened.

I was pulled from the writing and editing to work on the stuff that was going on in my own life. I was traveling and shooting thirteen episodes of a television show, while still seeing clients and teaching. And the hardest stuff of all—my twenty-year relationship and fourteen-year marriage to my best friend came to an abrupt end. We separated and divorced. Then, my father suddenly became ill, was hospitalized for four months, and then passed away.

The one thing that kept me going was my business as The Organizing Maniac™, which gave me a purpose—to serve my clients, do workshops, and share my teachings. However, at one lecture I gave, when I brought up the letting go of marriage and my recent divorce, it seemed that people were shocked to hear me talking about my stuff in public. Were people ready to hear me talk so candidly about my stuff?

The truth behind my stuff?

It has taken me a while to get truly grounded again. I had to forgive myself for thinking that my parents would be around forever. Many people had told me, "You will never understand until it happens to you, but it is surreal to have one of your parents pass away—the person who brought you into this world." They were right. I didn't think about it so deeply at the time, but my father's death still shocks me, and I wish he were still here to read this book. I can't believe he's gone, because I thought he was going to be around forever.

From what I learned from my father's passing, I am now at one with the notion that my mother will one day pass, and I have let go of the warped thinking that my mom will be around forever. I am no longer shoving that fear underneath my bed pretending it is not there, but instead I have confronted that fear head on and taken responsibility for this thought by embracing my mother—giving her love and being the best daughter I can be to her in the here and now. With my father, I thought I had said everything I wanted to say to him and did all I could do by visiting him in the hospital. But after he passed, when

I reread his letters to me telling me what a great daughter I was, I found myself wishing I could have spent more time with him and shared more with him, from my heart, about how truly grateful I was to have had such a wonderful dad like him. I realized that even if you tell somebody once, twice, three times, or more, you can never say "I love you" or "I appreciate you" enough.

I also thought that I would be married to the same person forever, that I would grow old with that person and would never, ever get divorced. I thought my visionary man would fulfill all my needs and desires, be my soulmate for life, make love to me every day like it was the first time, and fall more in love with me with every passing day. I still believe in love in this way, and so I haven't let go of that dream. This is part of what I teach as well.

I myself had to take action in letting go of a relationship that was no longer serving our highest good, let go of the "stigma" of divorce as a failure, and instead embrace my own perspective about my marriage, knowing in my heart that our marriage was, indeed, a success. I would have been married forever had I not confronted my own TruthLoveMeaningPurpose. I am forever grateful for the wonderful, loving relationship with my ex-husband in which I grew up, and the love we shared will forever remain a part of my heart.

I discovered that what was true for me might be very different from what was true for others, and the path to liberation included releasing any notions or beliefs I clung to that were based on society's dictums or somebody else's ideas. I have found that true liberation means coming from a place of peace within, knowing that my heart's desires were planted there a long time ago, even before I was born, and the fulfillment of those desires was mine to experience and manifest.

Also, over the past few years, I have also needed to get grounded in my new relationship. For me, feeling grounded in my relationship is paramount to being clutter free in my mind, heart, and consciousness so that I can be a clear channel for my life's work. Either I'm in this relationship body-mind-spirit-heart, or I'm not. So in this way, I have decluttered my heart over and over and over, to come clean to this relationship with an open heart, cracked wide open and left wide open, to experience true love again. It has been nothing short of remarkable, and with this true love grounding me, I feel like I can give love unconditionally to you, the reader, and to the world, and offer my gifts freely.

So here I am, feeling grounded again and connected once again with my TruthLoveMeaningPurpose. I feel I am now able to be a free and clear channel to share my teachings with you.

So with fearlessness, and with no holds barred, I'm putting it all out there. I am presenting this work to you. It is my gift to you from God.

teaching from my stuff. *still learning.*

i have not always been organized. I was not born organized. I "work and play" at being organized every single day. I organize because of the sense of peace and grounding it gives me. I declutter because of the sense of liberation that comes with letting go of the stuff I think I need but am keeping based on fear. I simplify because when things are too complicated, I get confused.

I become uncomfortable at the thought of someone calling me his or her "organizing guru." I like to think of myself as a facilitator, coach, and guide, coaching you to be your own guru and an expert in the field of stuff—namely, your stuff.

I believe in my heart that I can only teach you what I myself have learned thus far. I can only stand behind what I believe in if I have tried it and tested it, and it has worked for me. I can only speak with conviction and passion about those things that are working for me still, where I myself have seen, felt, and experienced measurable, perceptible results.

Luckily for me, I have what I call "selective memory," which has allowed me the ability to conveniently forget details about my past that are too painful to remember, such as how disorganized I was when I was younger! However, I will share what I do recall, which will give you a glimpse into the reason why I believe I was uniquely selected to be in this position to help you—wherever you are. I have no judgment about you, your past, your present, or future. I have been there. I have bought stuff, collected stuff, let go of stuff, held on to stuff, regretted stuff, been angry at stuff, been disorganized, organized it once, messed it up, organized it again, messed it up again, and finally learned what it takes to stay clutter free and organized for life!

And guess what? I can reassure you that simplifying, decluttering, and organizing is a life tool you can learn—that anyone can learn. Evaluating everything based on

TruthLoveMeaningPurpose is a way of life, and you too can use it to lead a clutter-free life. There is hope! I have tremendous compassion, faith, and belief that you can learn these simple mindset shifts, principles, and philosophies, so you can feel boundless energy and change your life forever. Soon you'll be screaming, like I do every day, "I love my life!"

As I've said before, and I'll continue to share stories to prove this point—I am not a naturally organized person. Organizing is not in my DNA. And yet I have learned and created simple systems through which I am authentically organized and living a productive, meaningful, and joyful life that honors my TruthLoveMeaningPurpose.

My intention is to share my truth—no holds barred, and without shame or embarrassment, because I know someone out there will be able to relate to what I have gone through and will benefit from my mistakes and lessons learned. I trust that the ruthless expression of my truth will activate you to confront your truth, too. And, I hope this will accelerate your journey to getting there—wherever you want to be!

growing up stuff. *still growing.*

a h, my childhood stuff. I remember a charmed life where I got everything my heart desired—a colorful, secure, happy life filled with security, love, and love of stuff. I felt very lucky having a mother who loved being a mother, and a father who loved being a father. They were very clear about their priorities and what was truly important, and hence they were very clear about their stuff and maintained clear boundaries on the stuff that was important to them and their roles in my life.

My first bedroom was painted a girly-girl blush pink, and everything in it was the same soft shade of pink: my bed was adorned with a ruffled pink bedspread and matching pink pillows, with a giant, pink, furry rug next to it, and a matching pink Kenmore play kitchen on the other side.

Years later, I remember coming home one day from school to a surprise in my bedroom— my parents had "made-over" my room with cheery yellow! They had bought me brand new yellow blinds, a yellow bedspread, and a yellow desk, bookshelves, cabinets, and chair. A pop of sunshine! I loved it!

Growing up, my mother would dress me up in beautiful, colorful dresses, whatever was in style at the time, and style my hair with colorful bows and ribbons coordinated to match every outfit. She sewed new outfits for me for Easter, Christmas, piano recitals, graduation, and whatever I wanted that I saw in fashion magazines. The most exciting part about starting school every year was going shopping with my mom for four brand-new outfits and matching shoes!

My mother was Supermom. She had a great sense of style, and when I look at the photos of her, I think, *How did she raise three kids while looking fabulous every day, wearing fabulous dresses with her hair in a bouffant hairdo?* For that matter, how did she host parties for twenty people every few weeks? Every summer, for one entire week, she would invite my three cousins to stay over. She baked cookies, arranged flowers, and had homemade snacks ready for us when we came home from school. She cooked up tasty meals in a pinch and made them look beautiful! The house was always pristine and organized, laundry neatly folded—how did she do it? I still think about this when I organize households and see mothers struggling with balancing the laundry, cooking, and taking care of the kids!

When I got older, I never had that "urge" to have kids. When I psychoanalyzed this, I think it's because I could never be a mother like my mom, whom I idolized as Supermom, so why even do it? I didn't have a passion for cooking, cleaning, flower arranging, or sewing. I realized later that even if I had wanted to be a mom, I would have been a terrific mother, as long as I did not compare myself to my mother or to other mothers and just tried to be the best mom I could be. For instance, I could share my passion for journaling, writing, and self-inquiry with my kids.

Now, every summer when I have my nieces over for a weekend, I practice being the best aunt I can be—not following some notion of what I'm supposed to do to entertain kids, but staying true to my idea of fun. We meditate, journal about what's important in life, journal about stuff we're grateful for, go to the bookstore to get inspiring books, read, bike to the beach and around town instead of driving, and do stuff that I love to do. And guess what? They have fun because I'm having fun, and they seem to enjoy activities they might not otherwise do at home. Now I teach clients who are mothers and fathers, "Be the best dad and mom you can be—don't compare yourself to your own dads and moms or other dads and moms! Instead, follow your passions and loves, and teach your kids from your hearts! Let go of the 'shoulds' and create space for your loves to inform the teachings you impart to your children."

.

Back to when I was little—I loved going over to my cousin's house because I loved being in her room. It was always organized and very neat, not a thing out of place! She wore the coolest clothes and was so stylish. I remember her white go-go boots, and I was always so excited to get her hand-me-downs! I remember when she gave me her favorite brown bandeau bikini—I was in heaven! Everybody called my favorite bikini "Band-Aids on June," because it barely covered my body!

The point is: I learned that someone else's hand-me-downs or giveaways that are no longer fitting their version of who they are may, in fact, be in perfect alignment with somebody else's version of their best self, and catapult them to a new level. I always had cute bikinis, but my brown bandeau bikini, given to me by my stylish cousin at age fifteen, made me feel like a different girl, and made me feel more beautiful than ever. So now I teach clients that giving something away is an act of love—you will never know the joy you are giving to somebody else who may use that item fully for what it was intended! This item could be exactly what they need to elevate their style, feeling, confidence, consciousness, and life, giving them a different perspective on who they are, allowing them to start attracting different miraculous experiences to themselves just because they are feeling differently!

.

I wasn't always so interested in being organized. When I was growing up, my mother was always organized, and it seemed effortless for her. I now know she inherited this as part of her DNA from my grandfather. My mom, younger brother, my cousin, and my niece have it. They were born with a gift for thinking and seeing things a certain way, and it doesn't make sense to them to leave stuff out, leave cupboards open, and leave shoes going in different directions at the doorway. All the shoes should be faced in the same direction, all trashcans should be emptied regularly, and all countertops should be wiped clean. From their perspective, it's simply the way stuff should be in the world—how else would you order the stuff? It's an easy and effortless way of living for them, based on their perceptions and how they see the world.

I was convinced of this theory, when in awe, I saw my then two-year-old niece sitting at the high chair wiping her eating area clean. I had never witnessed this act in her sister, who was five years older than her. And, interestingly enough, her parents told me she was never taught how to do this. I marveled at how she would close cabinets and put shoes facing the same direction. When my cousins from Japan came to visit, they were shocked when my brother was hosting a party at his home, effortlessly being the "host with the most," like my mother, making sure everybody was taken care of, and putting dishes and plates away as they were being used. They were stunned that his mannerisms were like that of my grandfather in Japan, and that he was "clearing" the stuff in the same diligent fashion as my grandfather would do. How could this possibly be, when my brother grew up here in the United States and had only spent limited time with my grandfather? This was a mystery, and yet it also cemented my theory that there are some who are born with "the gift of seeing, ordering, and organizing the world," and some who are not—and I clearly was not born with that gift!

For me, the process of learning how to organize and order my world, to see my world from a certain perspective, and to create systems that best serve me has been a lifelong education and learning experience, one that still continues to this day.

So you can imagine how surprised my parents and brothers were to suddenly hear how passionate I was about organizing, when their experience of me was quite the opposite.

It would probably startle you to get a window into my past and see my "cluttered" room with stuff everywhere! My room was injected with my personality, stuff that I loved and was passionate about, but with no rhyme or reason. I decorated my bookshelves with souvenir tchotchkes, hung up Bobby Sherman and Japanese teen idol Saijo Hideki posters on the walls, collected panda stickers from Japan, plastered my room with rainbows, ceramic unicorn figures, and Hello Kitty stuffed animals! Of course, this definitely was not the picture-perfect model of an "organized little girl's bedroom." Artwork was placed haphazardly, and stuff was strewn all over the room. The only constant was the bright yellow color peeking out amidst the dizzying array of my stuff's rainbow colors. Yet, I loved walking into my bedroom, which contained all the stuff I loved, and I remember my room being "happy!" I would have described it as sunshine!

I could never decide what to wear in the morning. I would try on one outfit after another, and leave my room in a heaping mess. Every day it looked like a tornado had hit. And every day, my clothes were neatly folded and hung by my mother who loved keeping the house tidy, neat, organized, and clean. I didn't realize later how much work this took until I actually had to do it myself! I think I subconsciously rebelled against my mother, who wanted me to keep my room clean.

I don't ever remember making my bed in the mornings, either—another key to success that I now practice and advocate so that you are set up for success when you return home! And, yes, I now advocate that parents teach their kids to create the appropriate "homes and paths" for their stuff, making it a fun game, rather than using it as a disciplinary tool, so the act of "clearing the clutter" and returning stuff to their "homes" becomes an act of joy and is about honoring the stuff, rather than something children simply do to obey their parents. We'll talk more about "homes and paths" in the Tools & Strategies section, but for now, homes are permanent spaces for all the "families" of stuff that share the same traits, purpose, and/or qualities, and "paths" either lead the stuff back to its home (like a clothes hamper) or out to another journey (such as the trash can or Giveaway Box).

I now also advocate a Weekend Basket for parents. You can try this yourself: If your children do not put their stuff away by the end of the day, put it in a large basket you call the Weekend Basket, so that your children cannot have access to that stuff until the weekend. You can imagine if my mom had that Weekend Basket, I would have been hanging up everything I had tried on, because I loved my clothes too much to be without them until the weekend! These are the kinds of simple tools and processes that will occur to you as well, as you get in touch with your own TruthLoveMeaningPurpose.

How could I have lived like this and functioned as a child? Was I totally oblivious that there was another way of living that could benefit me? I didn't know any better. And of course, the "disarray" was always temporary, because the "organizing" was done for me. I am so grateful to my mother for teaching me that having things in order when I arrived at home helped me to study in my room, go out and play, and enjoy my life. My mother set a gold standard of how things could be and should be, if I am to truly feel like I can soar with my other endeavors. Interestingly enough, when I moved out on my own, I maintained these standards that my mother had taught me—I always made my bed and put stuff away.

Now I teach others to examine their past and the environment they grew up in, because I guarantee you that if you examine your present behavior, you would discover that it is dictated by that past. You are cluttered up because you grew up in a cluttered household— you're simply used to that way of living, and you have never been exposed to another. Or, you are extremely organized and do not tolerate disorder because you grew up in a cluttered household and it drove you nuts, and you vowed that when you were out on your own, you would always have a home that's orderly and would never let things get out of control. Or, you are extremely organized because you grew up in an extremely organized household, and you are accustomed to that order and feel there is no other way to live. Or, like me, you grew up in an organized household, but you rebelled against that order because you thought somebody else was imposing ideas on you, and so you did the opposite of what would really serve you.

Do you know what drives your behavior today? Getting to the truth behind your present behavior will set you free because you will understand *why* you do what you do, so you can start changing your behavior to align with your desires.

Now I shudder at the thought of having to leave the bed unmade, clothes on the floor, or unfinished dishes in the sink. When I do this, it stays with me most of the day—I leave the house feeling like a mess and feeling like, *I don't have my s*** together!* It just starts my day off on the wrong note. If I'm at home, I cannot concentrate, relax, or get work done when I feel and see that things are undone and incomplete. I have developed and mastered my own personalized "clutter radar," and I am so sensitive to it that I can sense the clutter permeating the space even if I cannot physically see it. The unfinished stuff distracts me, and I have to complete it before I can focus on the task at hand.

．

When my mother and father would host parties for our relatives every few weeks—dinner for about twenty people, with all the dishes cooked by my mother—we would all be assigned various chores. I would clean the toilets, while my brothers cleaned the windows. I learned then that when you're having people over, it is a great excuse to get your house in perfect order! Now I advocate this to my clients: Set a target date of a party or get-together, so you are forced to set a goal and meet the deadline of having everything in its place before your guests arrive!

Let's take that concept to the next level. I know how stressful it can be to cook, clean, and prep for the party in a whirlwind before the guests arrive, so I thought, why not always have your house in order, as if guests could stop by at a moment's notice? If you have proper homes and paths for everything, then the act of putting stuff into these homes and paths is seamless and not a chore, and taking the extra minute to put stuff away every single day does not allow the buildup of stuff. It simply becomes a way of life. It's living your life as if it's a work of art.

Now, I just love, love, love the feeling of having things in order and being surrounded by things of beauty in the space where I reside. I am the "special guest" whom I keep my house in order for. I really try to practice what I preach; otherwise I would feel like a fraud teaching my clients to maintain this standard. I try to leave my house feeling like a million bucks from the inside out, because when my house is in perfect order and impeccable in my eyes, I walk out of the house feeling like a success, and I carry that feeling with me throughout the day!

It's as if the house is an extension of me, and even though no one else knows, I know inside that I am "in order" from head to toe! And, when I come back to the house at the end of the day, it takes my breath away—I feel so grateful and feel like a million bucks every time I walk in the door! No one else sees the space but me, but I know deep inside that I'm living and honoring the truth of who I am.

I now teach others that "grounding" comes from within. Are you in alignment from head to toe, from the inside to the outside, from the outer spaces to the inner spaces? Only you know what is true, and that's all that matters. You set yourself up for success when you do this every day! Live your life as if it was your ideal life *now*. Don't wait until you get the perfect furniture. Make do with what you have, and rearrange your stuff. Be proud of your stuff and display it proudly. Most importantly, do whatever it takes to love your living space now! And why not be proud of your space or home, so that you can entertain your friends and family if they happen to drop by at a moment's notice?

.

I know it may sound anal and perfectionist to many, but for me, I have learned that the smallest things I have control over that I don't manage here and now have a way of getting to me and catching up to me. These little things build up and cause explosions that suddenly erupt into volcanoes with stuff flowing over! Because I know I have control over the little stuff, I know I will feel better taking care of it now rather than later—and my day starts off that much better.

For me, this means not letting my mail and bills overflow. This means not leaving stuff out on my desk. This means not letting dishes pile up in the sink until the following day. This means picking stuff up immediately when it's on the floor and returning it to its proper home. This means unpacking after a trip. This means making decisions about stuff now rather than tomorrow.

Now I am aware that the reason why, as a child, I probably did not pick up after myself but threw everything more into disarray was because I subconsciously chose to rebel. No one was going to tell me what to do! My mother kept prodding me to keep the room neat and clean. Because she kept on repeatedly wanting me to do this, I kept doing the opposite. I thought, *She is trying to control me!* At the time, I didn't consciously think, *I'm going to do the opposite!* but in retrospect, I know this was what I was manifesting, trying to maintain control over my life and my physical space in my own way. Funny that "My Way" was my favorite song I used to play and sing on the piano back then. If I had the insight then that I do now, I would have realized that I was only hurting myself by doing the opposite of what was truly for my highest good. Had I listened to my mother and followed her systems, which were quite simple and easy to follow, perhaps I would have felt more grounded as a child and would have been comfortable in my own skin. I didn't know then that I was sabotaging myself by messing my stuff up, just because I didn't want someone to tell me what to do. This goes deep.

Where else did I do that in my life that I was not aware of?

I was on a constant diet when I was a teenager, trying to measure up to some impossible standard from reading fashion magazines. My favorite food in the world was ice cream. Feeling the smooth, creamy ice cream in my mouth go down my throat was soothing. Nearly every day, my parents and my brothers would try to help me stay on my diet: "Only one scoop, June; it's fattening!" However, I would rebel and shove two scoops of ice cream into my mouth. Intent: "Don't tell me what to eat!"

It's funny—I have this obedient, "good girl" side of me, and this naughty, rebellious, "don't tell me what to do" side of me, and I have had to reconcile these in my mind and heart. I have worked hard to declutter the subconscious beliefs buried inside of me that could sabotage me unknowingly, and keep me cluttered up physically, mentally, and emotionally. If you don't deal with them, they lurk underneath the surface, driving you to unwanted outcomes, rather than you consciously driving your behavior to successful positive outcomes. That's why I love touching physical stuff—it allows me to touch the mental, emotional, and spiritual layers it is attached to.

•

Without a care in the world, given everything my heart desired, I could have been described as a happy-go-lucky girl with a big heart. I loved boys and having fun, playing with my girlfriends, writing poetry, reading Nancy Drew mysteries, playing the piano, playing dress-up, playing in the clubhouse I created, and being a good friend and helping others!

I was also clumsy, klutzy, flighty, and forgetful! I would forget stuff everywhere, such as the time I left my brand-new, favorite white sweater at the baseball field. It was already gone when I returned fifteen minutes later. I lost the new aquamarine ring my mother gave to me on my twenty-first birthday—I was showing it to my friends at a restaurant and left it on the table. It was gone when I came back a few minutes later. I broke a chandelier at my aunt's house while swinging my arms around to tell a story. Stuff seemed to break when I was around, and stuff seemed to drop out of nowhere, like the glass ketchup bottle that would drop out of the refrigerator whenever I opened it. However, my dad would always say, "Don't worry about it!"

One summer, when I was thirteen, I went to this one-day charm school to learn proper etiquette, such as how to properly set a table, how to drink soup and eat from your plate properly, and how to walk gracefully. But I don't think I retained much. I'm sure many of my clients can attest that yes, I am not the most graceful person around, but is grace required for organizing, decluttering, and simplifying? No—thank God!

My experience with losing, forgetting, and breaking stuff at such an early age led me to have a detachment to stuff. I had to release my attachment to the importance of stuff, not lamenting the losses, but instead focusing on the wonderful stuff I did have. My parents would never get upset at me for breaking or losing stuff; they never scolded me because I think they knew that I was already hard enough on myself. They tried to teach me to take care of the stuff that I had and appreciate the stuff, but also that the stuff and the accumulation of stuff was not the most important thing in life. I would lend new clothes to friends that sometimes would be returned "worn out." I would forget to bring my homework to school, but I would remember to bring my snacks! My parents reminded me to ask myself before leaving anyplace, *Do I have everything? Am I forgetting anything? Look around . . .*

Now, I teach others the lesson I learned through these experiences of having forgotten and lost so much stuff: Stay in the present moment, because it is when you are thinking of being elsewhere that you forget your stuff. For instance, when I'm with a client, ending a session, and I take out my keys while I'm still talking to her and I leave the keys at her place, it is because I really should have been in the moment fully engaged with her, not thinking about my car and getting into my car, which would prompt the natural grabbing of my keys in my purse. Why was I ahead of myself, thinking about where I was going, rather than thinking about where I was currently? Think about what you need when you need it. Grab what you need when you need it.

Also, when something gets broken and lost, perhaps it is not meant to be yours anymore. The stuff was with you for a while: remember the memories of the stuff and the good feelings it gave you, and then let it go. Let other stuff in your life bring you joy, as it's not about the stuff, but about the love in your life, and the stuff should not be a replacement for true love and happiness.

·

I can't report any traumatic experiences that would have cluttered up my mind and heart in my childhood. I loved reading "Dear Abby" and "Ask Ann Landers" in the newspaper, and seeing how they would solve the problems they were presented with. I loved watching the soap opera *General Hospital*, and the dramas that unfolded. My life was pretty drama free, except for the occasional "Why did you bomb Pearl Harbor?" comment from ignorant kids, or "Are you really Japanese, and who are your parents?" from ignorant Japanese-American kids in Japanese school who didn't believe that I was really Japanese with my light brown hair. Being judged by how you look or for being a certain ethnicity is not a good feeling. This experience taught me to have compassion and tolerance for all people, no matter what color, age, gender, or ethnicity. We are all one!

·

In high school, I always carried a day planner with calendar, contacts, tasks, and notes, after my dad taught me to write everything down. He said, "June, I know you're smart, but just because you are smart doesn't mean you'll remember everything, so you should write everything down." This is something I still do to this day—only now using my iPhone and computer—and I advocate this to my clients. I took what he said to mean, "Jot down what's inside your brain, which is brilliant, so you can have room for other smart ideas and stuff to come in!" I have always loved creating lists, journaling, and doing these "mental dumps" ever since I was little, but I never realized how cluttered up I could get if I didn't have a system to manage it all! I am still a proud nerd trying the "latest and greatest" tech tools to see if any new tools will save me time. And, I have always been into time management systems, having explored every imaginable brand and system, because I just loved the idea of having a "planner" that contained "my life," including contacts, dates, projects, goals, and to-dos! I now teach others to have a special place to write down their goals and dreams. Mentally dump what's in your brain, so you can free up your mind/heart/consciousness. Get it on to the page, where you can see it and take action on it, rather than letting this "clutter" run rampant in your head and drive you crazy! Free up valuable brain matter for your visions, inspiration, imagination, and inventions! Figure it out on the page and take your next steps when you see it on the page, rather than trying to figure it all out in your head!

During high school, I organized events and was very involved in extracurricular activities, student government, and clubs. I helped organize the prom, edited the yearbook, and organized my own political campaign for student-body president. I loved helping friends with their problems. I loved volunteering my services to the convalescent hospital. I loved playing piano for Christmas carolers. Even though I myself did not have a serious relationship until college, people often came to me for advice on love, relationships, and life.

Before I went to college, I took a "college success" seminar, where we were given sheets with squares that represented time slots for the week. I learned how to schedule time in for classes, studying, social activities, and working out, and I still advocate this methodology to clients. I noticed that whenever I set my intention with clear boundaries on my time, and a target time for each activity, it seemed that all the angels in the Universe would gather together to help me get it done in that time period. When I forgot to do this, things just seemed to take twice as long.

■

During college, even after vowing to leave the socializing and extracurricular activity behind to get down to serious studying, I still became active in dorm government. Juggling my classes, studying, and activities was just a way of life for me, and now, with my new tools to manage my time, I felt empowered and in control of my time. As for clothes— wow, my dorm closet left little room for my wardrobe! I would change at least three times a day, depending on how I was feeling, and if I wore something that didn't quite feel like me, I would run home to change! I now teach people to let go of stuff that doesn't make them feel good, no matter how much they paid for it. One indicator of something you should let go of *now* is feeling like you want to go home and change, and thinking, *What was I thinking, wearing this today?* Wearing something that doesn't make you feel like a million bucks for even one hour of your life is not worth it! Life is much too precious!

I was still into rainbows and unicorns back then, so my dorm room was decorated like crazy with them, and I loved my rainbow bedspread! I bought about a hundred colorful ribbons to go with every one of my outfits, and I used the ribbons to decorate my bulletin board. Mom's influence of being dressed impeccably from head to toe, with matching accessories, had been passed on to me. However, I had not yet mastered "organizing." In fact, I had no clue about it!

I was into having fun, being social, learning, and figuring out what I wanted to be in life! I had some ideas about what might be great careers, but I didn't know exactly what I wanted to do. To help me sift through and declutter my career choices, I decided to do a lot of internships, as everything seemed exciting! I worked for companies specializing in animation, publicity, television news, producing, and multimedia entertainment, and I even toyed with acting, with my first onscreen role in a soap opera. The show was cancelled, and the episode never aired. Also, in my junior year in college, I became a peer counselor, helping my peers to navigate the ins and outs of classes, university life, and just life in general. I loved this job and couldn't believe I was getting paid to do what I loved to do—talk to students and help them!

Yes, I was still into my day planner, and by this time I couldn't find one to suit my needs, so my idea of fun was creating my own "calendars" and "task lists" with my best friend.

•

After college, I continued my pattern of leading an active and busy lifestyle by joining organizations, hosting charity events, planning fashion shows, being the editor of a newsletter, working out, and going out on weekends! I had many short-lived careers and jobs, too many to mention here, ranging from advertising, real estate, property management, and television news. One job I had was assisting an attorney in organizing his research bank, and he said to me, "You should be an attorney," as I was able to figure out how to organize the topics into the right categories. I did not know at the time that "organizing" could be a profession!

One day I was organizing one small makeup drawer in my bathroom. I loved taking containers out, putting them back in, trying to figure out the perfect configuration like a Rubik's Cube or jigsaw puzzle, making sure all "like-items," or related items, fit into one container, and all the containers fit perfectly together. I also touched everything once, twice, three times, asking myself, *Is everything in there something I'm using?* When all the stuff would not fit into the drawer, I would go over my stuff again and confront my truth of whether I really needed twenty lip glosses, toss the idea back and forth in my mind, try on all of them to see which ones I truly loved, throw out the shades that made me look like a clown, and then everything would fit! I learned then that if there's only a limited amount of space, and if I've decided what's going into that space, in order for it to look pretty and be functional, I must let go of a few items to make it all fit, and I must make some hard decisions. Little did I know that I would be doing this as a living—helping others to organize their drawers and ascertaining whether the stuff in there was important to keep or not.

•

After a brief stint in television news, I became an actress, and immediately began booking acting jobs and getting agents and managers because of my marketing and business skills. The acting school I was attending marveled at how quickly I built my resume, and I was asked to teach a class on how to be a working actress. I titled the handout, "How to Organize Your Acting Career." Little did I know that the word "organize" would play a significant role in this yet-to-be revealed career for me. I taught actors that the key to marketing yourself was staying organized and having systems for success! I had developed successful systems to submit myself for roles, for getting representation, for following up on leads, and even for letting go of apparent rejections and dead-end paths.

I couldn't get enough of acting and wanted to be the best I could be, so I studied the best acting techniques and read books by legendary acting coaches such as Stella Adler, Stanislavski, Lee Strasberg, and Sanford Meisner. When I read Meisner's book, it rang so true in my soul. I thought, *I must study with him!*

Studying for two years with Sandy, as we affectionately called him, changed my life! Not only did he help me to declutter a very important repressed memory from my heart, but he helped me come to terms with what I thought were my own personal limitations. I sobbed uncontrollably as I told him the story of how, when I was seven, a girl told me that I could not possibly play Cinderella because I was Asian and not blonde. I didn't realize that I had "clutter" in my consciousness regarding the issue of my heritage, and thus limitations on my own achievement and success! I didn't realize that I held clutter in my heart—resentment towards "those girls" who oppressed me from fulfilling my dream of being Cinderella!

Since then, I have done much work on myself to release this burden of fear of not being "good enough," practice forgiveness towards myself for holding on to this fear, and practice forgiveness towards those young girls who did not know any better.

I now believe that the clutter in our hearts and minds is what creates heavyweight clutter in our bodies, environments, and lives, preventing us from moving forward at an accelerated pace and achieving the success we desire! I also believe that our past experiences shape who we are today, for worse or for better, and we can choose to redefine that past by holding on to the important lessons we have learned and letting go of the rest. Recognizing this clutter and letting it go are the most important things you can do for yourself if you truly want to be free forever! I now teach others to rewrite their stories, telling their stories from the perspective of lessons learned, and looking for the miracles in any experience!

Sandy taught me that "Acting is living truthfully under imaginary circumstances." This lesson began my journey of going within myself to search for the answers of what's true and what's not. I asked myself, *What are my intentions behind my actions? Am I being truthful in this role? Am I being truthful in real life?* If I wanted to be a brilliant actress, I had better know my own truth, so I could respond from that truthful place in my roles as well as in life, instead of coming from a fake and phony space.

So my diligence in learning acting and getting to the truth behind my acting and my own life led me to declutter people and stuff from my life that were no longer in alignment with my truth. I realized everything was interconnected, and I could no longer pretend to care when I did not and/or pretend not to care when I did. I realized how deep this being "truthful" goes when I confronted my truth within—as nobody could know my truth except me, myself, and I. I went through my apartment and touched everything. I reorganized everything, including my clothes, paperwork, anything, and everything. I let go of old love letters from past boyfriends, old photos that I didn't love of myself, old paperwork pertaining to past careers. I felt great going through my stuff—the stuff I could control.

The life of a working actress was different from day to day. Sometimes I would only hear about auditions at 4 p.m. the day prior, and I booked jobs in which I was working the following day. I traveled out of state for jobs at a moment's notice. I realized that in order for me to feel grounded going on auditions where I am judged and asked to perform at my best, I had better be ready for everything and anything that comes my way. I had better feel great about myself and my life, so I could give my all in these auditions and jobs, and show up as my best true self! I had better be prepared in body, mind, spirit, and soul. I realized that the life of a working actress was not something I could control. I could not control whether they liked me or not, or whether I got hired for the job or not, nor could I control the rejections.

During my first year of acting, I got audited by the IRS! How could this happen? I was spending more money than I was making, barely making enough to survive! Instead of lamenting, however, I used this as an opportunity to shift my perspective of money, and learned from my mother and brother how to manage and organize my finances and keep track of money. And I learned the importance of keeping every receipt to back up my tax records. Little did I know that this teaching would later help me set up others on Quicken to empower them with their money, as well as help others to get through their audits without fear. I now believe that fear comes from not knowing what is going on, and feeling out of control with your finances. Confronting the truth of your money, being aware of where it is going, and organizing it with clear boundaries empowers you to make necessary changes to your behavior and take charge of your finances!

I also felt empowered when I decided to take charge of other areas of my life and to control what I could control. I could control the physical space in which I lived. I could control how much I rehearsed and studied. I could control my physical paperwork. I could control my nutrition, my fitness regime, and my physical body. I could control my thoughts and how I perceived every experience. I could program a proper mindset, thinking positive thoughts about myself and visualizing what I desired. The more I organized the elements I had control over, establishing clear boundaries and wonderful systems, guess what I discovered? I felt truly boundless with my life, imagination, and success! I felt unstoppable!

Now I teach others to reclaim the areas where they have lost control—to organize and establish clear boundaries with their physical spaces, relationships, and time; and to declutter detrimental thoughts from their minds, replacing those thoughts with more positive thoughts that are in alignment with what they wish to create, so they too can be free to be all they were born to be!

Sandy also taught us that relaxation and concentration are some of the keys to great acting. So I studied different meditation techniques, and finally learned how to practice Transcendental Meditation. This powerful and simple meditation technique I began practicing twice a day seemed to clear the cobwebs of confusion from my mind. Suddenly, with this tool, I felt like everything in my life was flowing—I could memorize my lines easily and effortlessly—I felt like I was a brilliant actress! I now crave meditation to still my mind, to go within, and to tap into Universal Intelligence. Meditation gives me more energy, inspiration, and guidance than any book or person ever could, so now I advocate this as a tool for many clients as well.

When things seemed so out of control, and I found myself thinking, *When will I get my next job—and my next paycheck? How do these casting directors or producers perceive me at an audition?* I would always come back to the stuff I could control, and organize that stuff and go deeper with that stuff so I could remain a clear channel for my work. I kept probing and going deeper: What more could I control and get clearer about? My image. My environment. My thoughts. My attitudes. My belief systems. Let's continue managing that, going through that, organizing that, decluttering that! That's when something came through from God. Four simple words.

Truth. Love. Meaning. Purpose.

Suddenly, I started evaluating everything based on these four words. Each word on its own was powerful, but it was clear to me that the combination of these four words took on a different meaning. My organizing, simplifying, and decluttering went deeper. My life went deeper. It became a way of life.

.

As I continued to work as an actress, I finally decided to do organizing "on the side," for fun, just because I enjoyed it so much! My husband at the time would call me "The Organizing Maniac," so I had business cards made at Kinko's. Prior to my acting career, I had successfully and confidently made money at other businesses I had started myself. So I just did what I had done before—I made business cards and started spreading the word, just by telling everybody I met, "This is what I'm doing now!"

Another passion of mine was the beauty business—I loved playing with makeup and pretending to be a makeup artist—first with my Barbie dolls, and later on with friends! I was the ultimate beauty hound, reading all the fashion magazines and trying out the latest and greatest makeup. It was fun doing "face art," learning how to create shadows and light on one's face, and creating different looks and styles. I loved organizing my makeup by type in my pink Caboodles box, and I eventually started doing makeup for friends' weddings and other events. I made my business cards, and suddenly I was in wedding photographers' books—and my services were in demand! I loved doing makeup for the bride, along with bridesmaids, mothers, aunts, and grandmothers, and making these women feel beautiful and feel like a queen for a day! Ultimately I made a tough decision not to do any more weddings, when I realized I was juggling three businesses—makeup, acting, and organizing.

I now teach clients to take risks and do what their heart is calling for them to do, to not be so "in the head" about how things are going to happen. Let God/Universe take care of the "how"—just follow through on their passion by taking action and doing something on the physical level. Because we are in a physical universe, and yes, we are spiritual beings in a human body, we cannot test our theories and concepts in our heads and hearts, but we must test out our thoughts in the physical universe, and the Universe will respond. This is the greatest journey—to put your stuff out there and to be conscious about your time. Time is your most valuable commodity, so what are the priorities that bring you the most joy? Focus on the activities that bring you the most joy, and money and success will flow in as you follow your flow of energy and bliss.

While working on a set in my first recurring role, I helped an actress plan her wedding and revamp her business. During this time, I also helped a friend raise money for and produce her short film, which went on to win many awards. I coached a fellow actress's husband, an investment banker in Beverly Hills, who got promoted shortly after we organized his office. I flew to Hawaii to organize the business of a friend who was a psychotherapist. Another friend, a professor, told other professors about me, and I flew to Northern California for a week, where they all fought over my services. I met an architect while training for the LA Marathon, and I organized his firm. I was working on a pilot with a friend, and we met a screenwriter who hired me to organize her office and who told other producers and writers about me. In acting class, I met an attorney, graphic designer, and rabbi who asked me to organize their respective offices. My hairstylist in Beverly Hills asked me to organize his hair studio. My facialist asked me to organize her business. I met a public relations CEO at an event, and he asked me to evaluate and organize his office in downtown Los Angeles. Actresses asked me to organize their families and kids. At the same time, a friend with a successful aerobics business told the city coordinator where she taught classes about me, and she asked me to teach an organizing class.

The business truly took on a life all its own, and I went on to speak in front of university hospitals, governments, companies, and private and public organizations to share my passion for organizing, decluttering, and simplifying to live one's best life. And that is how The Organizing Maniac™ was born.

what else? *it's all about the "what else."*

i share all this with you, because I want you to see that organizing was indeed a passion for me—not because I was good at it, but because I saw the benefits of transformation, liberation, and tranquility it offered!

Organizing became a tool in my toolbox to move my life forward. I organized my stuff every time I wanted to make a change in my life. If I felt my life was out of control, I used organizing as a way to get myself grounded. I remember cleaning up and getting stuff organized whenever I felt overwhelmed! I would touch my stuff and ask if it was still me, because I felt lighter when the stuff that was not truthfully me was no longer in my life. I felt lighter with less stuff. I felt lighter when I moved stuff to match the vibration of who I was at that time. I realize now, of course, that these actions were assisting me to process and move through not just the physical clutter but my internal clutter behind the clutter, and this system was a powerful catalyst for transformation and change.

Discovering that the organization of space and stuff can lead to organization in the mind and heart propelled me to come up with even more systems for my stuff and space that I believe have contributed to success and happiness in my life. Controlling what I can and letting go of what I cannot have led me to be boundless with my creativity, imagination, and ideas. I am able to containerize and create boundaries on stuff and space that I have control over, and let go of control in areas I do not, such as other people's stuff, lives, attitudes, thoughts, and ideas. I am happy controlling what I can control. I let go of all else.

So what do you have control over?

Your physical stuff.
Your physical space.
Your physical body.
Your physical mind.
Your thoughts.
Your mindset.
Your belief systems.
Your heart.

What do you not have control over?

Other people's stuff.
Other people's ideas, thoughts, and feelings about you and your stuff.
Other people's ideas, minds, and hearts.
Other people's opinions about you.
Other people's spaces.

Decades later, I am still just as passionate about what organizing, decluttering, and simplifying the stuff of your life, heart, and mind can do for you. I am just as passionate about how TruthLoveMeaningPurpose can transform your life.

Although my services as a professional organizer continue to be in demand, my work has evolved to include lifestyle coaching, life coaching, and business coaching, and helping people live a life they absolutely love! I have witnessed miracles flow into people's lives when they deal with their stuff, move their stuff around, release their stuff, simplify their stuff, put boundaries on their stuff, and create homes and paths for their stuff. I have witnessed miracles in one's health, finances, relationships, love life, and career, just by dealing with the stuff attached to it.

I love connecting the dots and seeing how all this is connected, because there is no such thing as a mere coincidence. The connection between your mind, heart, and your stuff is significant. Once you choose to accept this and see this connection as a powerful tool, then you can use the stuff in your life productively to serve you, and/or let it go if it is no longer serving your highest good.

The journey continues for me even today, as I exclaimed to my boyfriend this morning after meditating, "I have more to declutter!"

He exclaimed, "What else?!"

This book is about the "what else": the stuff you can't see behind your physical stuff that you will now touch and hold on to, or let go of, so you can be all that you were born to be.

Stay open as you go on this journey with me—touching everything in your life, evaluating your stuff, turning your stuff inside and out, and being happy with your stuff based on TruthLoveMeaningPurpose.

the only way i know. *sharing my way.*

W hen I first began organizing, I thought I should do my due diligence and do what the entrepreneurial books told me to do: Learn everything I could about the business I was starting, and be inspired by the successful businesses that are doing what I was doing. So of course, I got several books on "organizing," but the truth was, they left me more confused.

The books were not confusing. There were so many brilliant methodologies and philosophies about how to best organize stuff, paperwork, and time. Should I do it this way or that way, or do it my own way, as I have been doing? What was creating clutter and confusion in my mind was trying to incorporate all these brilliant systems—at once!

I know I could have probably picked one system, yet no one system or methodology resonated with me. I had to go and create my own system based on everything I had learned and read my entire life! Throughout this book, I will give credit to the books I have read that have influenced my teachings. I am so incredibly grateful for each and every one of these wonderful teachers!

So I discovered that the best way for me to help others was to share the systems I had developed in my own life. I had a solid foundation and belief in these systems I had tried and tested, and that had ultimately proven to be successful for me. I knew I could teach and preach these ways confidently and stand behind these systems.

With this surety of purpose, I am able to freely give my gifts.

And, when asked questions about something I don't know or have not heard about, I will happily and confidently say, "I don't know; I haven't tried it yet. Tell me about it. Try it and let me know."

When I let go of having to be the "expert" in all things to my clients, I release the need to know all things, and I release the fear of not having the answers. I release the fear of someone asking me something I don't know.

As I release having to "be in the know" all the time, I open up my mind and consciousness to more answers from Divine Source, or even from my students and clients, to flow in. Now I am at peace with being in the question and not the answer, and simply assisting others by just sharing my way.

As I deal with others' stuff and help others to arrive at the truth behind their stuff, I discover more about me and my truths regarding my stuff. As I see how much stuff people have that does not fit the truth of who they are today and does not fit the truth of their space, I am inspired to live truthfully with my own stuff. As I see how people are not truthful with themselves about their stuff, I am inspired to go within for the truth of my stuff. When I see how people are afraid to confront the truth of their true selves and their lives, I am inspired to confront the truth of who I truly am and express the truth of my heart and mind. When I see how people are afraid to deal with the emotional and mental stuff that comes up with their stuff, I am inspired to be courageous and deal with the stuff that comes up in my life. I am inspired to go deeper and search within for the truth of my life, heart, mind, and stuff when I see how people want to stay on the surface and don't want to go deep with their stuff because it's too painful. Perhaps they don't know what's there, or they don't know what else will come up—can they handle it?

Always, I have compassion for other people and their stuff, because I have my own stuff to deal with. The last thing I would do is judge others' stuff. How could I possibly be of service to that person and their stuff, with judgment taking up valuable space? How could I possibly partner with the best organizer in the world, God, if I stand in judgment of others and where they are in their journey with their stuff?

Now I know leading a clutter-free life in my heart, mind, and consciousness requires a day-to-day, moment-to-moment vigilance by me, myself, and I. It's all about me and my stuff.

YOU
&
YOUR STUFF.

ready, get set, go! *get all fired up!*

do you want to make a radical shift in your life?

Then get excited!
Get enthused!
Get fired up!

Are you willing to let go of some stuff to lead the life you always envisioned?
There is a way—a simple way—to do this.
Just step up to the plate and decide right here and now that you are willing to do the work to get there.

I will be your coach during this journey.
I will speak the truths you will need to overcome those seemingly insurmountable obstacles and challenges along the way.
I will remind you of your true self, your courage, your greatness, and the fact that you can do this.

All I need from you is:

Your truth.
Your heart.
Courage.
Fearlessness.
Willingness to look within and confess the truth to yourself.
Willingness to release your fears, doubts, and worries.
Willingness to do something differently.

Willingness to view your life differently.
Willingness to view your stuff differently.

There are no accidents. You are reading this because you are ready to radically transform your life—and you can!

I believe in you. I believe in your ability to shift and change the landscape of your life to one filled with miracles, because I have witnessed so many miracles myself and have been the lucky recipient of my own miracles!

My prayer for you, the reader, is that you, too, will receive miracles upon miracles by reading this book and taking action regarding your stuff! And that you will start seeing the beautiful stuff you are already made of, and fearlessly let go of the stuff that is no longer serving your highest good! Remember, you are already a masterpiece, and your life is a work of art. So what kind of art are you creating?

C'mon, you are here reading this, so start here and now by doing something active from the start! Don't just read the book; do something differently! Get up in the middle of reading—now and throughout the book—and start touching your stuff and letting it go! Do whatever strikes you at that moment, and don't worry about being right! Whatever action step you take is the right action step for you, because you are following your heart! Call whomever you feel compelled to call to express your heart! Write in the margins, highlight every word that resonates, and re-read it over and over until it sinks in—and then, take action.

Because we are in a physical universe, you must take some kind of physical action to match what's going on inside of you emotionally, mentally, and spiritually—to move energies in the Universe so miracles can pour forth!

You can do this.
You can live the life you have always wanted to live.
But you must do the work.
The work can be easy and effortless, and even fun, if you follow the flow of energy.

The flow of energy is whatever you feel in your heart you want to do in this very moment. Don't get caught up in your head. Don't overthink it. Don't wait for everything to be perfect before taking action.

All you need to do is tune into your gut, heart, and feelings. What are you feeling in this moment? What positive action can you take with this feeling? Check in. Don't just shove your feelings down and under. Please, this time, do something differently, and deal with whatever comes up to the surface. Deal with it once and for all.

Let go of the clutter from the past. Instead of being cynical and thinking you have read so many books on organizing and self-improvement, you have taken so many seminars and done so much work already, blah, blah, blah—why not this time be a bit like Pollyanna? Be optimistic, and believe that *this* time things will change. Why not have hope and faith that this time, things are on the upswing for you? Things are shifting for the best.

Perhaps, just perhaps, now is the time you will change—permanently. Now is the time you will do something, just one thing, differently, and suddenly you will think differently and act differently. Suddenly things will *look* different.

This time, instead of thinking, *I know,* instead think, *Maybe I don't know,* or *I know there may be another way.*

The scariest place to be is where you think you know. You are living so much in the answer that you don't know what you don't know. Why not think instead that you know a lot, but perhaps there is more to learn about you, your stuff, your world, and your life.

So as you read this book, keep confessing,

> *I am willing to change.*
> *I am changing.*
> *I am willing to see what is holding me back from a life I love.*
> *I am taking just one action step to create space for miracles!*
> *I am changing for the best.*

As you confess this, see what physical action you are prompted to take. Just go with it. Again, don't overanalyze. Don't process just yet.

Right now, my goal is to get you to take action, some kind of action, to move you forward.

Of course, I don't want you just to spin your wheels. I don't want you to be on the treadmill of life, just being busy for the sake of being busy.

That's why by going on the ride with me and following these simple action steps, something will change in your life, and that change will inform your next step.

Do you get it? The Universe cannot give you the change you want if you are not willing to take that first step. Angels are lined up at the door of your life, waiting to come in to help you—if you allow it and you ask for it.

Whenever a fear comes up, believe you can overcome that fear.

Believe you have the courage to change.
Believe you have the courage to face that fear, stare it right in the eye, and know there is a divine solution.
Believe that divine assistance is available to you here and now.
Believe that messages for you are pouring forth in abundance.
Believe that anything and everything is possible.

Believe there is nothing you cannot do.
Believe in yourself and your divine destiny.

You were put here on this earth with a divine mission—to be and live your authentic self, to be supremely happy and supremely prosperous, to love yourself and your life.

The only thing standing between you and the visionary life you desire is yourself and your belief.

Get out of your own way. Get the stuff out of the way that is clouding you from seeing the truth of who you are, and from living the life your heart desires and deserves.

So, let's take a journey into yourself, first and foremost, and figure out if you know who you are, and if the stuff in your life is in alignment with who you truly are.

Stay in the question and don't be in the answer.

If you think you know who you are, great. But you're reading this book for a reason, so there's probably a sliver of stuff still in your life that needs to be released, stuff that is clutter and not part of you. So perhaps you don't know yourself as deeply and as well as you thought you did. Perhaps you thought you knew who you were, but you don't anymore. Perhaps you are changing your perception of who you are and changing from who you were some time ago, and you need help defining that and making sure the stuff you have now is in alignment with this new person, this new you.

Whatever the reason you're reading this book, it's all about shifting your perspective about you and your stuff.

I'm praying you will receive miracles and powerful insights that will give you just one clue and just one action step that will radically transform your life for the best!

Ready. Get Set. Go!

.

exercise. *get in touch with your feelings, heart, and highest vision for your life.*

Journal about how you are feeling as you begin this journey.

How do you feel right now, with all your stuff around you, disorganized and cluttered?

This is *why* you are on this journey.

Now imagine that you have finished this book and are motivated enough to become completely clutter free and organized.

How would you feel? Journal about this. You can begin by simply writing things like:

I feel alive, full of hope, filled with joy. I feel free.

This is *why* you are on this journey.

Whatever comes to mind, this exercise is intended to help you tune into your feelings now based on where you are, and how you *would* feel if you were living the organized and clutter-free life you desire.

How would you live? What would you do? Would you do things differently? Would you act differently?

This is about remembering *why* you have embarked on this journey, and connecting you, your heart, and your feelings to your highest vision for the life you want to live.

Just remember: every step forward is a step in the right direction. As you move forward, if you are moving closer and closer to feeling good and find yourself feeling better and better every single day, then you are on the right path.

you are special. *honor your unique gifts.*

Y
ou were born to do something special.
God created only one of you.
I believe God created you as a perfect being—a masterpiece work of art.

You came into this world with fresh, new eyes with a fresh perspective, full of hope.

Do you think God put you here on this earth just to plod along, accepting the circumstances of your life, accepting all that is?

How can you think that you are here just to accept where you are?

Are you living in your passion?
Are you truly happy?
Are you truly excited to start the day and give yourself to the world?

Striving?
Good.
Moving forward?
Good.
This is your journey.

Remember that your journey is a treasure hunt, where treasures abound!

As you go to and fro, you will discover that the treasure chest you were seeking your entire life was right inside of you. As you dig deep and mine the treasures buried within—finally discovering the gold mine that is your unique life purpose, and learning to use the gems you have been blessed with—a whole new world will be unleashed.

The life purpose and life assignment you have been given is available—right now—for you to manifest.

You have been given everything you need to handle whatever comes your way.

Use the talents, gifts, and skills you have been blessed with.

How is it that we forget what we were born to do and what gifts we came into this world with?

From the minute we are born, we are bombarded with rights and wrongs. We are bombarded with our parents' stuff, our teachers' stuff, and other people's stuff.

I believe it is often other people's clutter that causes us to forget our purpose and our gifts. Other people's clutter becomes clutter in our own lives, and then we can't see clearly. Layers of others' opinions build up and create a cloud around us. We start living life in a fog. We just put one foot in front of the other, and wake up each morning without checking in with what sings to our heart and what we were born to be and do.

Other people's clutter, other people's belief systems, our parents telling us this is right and this is wrong, and our teachers telling us this is correct and this is not, all can create clutter of the mind. Don't get me wrong—I am the first to admit that if it were not for my parents and their guidance, I would not be where I am today.

Guidance can be tricky for parents, because there is a fine line between teaching kids to believe in their own voice and listen to their own intuition and trying to force kids to follow the path of what parents think is best. How do your parents truly know what path is best for you? They don't. How can they advise you if they themselves are not happy and living in their passion? How can anyone know what's best for you? Only you know on the inside, once you clear the clutter of others' voices out of your mind.

So if you can, just for today, check in.

What do you think you were born to do? Pretend for a moment that you truly knew what gifts God anointed you with when you were born.

If you knew that failure was impossible, and you would be successful doing whatever your heart desired, what would it be? If you could make all the money in the world doing something, what would it be? What would make you happy and beyond?

Take a minute to think about it, and don't just rattle off the answer you have been giving your entire life.

Seriously check in with your heart.

Open up your heart to the possibility that you can make money, lead a happy life, and find joy in doing what you came into this world to do. If you choose, you can release the clutter of shoulds in your mind and follow your heart to fulfill your passion. This is the divine destiny you were born to fulfill.

Don't clutter up your heart and mind with "I can't" or fear.

Let go of the fear and leap into the realm of possibilities where your dreams can come true.

Don't leave unfinished business behind in this lifetime.

What are you saving for? What are you saving yourself for?

Create a "love your life/love yourself" vortex around you. Start with the little actions of loving yourself and the way you are. Start by saying yes instead of no to you and your heart. Start by saying yes to you and your true self—uncluttered by others' beliefs telling you to be careful, to worry, to doubt, to believe the world is a scary place.

Say yes with love today to what your heart desires.

Say yes with love to your dreams, and pursuing a particular dream you have always longed to achieve.

What you choose to say yes to makes you exactly who you are. Embrace that. No shoulds. No have tos. Just "I love."

Your unique loves make you special. There is only one of you with your unique loves and your unique heart.

.

exercise. *three dreams.*

Is there something you've always wanted to do or be in this lifetime? Name at least three dreams and/or desires you have that you have not yet achieved. Name three reasons why you have not pursued these dreams/desires. Name three reasons why you should just let go of the shoulds and go for it.

exercise. *your unique qualities.*

Write down ten qualities that you feel make you unique.

Write down three action steps you can take *now* to signal to yourself that you are special, that these unique qualities are special, and that you are now going to go after your loves.

the puzzle of you & your stuff.
the most important puzzle to solve.

s a professional organizer, I have been privileged to get an inside look at people's stuff—their minds, hearts, lives, homes, offices, families, and much more. The main question I ask over and over again, as I help clients examine their stuff, is, "What is this?"

If I were in your house, picking up and touching all your stuff, you might find it scary at first to open up to me—a total stranger—about your life. But once you make the choice to just go on the ride with me and open up, all the stuff you have been keeping inside your heart and mind comes spilling out in response to that simple question, "What is this?"

You might fumble in your consciousness for the truth of "What is this?"

It might trigger a need to explain to me the purpose, meaning, and truth about your stuff, and why you have it in your life.

You may feel it is an inquisition. You feel this compulsion to defend the stuff, acting as if the stuff has rights. You begin to espouse to me why the stuff has the right to be in your life. You share with me its acquisition, its history, its significance and your feelings about the stuff.

What I have discovered is that often you may not know your intentions in having the stuff, not because you are not smart, aware, or even self-actualized, but because no one ever questioned you in such depth—and most importantly, because *you* never asked yourself the truth about your stuff.

If you live in a big house with many rooms, you have plenty of room to house the stuff. If you live in a small house with a garage, you have plenty of room to house the stuff. If you live in a smaller space, and you have lots of stuff, you cram the stuff into every space you have.

The only time it becomes a problem is when you, the owner of the stuff, living amidst the stuff, begins to feel like the stuff is taking over your space and controlling your life, rather than you controlling your stuff and your life.

When the stuff is not organized and labeled, then the stuff is possibly sitting in boxes or jumbled up, crumbled up, stacked up, piled up—the stuff doesn't get tended to and just sits there collecting dust. You pile more stuff on top of that stuff, and you forget about the stuff behind the other stuff, and you go out and buy more stuff. You forget about the stuff in your garage or storage unit, and you go out and buy duplicate stuff.

What is the truth about your stuff?

You didn't make the time to organize the stuff. You spent lots of money and time collecting the stuff. Yet now you don't have the energy to deal with the stuff, let alone organize it! You are overwhelmed with the stuff! You don't have the heart to go through it now—and besides, it's just much easier to get new stuff and use the new stuff!

It doesn't become a problem if you have rooms or spaces that can be dedicated to the housing of the stuff. You can shut the door and pretend the stuff is not there. You can store the stuff in a storage unit far, far away, pay money every month for the housing of the stuff, and pretend it is not there. You can even house the stuff in a prime storage space closer to home, pretending you will go there to get the stuff, but will you truly?

If money is no object, then you can pay to store the stuff, and the charge can automatically be debited from your account. Your accountants see the debit, you never do, and it is just part of your monthly expenses that add up to your "cost of living." Your space gets cluttered up with more stuff, and you conveniently move some more stuff to storage. You promise yourself you will deal with your stuff later, but you never do. Life is too exciting with the current stuff you have in your house and life now; why would you take the time to go through your old stuff?

The time comes, however, when there is a death in your family, a divorce, a career change, a change in your finances, or another event that causes you to start questioning whether the money you are paying for the storage of the stuff is really worth it.

You never use it. You don't touch it. You haven't missed it.

Do you really need all this stuff?

relationship stuff.

Yes, you could just dump the stuff without taking a look at it, because the truth is you don't really know it's there. Some of the stuff was from two relationships past—and you convince yourself it isn't really that important.

But if it wasn't important, why didn't you dump it immediately after that relationship was over?

Because, at that time, you were still getting over the relationship, holding on to the hurt, healing your heart, and you needed that stuff to comfort you, like babies need a pacifier or their favorite stuffed animals to comfort them. The relationship is gone, and you still feel empty inside. However, you still have some of the physical stuff—or if you don't have the physical stuff, you still have the emotional and mental stuff, the thoughts, feelings, and memories hanging around—which makes you feel a little bit better. You don't feel so alone.

Years later, while going through your stuff, you may become aware of the stuff you do have that is connected to the past relationships, but you choose not to touch it, and not to deal with it. Why can't you just dump it?

Why not just deal with it, once and for all?

Because it's too painful.

When going through your stuff, often it is much easier just to dump all the stuff without taking a look at what lies beneath it.

However, this time, I'm encouraging you to use your stuff as a therapeutic tool to get through your emotional, mental, and spiritual stuff. Open up the boxes and containers, and pay proper homage to the past, present, and future. By doing so, your heart/mind/consciousness/soul/spirit gets to pay its own respects to the experience, taking away the good stuff such as lessons learned, and letting go of the bad stuff. Get it?

It was not only the physical part of you in that relationship.

Your heart was into it.

Your mind was into it.

Your spirit and soul were into it.

All parts of you were into this relationship. When the physical relationship ended, when you stopped seeing this person, and this person stopped being a part of your life, you moved out, left the house, and took your stuff. But there was still a part of you—your heart, mind, spirit, and soul—that was left behind.

So, if you're following this train of thought, think about this:

You took the physical stuff.

You perhaps dumped it into your garage.

You perhaps dumped it into the storage unit.

You perhaps even dumped it into the trash.

Or perhaps you stored it away somewhere else to be forgotten.

But what about the feelings, emotions, and thoughts attached to the relationship?

If you didn't process and touch those feelings and thoughts completely, you left those behind, unresolved, and you're still carrying them inside of you—in your body, heart, and mind.

Just getting rid of the physical stuff alone will not get rid of the emotions and feelings attached to it. However, the physical letting go is an important beginning, providing a powerful impetus to touch that part of you inside—the pain, emotions, feelings, memories, and lessons.

So this journey you are taking can be life-changing if you truly get in touch with the mental, emotional, and spiritual stuff behind the physical stuff. If you get in touch with the thoughts, emotions, and feelings attached to your stuff, you will be light years ahead when you are tackling your physical stuff. Just remember, the physical stuff is the first layer—the surface—of what you are truly tackling. The reason the physical stuff can feel so dense and zap your energy is because of what lies underneath the stuff.

If you are ready to hear the truth, choose to fearlessly examine the truth behind your stuff, and prod your inner self to bring that truth to the surface, then I guarantee that everything and anything related to this stuff that needs to be touched and released will come up. Then you no longer have to stuff away those feelings in your body, heart, and mind. You can instead let go of them once and for all.

You can forgive yourself, forgive the other person, and mourn the death of the relationship that taught you so much. You can celebrate the lessons, and applaud yourself for opening up your heart in this relationship and giving it your all and doing your best. You can be grateful for everything you learned, because you are the person you are today because of this past relationship.

Keep the positives, and leave the negatives behind. You will finally take the stuffed feelings all the way through to their end, and let them go. They will no longer possess you and take up valuable space in your body, mind, and heart, and pollute your other relationships. You will finally be free of the stuff, inside and out, and close this valuable chapter of your life with grace, faith, and trust in your present and future.

You are still here: breathing, resilient, desiring to change, reading this book.

You will no longer be living as a prisoner of your past and your hardened heart.

You will be moving forward, free from your past and with an open heart.

body stuff.

What about body stuff? If you are following my train of thought, and you get how the physical stuff is connected to the mental, spiritual, and emotional stuff within, then the body, the physical house for our souls and hearts, must be affected by what we think, how we think, and what we feel.

Many diseases in the body, I believe, result from holding on to the mental, spiritual, or emotional stuff that has been stuffed away into our bodies. From years of doing yoga, visiting holistic health practitioners, and reading Louise Hay's book *Heal Your Body* time and time again, I have learned that it is all connected. Perhaps my fear of moving forward is causing my foot issues. Or my tight shoulders are the result of the burdens I feel I am shouldering.

Because we are spiritual beings born into a physical universe, it would make sense that our physical body is the container housing our soul, and would contain all the answers and questions to our existence, as well as contain past experiences we have not yet dealt with fully. When we have mental, spiritual, or emotional clutter, and we have not reconciled it in our minds and hearts, it stays lodged in our bodies.

When we hold a grudge, we hold it in our bodies. When we hold on to resentment, we hold it in our bodies. When we hold on to past grievances and hurts, we hold them in our bodies. The destructive thoughts we carry are buried in the darkness within our body, and are tentacles preventing us from a life of love, liberation, and freedom. The mind-body-spirit connection is so powerful that what we think is what we create—literally—in our bodies, experiences, and environment.

That means whatever stuff we have not fully processed is living in our bodies, lodged in our bodies, stagnant yet growing, like mold on a rock. The stuff is rotting in the dark. To declutter it from our bodies, the stuff needs to be brought into the light to be examined, dealt with, and fully let go.

To deal with this buried stuff, confront it head on and heart on and ask, "What is the truth of this feeling or thought, and why has it surfaced?" Then befriend that truth. Allow it to bring up all the tears, frustration, or whatever else has been buried to the surface. Allow the pain to touch you. When the pain has fully come to the surface, out into the light, welcome it. Communicate with it. Thank it for being in your life and for teaching you. And then release it fully.

Keep only the lesson and the blessing behind that feeling or thought, so that all that remains in your consciousness is the lesson learned—the blessing.

Just "asking" for the stuff to come to the surface could remedy the clutter. Setting a clear intention and declaring to the Universe that you are ready to deal with the clutter in your body will bring it to the surface.

But get ready to deal with it.

Don't shove it under again.

Don't be afraid of it.

Ask for truth and love to flood your consciousness. Ask for the truth of your body to come out of the darkness to be dealt with, and do not be afraid to shine a bright light on the truth of your body. Allow all the secrets you've kept locked up inside to come to the surface. It's okay. Allow all the inner desires, goals, and dreams you've kept behind closed doors to come out and be shared with your true self desiring to lead a clutter-free life.

Why do we not ask for the truth?

Oftentimes we are in denial, fearing we will not know how to handle the truth when it does rise to the surface. We do not trust our body's divine wisdom to deal with the information and heal itself of its clutter. We may be afraid of confronting the truth of those thoughts, feelings, or fears that we've kept shoved away in our bodies for so many years.

Trust that you will have everything you need to deal with the clutter of your body once you decide to ask for the truth to reveal itself to you. Trust that you can let go of the clutter in your body and the accompanying mental and emotional clutter, the thoughts and feelings, so you can lead the life you envision! Envision a new way of life without this clutter, and visualize yourself as whole, healthy, happy, healed, and free!

•

exercise. *solving the puzzle of your stuff.*

To understand the puzzle of your own stuff, you must become a connoisseur of your own stuff: embrace it, confront it, and then, finally, make a conscious choice to let it go or keep it. Journal about the following:

What do you most need to figure out regarding the puzzle of your stuff?

What do you feel is the most cluttered area of your life? Your relationships? Your body? Your physical stuff? Your storage? Your home? Your office? Your bedroom?

What are you scared of facing? What are you scared of letting go?

Do you feel that the clutter in your environment is connected to some kind of clutter in your body and/or relationships? If so, how?

the birth and foundation of your system. *know thyself.*

i shared with you the journey of my life and how The Organizing Maniac™ system was born. I shared with you my journey of looking carefully at everything in my life to see if I was leading an authentic life honoring my truth. I shared with you that the best path for me was following my way of doing things, and that it was dependent on me and how well I knew myself. I could research all the latest and greatest organizing tools, and learn about the greatest organizing systems, but the most important system I had to master was my own.

I shared all of this with you because I believe that you, too, can master *you,* and you can come up with a system tailor-made to you that can honor your truth. And you can use this system as your foundation from which to leap off and do anything you want to in life. With your system rooted in the foundation of *you,* I believe you can lead a life you absolutely love that includes the stuff you love!

Once you get it right, you won't have to organize, reorganize, and reorganize again, because a great system stays organized! You will, however, need to refine the organizing and decluttering based on who you are day to day and year to year. But that is the fun part—changing your systems with the ever-growing, ever-evolving, wonderful you and your amazing life!

Accept your issues and experiences as unique to you, and worthy of your love. Accept your past as the blessed vehicle that brought you to where you are now. You are who you are today based on your past, your past choices, your past belief systems, and your past attitudes. In your past, you may see victories to celebrate, as well as losses you wish to forget. Nevertheless, accept *everything* that has ever happened to you as a celebration of who you are. Every single experience is one you have chosen to participate in, every single relationship is one you chose to engage in, and every single item is what you have consciously brought in. No more lamenting, no more whining, no more berating yourself, no more getting angry at yourself, no more playing "poor me"; just accept where you are today.

Vow to do things differently now to create a new future. Vow now not to have any stuff in your life whose only purpose is to make you feel badly. Vow now only to have stuff in your life that lifts you up, empowers you, and makes you smile!

Vow now to create a new way of life, celebrating the unique you.

No one like you will ever be born here on earth during this lifetime. There is only one of you, with your unique stuff, qualities, essences, likes and dislikes, and past history.

There is only one of you, with your unique perspective on life, your things, and your experiences. How do you honor this uniqueness? How do you honor your true self? How do you get to the truth behind your stuff?

Ask the right questions, listen to your answers, and based on those answers, go even deeper for even more truthful answers.

Getting to the right answers within yourself will allow you to begin to establish the right systems and the best systems for *you*.

Why try to replicate another person's system? Do you have the same heart, mind, soul, and spirit as the person next to you?

So the greatest mystery and puzzle to solve is *you*.

The greatest trip you can ever take is going within you to get to the true beauty of you.

Once you figure out who you truly are, are willing to admit the truth of who you are, are willing to be at one with the truth of who you are, and are willing to lead your life and the truth of who you are in an open and truthful way, the rest is easy.

You must confront *you*—the true you that is hiding behind your stuff and/or using your stuff to pretend to be someone you are not, or thought you were, or thought you were supposed to be according to society, your parents, or television.

You must reveal the true you and be willing to live with the stuff of you, displaying the true you, being the true you, without caring what someone else will think.

Lastly, you must be willing to part with the stuff that is not you, have only the stuff that is you, and love all the stuff that is the true you.

The key to happiness is to love you, your stuff, your work, your passions, and your loves—and then, you will love your life.

You, you, you—what you feel, what you think, what is important to you, and your stuff—is where it's at.

So this system I'm advocating and sharing is a very simplified approach to decluttering that encompasses your body, mind, spirit.

It is, in fact, a journey of opening up your mind, consciousness, and heart to a new way of thinking about you and your stuff.

This journey is about *you*. It's not about your neighbor next door. It's not about your boss, colleague, husband, wife, child, or friend. And most definitely it is not about me. I share my journey with you to inspire you and help you realize that I am not much different from you.

If I have done it and can continue to do it, you can do it. Yes, I went through it, I am now loving my life, and I am sharing my "secret" for success/love/life with you that I stumbled upon and that everyone can apply to their lives!

I'm merely your facilitator to help you think and feel deeply about your own life in relation to your stuff—the stuff that is potentially holding you back from great relationships, a better career, a better job, more money, promotions, or finding the perfect mate.

Let go of the stuff that is not you and is holding you back from being all you can be and fulfilling your greatest potential here on Earth in this lifetime.

Let's unearth the treasures within you and your stuff.

Let's pay proper respect to your past and the stuff that did serve you in the past.

Let go of the stuff that is robbing you of your vitality.

Let's together find the best you, buried amidst your stuff.

Let's unveil the new you, full of vigor, love, life, and light!

Let's peel away the layers of stuff covering up the beautiful you, with your TruthLoveMeaningPurpose!

·

exercise. *know thyself.*

Journal about how things were when you were growing up—disorganized or organized, neat or messy. Were you expected to be a certain way or to keep your room clean? How did that make you feel? Did you enjoy being organized, or did you create messes? Understand where you came from. Understand why you do the things you do. Are they products of your upbringing? Are they learned behaviors?

Journal about why you think you are the way you are, based on the childhood/upbringing/environment you were raised in, and/or what you have learned.

What's holding you back from living your best life?

What is it about your life that you absolutely love?

What stuff do you have that represents the "true" you?

defining you. *it's all about you and your story.*

t he truth of who you are. The truth of your stuff. Are they in alignment?

What kind of story is your stuff telling? What story are you telling yourself when you walk into your space or life? Are you running away from your life because you want to be in another's life or story?

A great story depends on the 5 W's and the 1 H:

Who?

What?

Where?

When?

Why?

How?

who are you?

Today. Not yesterday. Think about your roles of today and compare them with your roles of five years ago. Some of them will be constant throughout your life, but if you are shifting, growing, evolving, and transforming, then perhaps your passions and loves of five years ago have shifted, too. In order to stay clutter free, you must stay current with who you are today. Let go of the past roles and use the tokens from that past as a way of honoring your past, but don't hold on to them based on fear. Let go of the past roles to create space for the new roles to fill up your life.

what do you have?

What kind of stuff do you have based on who you are today versus who you were in the past? Examining this will liberate you as you come to realize that the stuff for your journey is defined by who you are today as well as dreams of who you want to become in the future as well as who you were in the past. How do all these items make you feel? Getting in touch with what the stuff represents will assist you deciding whether to hold on or let go.

where are you?

Look truthfully at the space you are in now. Yes, you have dreams of moving to a bigger house and filling it up with the decorative items you have collected, but when is this happening? We fill up our lives with stuff for the future and/or keep things based on the past, without thinking about the most important thing: where are we now? Confront the truth of your current space. Once you do, you will be liberated, because you will appreciate where you are now, and be happy with your space.

when?

This is key. Now. Today is the present. Stay with the present.

The stuff in your life has to match up with who you are today, not who you were years ago or even months ago.

why?

Examine your need to organize, simplify, and declutter a particular area of your life and space. Why do you want to organize, simplify, and declutter?

For example, I have too many clothes, and I need to declutter because I don't feel good walking into my space and looking at my closet.

how?

Examine your criteria for evaluating your stuff. How do you decide what to keep and what to let go? How do you let go? How do you hold on?

Delve deep. Why are you here? How did you get here?

Without self-awareness and delving within for the answers, even if someone took all the stuff away for you, you would simply create the stuff again.

.

exercise. *get in touch with you.*

With this simple exercise, you may realize that you are living in the past or the future, but not in the present. You may realize that you are holding on to a lot of stuff from the past, or for futures you envisioned that are no longer relevant. No one can do this exercise for you, because you are the only one who knows who you are on the inside—your dreams and passions—and only you can confront the truth of you and the stuff you have. Perhaps you may see that the You of Today is somebody you do not like, and the You of Yesterday was somebody you loved. Then incorporate those qualities into your being. This isn't just about stuff, but the core of who you are today versus who you were in the past and who you will be in the future. You can be anyone you choose to be, and do whatever you choose to do, once you gain clarity.

Who are you? List ten adjectives (e.g., lovable, compassionate, passionate).

Who are you? List seven roles you play in life (e.g., mother, musician, traveler, attorney, student). Under each of these roles, identify the sub-roles you play (e.g., advisor, playmate, scheduler, guidance counselor, babysitter, laundress, chauffeur, homework helper).

Who have you been in the past? List the roles and passions of the past that you no longer play now (e.g., Starbucks barista, roommate, schoolteacher, baby mother, angry, unforgiving, bitter).

What roles would you like to play in the future? List the roles you envision yourself playing (e.g., husband, father, business owner, actress, loving, prosperous, generous, compassionate).

What are your goals related to each role? (As household CEO, your goal might be to have an organized, streamlined household where everything is in its place and everyone is co-existing together harmoniously. As manager, your goal might be to feel successful at work. As a father, your goal might be to be a present dad. As a mother, your goal might be to be a patient mom.)

What are your intentions? Your intention is the "why" and the TruthLoveMeaningPurpose behind the goal (e.g., I am doing whatever it takes to clear up my clutter once and for all, and feeling great about myself and my life).

laser-like focus on you. *rescue yourself first.*

While you are on this journey, stop yourself when you think about someone else.

As you read this book, have laser-like focus on you, and only you.

Stop the obsession to want to rescue, help, or serve someone else.

For just this moment, be a little selfish.

I want you to be absorbed with yourself.

The journey of self-awareness and going within is sometimes difficult because we don't want to look within. What comes up may be painful. What comes up may be ugly.

But if you take this journey, I guarantee that you will start honoring the beauty within the ugliness, and define everything about yourself and your life as beautiful, because it is uniquely you. You—who you are, your likes and dislikes—are all beautiful!

So right now, stop thinking about, "Oh my goodness, so-and-so must read this book. This person would so benefit from reading this. So-and-so needs this information."

Right here and right now, focus on you and solely you.

This obsession with other people's journeys and pointing fingers at somebody else takes the focus away from your need to take personal responsibility for your own journey and what needs to be adjusted on your journey.

By the way, I use the word "adjustment" or "refinement," because I believe we are all perfect, divine beings that came into this world perfect *as is*, and your soul is uniquely different and beautiful in its own divine way.

What got in the way of living out your perfect divinity were other people's judgments and belief systems, the world telling you how you have to act and what you have to do and what you have to believe to be accepted. Such as, the world is a bad place, so you must protect yourself. We have enemies in this world whom you need to know about. There are things to watch out for. You better be careful or else you will get hurt and beaten up.

Do this. Don't do that. Don't cross that line. You should do this to be a good person. You'd better do this, or you won't be accepted by society. You'd better do this, or your friends will think you're weird, nerdy, not cool. You'd better follow the crowd, or else. You'd better do your own thing, or else people will think you are a follower.

How many of these things have we been told throughout our lives by well-intentioned teachers, parents, family, friends, acquaintances, and even strangers? How many of these ideas are still residing in our consciousness?

Let go.

Today, start decluttering your consciousness of the shoulds.
What rules have you been following?
What commandments have you set for yourself?
How are you punishing yourself?
How are you rewarding yourself?
Are these rules the true measures of your success and happiness?
Does following the rules and not doing certain things make you a happier and better person?
Do you feel more alive following these rules?

The truth is that you don't need others' rules. All you need are tools to set your own rules. And the only tool you need for your success and happiness is TruthLoveMeaningPurpose.

And even then, remember to always go back to you. Not somebody else.

Everybody's TruthLoveMeaningPurpose will be radically different.

But because we all come from the same Source, I believe there is a commonality and synchronicity within each of us, because we are all connected. We are all one.

The heart connects us all.

As we start honoring our own TruthLoveMeaningPurpose, I believe there will be less war on this earth. We will strive less for resources and compete less. We will compare less. We will show less judgment and more compassion for everyone's unique journey, including our own. We will be able to tolerate differences, for the differences are what make each one of us unique.

Why try to imitate someone else? Why covet what another has? Be proud of your stuff and your unique journey. Honor your unique stuff and your unique journey. Let that unique stuff and unique journey inform you and reveal more of who you are deep inside.

Once again, stop pointing the finger at everybody else and thinking they are the ones with the issues. It's all about you right now. They are merely messengers for you on your journey to teach you more about who you are. They are triggers for you, triggering you to go deeper within to understand the truth of who you are. They are mirrors of you: your beauty, your ugliness, and everything in between.

Embrace and love all of who you are.

•

exercise. *focus on you.*

Every time you notice yourself thinking of somebody else while reading, put an X at that spot—right here in this book.

Every time you catch yourself thinking, *OMG, so-and-so should be reading this,* put an X.

Every time you think of yourself and how a statement relates to you, circle it.

Focus on the circles, and note that these are the areas you must first work on.

Then focus on the X's: you are guilty of these as well, and these are areas you can work on also. You may have heard the saying, "If you can spot it, you've got it," which means you would not even be able to spot the issue in someone else unless this issue was somehow related to you.

At the end of the book, notice how many circles and X's you have. If there are more X's than circles, just be aware of how you shift your attention away from yourself to rescue others, when your time and energy might be better spent first working on yourself.

what do you really need? *honor what's important to you.*

When Hurricane Katrina hit New Orleans, watching the tragedies people suffered and the losses they endured on television forced me to look at my life differently. Those events shifted my perspective on my own life. It made me think about stuff differently and what was truly important.

How would you feel if you lost your home and belongings? What are the three things you would take with you if you had to leave in five minutes and were forced to evacuate?

Me? I would grab myself, my boyfriend, and my phone. What about clothes? I could replace them. My photos and papers are archived in cyberspace. Having lost things along the way during my life, if anything else was lost or gone, I would probably think, *Oh well, it's probably meant to be.* My loved ones and staying connected to the most important people in my life are the most important stuff to me now.

Some clients have told me that they secretly wish something, such as an earthquake or a fire, would wipe out everything they had, and then they would have to start all over. Then I tell them that the mind and the Universe are powerful in bringing forth your desires, so if they wish for that too hard, it might come true.

At a wedding I attended, I talked to a couple whose basement flooded. The water ruined everything in the basement, including important family photos, antiques, and records. They shared with me that they were secretly relieved, because they had been wanting to go through the basement for years but never got around to it. They figured it was nature's way of taking care of them, saving them time in dealing with their stuff.

What stuff are you holding on to that you truly don't need or wouldn't miss if it were gone? What are you are hoarding, and what could you be passing on to people in need? Have you abandoned any "precious" items you wanted to hold on to, letting them sit around collecting dust? Is it fair to these items, which worked so diligently to fulfill their purpose when purchased, to neglect them this way, leaving them to die, wilt, or rot?

Today, think about your stuff differently. Do you know which items you cherish and value the most? Would you really be that upset if that item you thought was so important was gone? What is the worst thing that would happen? Where is this item that you treasure so much? Are you taking care of it as the treasure that it is? Take care of it, truthfully, if it is that important to you!

What items have you relegated to the "just in case, maybe, kinda-sorta" pile? Why have you not made a decision about it? If you decide in this moment, today, to keep it, then take care of it and find a proper home for it. If you cannot decide and do not really have an opinion either way, then be fearless and let go of it! Do you really think you will miss it later?

Confront the truth today. Be fearless in your choices. Trust that you will be fine, no matter what. Trust that whatever decision you make today is serving your highest good.

·

exercise. *the three most important things.*

If you had to leave your house right now and could never come back, what are the three most important things you would take with you? Writing down your answers to this exercise can help you gauge what is truly important to you and what is not.

exercise. *three neglected things.*

Pick three items in your home that you consider precious but have neglected. Take the time to touch them, talk to them, dust them off, and find a home for them. You should immediately feel better taking care of the stuff you declare is important to you.

exercise. *three ambivalent things.*

Pick three items you are ambivalent about. Take the time to touch each one and ask yourself if it is something you still treasure, and why. If you cannot come up with a great reason, or you feel you must make something up (you'll know if you are doing this!), then it is time to let it go. Let it go. Repeat this process with the other two items.

It may feel awkward or unnatural to do this at first, because you may have a tendency to hold on to something if you are unsure or if it's a maybe. But I'm trying to get you to exercise your "decision-making muscles." Instead of erring on the side of holding on to something when you are indecisive, I want you to err on the side of letting go.

The truth is that if you continue this process with more items in your home, you will feel lighter and more vibrant, and your home will exude a positive vibration, because the things you decide to keep will be definite loves and yeses! Your life will be singing "love, love, love" and "yes, yes, yes" to Life itself! Get it?

deal with your stuff. *align with the true you.*

figuring out what is your stuff and what is other people's stuff can be a lifelong journey. We are taught, from the time we are young, what is right and what is wrong. In every society and culture, there are rules and ideas about what is acceptable and what is not, what is approved and what is not, what is politically correct and what is not. By the time we are children, we have already formed ideas about who to be, what to do, and what to have.

In my work, I have been fascinated to discover that even kids as young as three years old can have clutter. How do kids so young accumulate clutter in their physical stuff, in their heads, and in their hearts? Because of the input they receive from their parents, environment, television, and friends.

So it makes sense, of course, that teenagers and adults have clutter too, and that this clutter can be magnified if we do not address it as we get older.

Clutter will continue to grow like ivy, resistant to disinfectants or pesticides, because the gook around it builds up and hardens. The growth of clutter accelerates, and gets exponentially heavier with time. Clutter weighs us down and brings us down. Our bodies get heavier, our breathing becomes shallow, and we start carrying the effects of clutter with us as we leave the house. We are inundated with clutter, but we don't even know it.

How can we carry clutter with us without knowing it? Because we become immune to clutter and the way it ravages our bodies, minds, hearts, and souls.

People don't even realize they have hardened souls and spirits, and that they have warped views about life and their stuff, because they're mired in their stuff. They cannot tell the difference between the forest and the trees. Because they are in the forest of their stuff, they cannot see the darkness that the stuff brings, and they cannot see the bright light trying to peek through to their spirits. Their stuff is screaming at them to do something about it, but they cannot hear it because too much stuff is screaming all at once, like a rock concert with many different bands blaring different tunes, all trying to get the attention of the audience. You are the audience held captive by your stuff, enraptured with your stuff, mesmerized by your stuff, paralyzed by your stuff.

Because there is so much stuff, you cannot breathe properly. You crave more breathing space, but instead you fill up your space with even more stuff. You want to feel the stuffed-up feelings you have, but instead you crush your feelings with more stuff so you don't have to feel it, because it's too painful. You feed your body with stuff. You drink stuff to make you feel better. You take other stuff to take you to a different head space. You run away from your stuff by buying more stuff or buying stuff for others. You want to let go of the stuff, but you're too afraid you might need the stuff someday. Your mind keeps filling up with stuff that could possibly happen, or thoughts about the stuff you spent so much money on, so that you start stuffing yourself up with guilt. Guilt about how much money you spent on the stuff you don't use, guilt about how much stuff you have compared to others, guilt about how much more stuff you want compared to the people on television who have good stuff.

You worry that something might happen to your stuff, so you lock it up. You want to make sure that the stuff stays in good shape for a long time, so you protect it with plastic, and tell everyone to be careful around it, because you want it to last for a long time. When someone admires your stuff, you get upset that someone touched your stuff and didn't put the stuff away properly. God forbid they break your stuff. The people who come to visit you every week aren't good enough. You don't use the good stuff, because you want to save the good stuff for a special occasion when you have special stuff and special people around you. You look into your closet full of stuff, and you think you have nothing to wear. Your stuff is a mess, and you wish somebody would organize it or clean up your stuff. Perhaps if your stuff was organized, clean, and neat, you would use your stuff. You might secretly wish for a fire or disaster and that the stuff would—poof—disappear.

Or instead of dealing with your own stuff, you blame others for your stuff.

You rationalize: It's not my stuff. I had my stuff organized, but it got comingled with others' stuff, and now it's our stuff—and what a mess! If it was my stuff, it would be easy to deal with. If only they didn't have so much stuff, I could easily organize my stuff. If they took care of their stuff, it would make it easier for me to take care of my stuff.

Instead of looking at your own stuff, it's easier to point at others' stuff and do something with their stuff. Their stuff is easier because then you don't have to go within to see your true stuff and what's behind your stuff.

Wait.

There is a way out of this mire.

There is a way to figure out the puzzle of your stuff.

In fact, figuring out of the puzzle of your life and your stuff may be the greatest key to happiness, joy, prosperity, and a life you love.

What if . . .

What if there were a simple way to discern what is your stuff, what is not your stuff?
What if there were a simple way to sort out your stuff?
What if there were a simple way to get rid of the stuff you didn't need?
What if there were a simple way to have only the stuff you truly wanted and needed?
What if there were a simple way of living your life with stuff you loved?

Just take a moment to entertain the thought of leading a life surrounded with stuff you love.

Can you imagine it?

If you can, good for you.
That means there is at least a part of you that knows who you are, and what truly brings you joy.

If you cannot, that's okay. That just means you have to get to know the stuff you are made of, which will help you let go of the stuff that isn't you, and keep the stuff that is.

What is the real stuff that matters?
Your stuff. Your life. Your loves. Your passions. Your desires. Your dreams.
This is about you.
This is about your life.
No one can decide for you what your stuff is.

So what is important to you?
What do you love the most?
What is the most meaningful to you?
What of your stuff serves a purpose?

You and only you can make these decisions and choices, and once you begin making these tough choices and deciding for yourself what your stuff is, your life will become simpler.

Why? Because you will no longer need to look to some book, idea, or role model to tell you the right stuff or wrong stuff to do and be.

You will know from a place deep inside that your stuff is not just good. Your stuff is not just okay. Your stuff is not just ordinary. Your stuff is great, extraordinary, and unique!

When you are in this special place, feeling on top of the world about yourself, your life, and your stuff, you will be unstoppable in reaching your goals.

This place will make you feel grounded and centered as you live your life.
This place is filled with *your stuff* and only your stuff.
This place is filled with your TruthLoveMeaningPurpose.
This special and priceless place will give you limitless joy, happiness, and prosperity beyond your wildest dreams and imagination.

When you live in this place, you will know that there is nowhere else you would rather be, no other stuff you would rather have, no other life you would rather live.

You will claim your stuff, and you will love your stuff!

You will scream from the mountaintop, "I LOVE MY LIFE!"

So get ready for the ride of your life!

Let's deal with your stuff *now*! Let's create a life that honors you and bring your stuff in alignment with who you truly are.

Not tomorrow, not next week.

NOW.

All you need to do is say *yes* now to this amazing ride you will take.

■

exercise. *your stuff.*

Journal about what you know is your stuff.

exercise. *others' stuff.*

Journal about what you believe is others' stuff.

exercise. *take responsibility for your stuff, and only your stuff.*

Do you blame others for where you are today? Journal about the ways you are now taking responsibility for your stuff and where you are today. Journal about the ways you can focus on your stuff and take action on your stuff, and stop pointing fingers at everybody else.

belief systems. *figure out if they are yours or somebody else's.*

t he stuff we have in our life is based on our belief systems. We have convinced ourselves we need this stuff, "just in case"—just in case there is an emergency, we better be prepared for whatever comes our way.

Many people have full-blown earthquake preparedness kits in their homes, closets, and cars. Some of them have never endured an earthquake, but they were told that when you move to California, you'd better be prepared, because California is an earthquake state! The city of Los Angeles advocates that every household should have an earthquake kit, because Los Angeles has been hit by earthquakes in years past. One of my clients actually went through the Northridge Earthquake, one of the biggest earthquakes Los Angeles has ever seen. Her apartment collapsed around her so that she couldn't get out, and having survived the ordeal, she learned that it is wise to always have an earthquake preparedness kit. Acquiring stuff and belief systems in this way comes from wisdom gained from experience: "I've been there. I've learned. I'm smart and prepared now."

However, what about those who have not gone through ordeals like these, and yet have stuff attached to certain belief systems?

I have clients whose parents went through the Great Depression, when food, money, and virtually all other resources were scarce. Their parents suffered a great deal, and having learned from that era, they held on to everything just in case there was another Great Depression. But interestingly enough, many children of these parents held on to that belief system as well.

When clients come to me with this issue, I always ask, "Have you gone through this struggle of lacking basic resources?" "No," they respond. "So, what is causing you to have

65

this belief system?" I ask. They realize that a whole belief system, based on the core belief that "resources are scarce," had been passed on to them, and they hadn't realized it until they were asked about it. They, too, had been living in the shadow of the Great Depression, even though it was more than ninety years ago. Powerful, huh?

So what belief systems do you hold on to that are not even yours, but have been passed on for generations? This legacy of belief systems can be burdensome and weighty. Do you want to lug all this around in your consciousness for a lifetime, and then pass it on to your kids as well? Or do you want to deal with these mindsets here and now, lighten the load, and shift some of those belief systems that have been subconsciously dictating your behavior?

So, check this out. See how deep this runs.

For example, while growing up, perhaps you witnessed your mother holding on to rubber bands. She would say, "If you can get them free, that's good. Then you can spend your hard-earned money on other stuff you really need. The free rubber bands are golden. Better keep them. You never know when you'll need them."

The child hears her mother say this repeatedly, and extrapolates that simple thought to the following belief system: "Rubber bands are scarce. Rubber bands are valuable. Rubber bands have many uses. Money is hard to earn. Hold on to your hard-earned money. Getting stuff for free is great, and you better hold on to the stuff you get for free. Only spend your hard-earned money on stuff you really need. Keep rubber bands. Keep stuff, because you'll never know when you'll need it."

So the child grows up and keeps rubber bands. She picks them up when she sees them on the streets, she starts a collection of all kinds of rubber bands, and we find them all over the house. The child also only spent money on stuff she really needed, rather than on stuff she wanted. She kept everything just in case the Great Depression hit again. But the child had absorbed this belief system early in life, and she was unconscious about its source until she examined it more in depth.

As you question your belief systems, look behind them to find the source. Where did you learn that? Where did you get that from? What led to that belief system?

To go deeper and to question the truth behind the belief systems will help free you of those belief systems that are no longer serving you—just like the Rubber Band Girl, whose house was littered with rubber bands, and she had no idea why.

Once the Rubber Band Girl realized that it did not make sense even to her why she was holding on to the rubber bands, she chose not to let go of the thousands of rubber bands, but instead chose to make a beautiful modern sculpture out of them, paying homage to her mother and her love for her. Then she was able to transform this belief system into a piece of art, using it for a different purpose than what her mother intended and redefining the purpose to suit her. She was honoring her TruthLoveMeaningPurpose.

.

exercise. *belief systems.*

Is there something in your life you are attached to, and you don't know why? Is there something in your life you collect, and you don't know why? If you had to throw it out, how would you feel about it?

Start writing about how you would feel giving away or throwing out something you have never used. How does it make you feel? Do you feel wasteful? Do you feel badly letting it go?

Where did that feeling come from? Go deeper. When did this thinking begin? And what did this thinking trigger for you that caused you to act differently? Getting to the source of the issue is key here. Once you figure out what belief systems your actions came from, then you can work on shifting that belief system to get different results.

Remember, your subconscious mind follows the orders of the conscious mind. In order to change the subconscious mind, you must start consciously affirming a new belief system, take physical action to align with that new belief system, and then your subconscious mind will follow suit.

you are enough. *let go of stuff envy.*

d o you envy others or their stuff?

Why?

Do you think their stuff is better? Do you think they are made of better stuff than you?

Why?

Do you think their life is better with the stuff they have? Do you think that the stuff they possess makes their lives better? Do you think that the stuff makes them feel better? Do you believe that their lives are easier with all the great stuff?

Do you feel that your stuff is not good enough?

If you had access to their stuff, then of course you could do something with your life. You could make something of your life. If you had the house they lived in, you would feel like a success. If you drove the fast sports car he did, you would be attracting the mate of your dreams. If you had a collection of fast cars, you would feel like you had arrived. If you were wearing the Louboutin shoes with the red bottoms, you would feel like you had arrived. Then you would really make an impression at your meeting with the CEO of that luxury brand. You would feel great driving up in your six-figure convertible, and you would land that account.

Why not feel that way *without* the stuff? Why not be that person now without the stuff? Driving that car or wearing that designer dress would look and feel differently on you anyway, since you are a different person than the one who has the stuff.

You make the stuff. Not the other way around.

Do you get how powerfully deep this goes?

Swinging that luxury-brand golf club is not going to make you Tiger Woods. Swinging that luxury purse while shopping on Rodeo won't suddenly make you red-carpet worthy.

You are all that you are without the stuff.

Why can't you carry the energy of that stuff you are coveting within?
What exactly is it that you are coveting?
The energy they are radiating while carrying or driving or possessing the stuff?
There will always be someone prettier, more handsome, smarter, richer, and thinner than you.
Why torture yourself and compare yourself to what everyone else is doing, being, buying, wearing, and eating?

I believe we compare ourselves to others when we feel less than, and not the other way around.

We compare when we feel that we are not enough.
We compare when we feel that we are not skinny or muscular enough.
We compare when we feel that we are not pretty or handsome enough.

Believing "I'm not enough" is deadly. It poisons and infects every good thing about you. When you begin thinking in this vein, you begin to question the good stuff about you, and you can no longer see the goodness of who you are and what you were born with. In fact, envying other's stuff blinds you to your own good stuff, and you forget about who you are.

When you start envying somebody else, you wish you had their life, their body, their face, their boyfriend, their house, their stuff.

This is why it is crucial to get in touch with *you.*

Honor you.
Fall in love with you and what makes you great.
Fall in love with your body.
Fall in love with your life.
Fall in love with your house.
Fall in love with your partner.
But always come back to you.

You. You. You.

Once you acknowledge the truth of who you are, let go of all that is not you.

Let go of wanting to be somebody you are not.

Let go of wanting to be all things to everybody and trying to fulfill some kind of ideal.

This will save you the grief and heartache of a lifetime chasing dreams that are not really you.

Stop coveting other people's stuff.

You do this because you feel like your stuff isn't good enough.

You are enough. You are enough without the stuff.

The only metric you need is TruthLoveMeaningPurpose—which is sooo you, and all about you.

Remember this.
You are happening.
Where you are is happening.
Where you are headed is happening.

Yes, get in touch with the stuff you envy—except use that stuff as markers on your journey of defining what is you and what is not. Once you become at one with who you are and accept all parts of yourself as beautiful, and accept those things as you, you will stop envying others' lives, and love exactly what you have, where you are, and who you are.

Love your life, because this life is yours. There is never, ever going to be a life that has the same unique twists and turns, the same bumps along the road, the same laughs and joys as yours will. Love your life, because there will never be a life that has all the stuff you have, and all the stuff you love.

Love where you are. Love who you are. You are enough.

.

exercise. *let go of wanting to be someone else.*

Think about a time in your life when you have envied somebody.

Why did you want to be like this person?

What qualities did this person have that you wish you had?

First of all, let go of wanting to be that person.

Instead, thank that person for being a gift and marker for you that inspires you to incorporate some of their essence into your own being and daily living. For instance, if this person was always optimistic, thank this person for being full of sunshine, and make a choice to start each day full of hope and optimism, seeing only the good in things.

exercise. *let go of wanting to have something else.*

Think about something you wish you had that another person has.

Why is that item so precious to you?

Why do you want it?

Now, let go of wanting to be that person with that item. Instead, thank that person with that item for inspiring you to include that item into your own wish list.

Think about the qualities of that item and think about the items in your own life, and see if there is already something in your life that resembles that item.

If not, put that on your wish list of items you wish to attract to yourself.

exercise. *you are enough.*

Write down ten things you love about yourself.

Write down ten things you love in your life.

Write down ten reasons you love being you.

These exercises are about exploring the reasons behind our stuff and what drives our needs and desires. Are they coming from an authentic place within you? Remember, rather than envying or coveting, shift your perspective and allow those people/items to be messengers for your journey. Do you want to include this quality or item, or not? Is it authentically you, or not?

Loving yourself and everything about you is the first step in letting go of wanting to be somebody else, or wanting somebody else's life or stuff. Cultivating love for yourself and honoring what makes you truly special will help you let go of comparing yourself to others and wanting what others have. You will begin to appreciate all the subtle and beautiful nuances of what makes you who you truly are!

honor you. *don't compare.*

Comparing is a "lose-lose" battle.

The only journey to be on is your own journey of self-exploration, self-development, and self-actualization.

Be the best you can be.

Let everything else go.

Don't worry about anyone else.

Don't worry about what anyone else is doing.

What they look like.

Where they are living.

How far they have come.

Where you are in comparison to all of the above.

Be supremely confident in your own journey.

Be grounded in your likes, dislikes, passions, and loves.

Be passionate about your dreams, desires, and goals.

Fall in love with you and your journey, and get excited about your life!

Once you do this, you will stop comparing and stop judging yourself.

You will stop looking around at everyone else and wish you were living their lives.

You will love your life, because you are doing the very best you can every day.

You will follow your own ten commandments about how to live your best life.

You will listen to your own heart about what next best step to follow.

You will be tuned in to your own "radio station" of life, not listening to others' opinions about what you should be doing.

No one knows what is truly best for you but you.

If you are ruthless with yourself, the truth will come to the surface.

If you ask for the truth to be revealed, the truth will come up.

If you seek the truth, the truth will arise.

Be open to what the truth is for you.

You may be pleasantly surprised to discover those things that are your truth and those that are not.

Today, check in.

Is this really you?

.

exercise. *be aware of how much you compare.*

Do you compare yourself to others?

In what areas of your life do you do this? (For example, in your career, do you think: *How old were they when they achieved success, and how old am I?* In your personal life: *Are they more attractive or wealthier than I am?* Or in parenting: *How are their kids doing compared to mine?*)

exercise. *make choices without comparing.*

What do you feel like wearing, eating, buying, or doing today? Check in with your heart, and see if you make different choices now that you are aware of how much you compare or base your decisions on what somebody is doing, wearing, or eating!

exercise. *order without comparing.*

When you're at a restaurant ordering your food, rather than asking everybody else what they're ordering, check in first. Go within. What do you truly want today? What do you truly feel like? Even if it is breakfast, why not eat dessert?

Doing this every day in small ways will make you acutely aware of the choices you make on automatic pilot, rather than truly checking into the truth of who you are.

only you know. *and it matters.*

i t doesn't really matter."

What are you saying when you say "it doesn't really matter?"

When I ask someone why they have an item, whether they really need it, and why is it important, item after item, they get tired of answering the question. These are some of the typical answers: "I just know I need it. I spent so much money on it. Of course it's important; my mother gave it to me. I'm keeping it because I want to. I bought it for my white water river rafting trip seven years ago. No, I haven't worn it, but I think I'm going to again. Of course I need it, just in case. I don't want to spend the money to purchase it again. My husband who passed away gave it to me; of course I need it. He gave me that, too. And that. I need it all."

To each of these answers, I can ask you even deeper questions to help you delve within for the truth behind the answers.

Many of us stop at the surface and don't want to go deeper.

Why?

We're scared of facing the truth of the answer.

We're scared of the pain that will arise.

In other words, we're scared of the truth of who we really are. We're scared of knowing the truth about what really matters. Because to admit it matters means we must start making conscious choices about our stuff.

The truth is that it *does* matter, whether or not you choose to slough off that question and pretend it does not matter.

Why you have your stuff matters.

If you have stuff and don't search within for the answers behind your stuff, you will continue accumulating stuff at an alarming rate.

You will never feel fulfilled with your stuff.

You will always look inside your closet full of clothes and say, "I don't have anything to wear."

You will always look inside your fridge and pantry filled to the brim with stuff and say, "I don't have anything to eat."

You will be in your living spaces filled with books and games and say, "I'm bored. I'm feeling restless. I don't have any good books to read."

You will be in relationships that don't fulfill you or bring you happiness or joy. You will settle. You will compromise. You won't go for what you truly desire because you're so scared to admit that *it really does matter.*

If you can relate to any of the above, you are not in touch with what fulfills you at your core. And I encourage you, right here and now, to begin letting go of stuff that no longer resonates with the truth of who you are today. Ask yourself the hard questions so you can let go of the stuff with false belief systems behind it. Honor your life and where you are right now by just keeping stuff you truthfully love right here and now, and you are truthfully using right now.

Yes, you care.

Yes, it matters.

.

exercise. *get in touch with the core of who you are.*

Get in touch with the core of who you are and what matters. Get in touch with what brings you joy. Pick one item you love and complete the following statements in your journal:

I care about this because . . .

This really matters to me because . . .

Then, pick one item in your life you don't really have an opinion about. Write down your answers to the following questions:

I don't care about this because . . .

It doesn't really matter to me because . . .

Now, let go of that item with love and light.

Say out loud:

> *I am now choosing to get in touch with what truly matters to me.*
> *I will now have stuff in my life that really matters to me.*
> *It all matters.*
> *I truly care about touching all the stuff in my life and seeing if it is something that really matters to me still.*
> *I am fearlessly letting go of that stuff that no longer matters to me and that I no longer care about.*

your change triggers others. *just be.*

beginning this process of dealing with your stuff can activate lots of fears within you. Not only is this a lot to deal with in itself, but this process can also activate fears in others around you.

Specifically, the fear of change.

As you begin your journey of simplifying, decluttering, and organizing, people around you may feel extremely threatened by your desire to change, and may even try to sabotage your forward progress by questioning your intentions and making you doubt your own process. Even though they may not be "doing it on purpose," and even though they may not be consciously preventing you from moving forward, the constant questioning and judgment from somebody else still makes you question whether you're on the right path. In truth, their questions are simply reflecting the fears that are within you and mirroring back to you what's also going on inside you.

During this time, when you have decided to change in a radical way and are taking your first steps forward, I urge you to keep your "changes" and "desire to change" to yourself. As Venice Bloodworth says, "Silence is golden." This is not the time to be clashing with naysayers. However, when confronted with negativity or doubts or fears, you must confront them so your intentions stay clean and clear, demonstrating to the Universe that your convictions are strong. Believe you are doing this for your highest good. Believe you have arrived at a point where you must do something differently to get different results, and must change in a huge way.

Even if you don't share what's going on with others, some will undoubtedly sense that a shift is happening inside of you. They may think you are unhappy with the way things are—and yes, you are unhappy with the results you have gotten thus far, and that's why you are doing something differently.

As you shift your environment and change the way you look at things, they may feel threatened. They may believe you will change without them. They may believe you will look at them differently. They may believe their role in your life may change. As you change your physical environment, will you try to change them, too? You are letting go of those things you are no longer using, or serving your highest good, and they may begin to wonder, "Will they let go of me, too? Will they leave me behind? Will they change? I don't want them to change. I want them to stay the way they are. That feels comfortable to me."

Being acutely aware that others may feel threatened by your changes—and being prepared for it—will help put you into the proper frame of mind, so you can respond with a surety of purpose, a passion for life, and a conviction about this desired change deep within your heart, rather than merely react to their fears. I recommend that you merely tell the people you're closest to, "I am shifting something in my life, and I still love you." They may still go on and on, but all you need to say is, "Thank you for caring and letting me know how you feel. I must do this! I'm following my heart and soul. I love you."

The greatest fear others may have is that you will stop loving them, so keep on allaying their fears by saying, "I love you." Stay in the flow of love. Come from love. Be love. This simple prescription does wonders for any relationship.

But don't stop doing what you're doing because you're afraid of change—and certainly don't stop moving forward because those around you are afraid of change. This desire to stay in the comfort zone of our lives is deadly. Be at one with the fact that the only constant in life is change. Change is dynamic. When you accept the fact that everything is always changing, you can rest assured that you can handle whatever changes come your way.

Yes, indeed, you can handle whatever comes your way. You can handle the fears of others by accepting others as they are, and realizing that the only person you can change is yourself. You cannot change how others are going to respond, act, and live, but you can change yourself and how you are going to respond: the words you speak, the actions you take, and the way you live your life.

This journey is not just about moving stuff around. It's about change. Changing the way you see the world. Changing the way you interact with your stuff. Changing the way you see the stuff in your world. Changing the way you do stuff and how you deal with your stuff.

Embrace change!

exercise. *one action step towards change.*

Write about any fears you have surrounding your change, particularly about what changing who you are might do to your life or others' lives around you.

Now write about how much you want this change. Write about how tired you are of staying the same and how you feel this change will dramatically alter your life, as well as others' lives around you.

Now, take one action step that shows the Universe you are willing to take action on this change you are desperately seeking. Seek the change just by taking action, and don't analyze it.

exercise. *express your feelings to one person.*

Do you feel someone is trying to stop you from changing? Express your feelings to this person in the form of an e-mail or letter. Start the letter with "I love you," and ask for their support in making this change. No need to ask for permission and/or explain the change. By decluttering your heart of any guilt about moving forward, you are clearing the pathways for the change to occur. Let go of their reactions, and don't rely on their actions or reactions to dictate how you are going to act in your own life. Let them be and love them where they are. Love yourself where you are, and love the changes you are activating.

your life assignment. *yours is unique.*

W hat if you were told that you were given a special assignment the moment you were born into this world? What if you were told that you were given your unique qualities, essence, personality, talents, and gifts to accomplish this unique life assignment? What if you were told you don't need any additional stuff to accomplish this life mission other than your heart, mind, and body?

Yes, your life assignment is your life purpose, your life mission, your divine destiny. Your life assignment is unique to you and your heart; it is what makes you tick, what makes you happy, what turns you on, and what sets you apart from everybody else in the world. The unique combination of your truth, love, meaning, and purpose of your life is what makes you so special!

It's not about all the stuff you buy, accumulate, or possess! Our priorities have somehow gotten all screwed up. We get stuff and buy more stuff, thinking our stuff is part of our life purpose, when actually all this stuff is preventing us from moving forward in living our life purpose, and to just live a life we *love*!

What if God told you that if you use all the gifts that God has given to you, God will reward you with all the stuff of life your heart desires?
What if God told you that you don't have to know how you will get there, but that all you need to do is listen to your heart, and do whatever makes your heart sing?
What would you do differently today, if you knew this?
What would you change about your life?
What would you do if you knew that you could not fail?
What would you do today if you knew that you would succeed, no matter what?

80

What would you do today if you knew that doing this life assignment would bring you everything, and make all your dreams come true?

God did not put us here on this earth just to plod along, to accept the circumstances of our lives, to accept everything that happens, and to live mediocre lives.

We came into this world with fresh new eyes, a fresh perspective full of hope!

You were born to do something special, to have special stuff to make your journey fun, and to have beautiful stuff to make you feel great every single day!

You are here to lead an extraordinary life because you, with your heart—with your unique loves, passions, and purpose—are extraordinary.

There is only one of you.

Do you believe that you are here just to accept where you are? Are you in your passion? Are you truly, truly happy? Are you excited to start the day and give yourself to the world?

This is the journey: embracing all of yourself in all of your glory.

You have been given everything you need to handle whatever comes your way.
You have been given everything you need to succeed.
You have been given everything you need to fulfill your greatest potential.

Embrace that thought.

Use everything you have: your talents, skills, and gifts.

Your stuff, then, should only serve your life purpose. You don't need extra stuff, because everything you need is within you.

.

exercise. *the infinite possibilities of your life.*

This exercise is about opening you up to the infinite possibilities of your life. I believe anything and everything is possible, if you truly believe. First, however, I want you to get in touch with your dreams, hopes, and goals. Write down your answers to the following questions:

If you knew you could succeed at anything, what would you be doing?

What have you been told that you're good at?

What do you love to do, even for free?

What do you want to change about your life?

What brings you joy and happiness?

Do you honestly feel you are fulfilling your potential here in this lifetime?

Are you using your true talents and gifts in this lifetime?

exercise. *life assignment stuff.*

This exercise is about checking in to see if the stuff you now have is in alignment with your life assignment, purpose and destiny. Journal regarding the following questions:

Is the stuff you have in your life right now helping you to be and do what you really want to be and do?

Is the stuff in your life serving your hopes and dreams?

Is the stuff in your life contributing to your happiness and joy?

Do you have stuff that you really don't need anymore, because it was connected to another passion or career that is no longer your career or passion anymore? If so, let it go. Create space for your new dream, new job, new career, and new passion to be born.

TRUTH.
LOVE.
MEANING.
PURPOSE.

foundation for you & your life. *feeling grounded.*

What are you standing on?
Do you feel grounded?
Do you feel centered?
Do you feel unshakable?
Do you know who you really are?
If not, you need to find the foundation for you and your life.

TruthLoveMeaningPurpose.

What if I told you that these four words—TruthLoveMeaningPurpose—can help you solve any problem and can bring magic and miracles into your life? What if I told you that these four words can be applied to anything and everything in life? What if I told you that these four words put together comprise your own personal formula for success, and will help you to make better decisions and choices with your stuff, big and small?

Yes, yes, yes! Believe it. I have seen it time and time again. When I ask my clients to remember these powerful tenets, they come back to me and tell me these words simplified their life. I myself have come back to these four words many times to remind me of what is truly important.

The combination of these four powerful words can liberate you and help you lead a more authentic life by simplifying all your choices and distilling them into a life that reflects who you truly are. The following kinds of questions can help you confront the truth of who you are now, and then dig deeper into your heart and mind for what you stand for and who you were born to be.

truth.

Is it truthfully me today? What is the truth of this space now? What is the truth of this situation now? What is the truth of this stuff now? What is the truth of my life now?

love.

Do I absolutely love it now? Do I love it with all my heart now? Do I love my life? Do I love myself?

meaning.

Does it have meaning for me (not somebody else)? Does it have meaning for me right now, or did it have meaning for me in the past? Does my life have meaning?

purpose.

Does it still serve a purpose in my life? Is it serving a purpose here and now? Where does it serve a purpose? What purpose does it serve? Does it serve a purpose for me, or for somebody else? Do I live on purpose? What is my life purpose?

We activate miracles and magic once we start honoring our TruthLoveMeaningPurpose, because we start easily and effortlessly attracting what our heart truly desires.

Let's reconcile the materialism of life and the spirit of life!

I believe your entire life should be filled with meaningful stuff you love, and that bringing order to that meaningful stuff that is truthfully you is an act of love. I would love for you to love the stuff of your life and to therefore fully love your life.

The stuff of your life includes the relics, reminders, and records of your life, connecting you to your memories. It should truthfully express your soul and spirit. It should freely transmit your love, both to others and yourself. Its purpose should be to make our lives easier. It should be meaningful to you. In short, it should be filled with . . .

TruthLoveMeaningPurpose.

Keep repeating these words.

Let these words sink into your consciousness.

These four words are the keys and magical miracle elixir to dealing with your stuff on all levels.

You can create whatever life you desire and whatever stuff you want in life if you figure out the *truth* of who you are and make sure the stuff in your life truthfully reflects who you are now, if you truly *love* your stuff, if your stuff has *meaning*, and if it serves a *purpose* for you.

TruthLoveMeaningPurpose.

．

exercise. *discover your unique metric: TruthLoveMeaningPurpose.*

Let's start exercising your TruthLoveMeaningPurpose muscles.

Without thinking too much, write down a few truths about who you are. Start with "Truthfully . . . " (Truthfully, I love crying and feeling deeply. Truthfully, I love almonds! Truthfully, I love kissing! Truthfully, I love people!)

Name some truths about your situation. (Truthfully, I am not the same person I was years ago. Truthfully, I am living with my boyfriend. Truthfully, two people are living in this one-bedroom apartment, and I must let go of more stuff to create space for his stuff.)

Name some truths about your stuff. (Truthfully, I don't like half my stuff. Truthfully, I feel my stuff is dead. Truthfully, I haven't touched those purses in years.)

Name some truths about your space. (Truthfully, my space feels too small for me. Truthfully, I have too much stuff for this space.)

What do you love, love, love? (I love anything furry. I love cycling! I love the color blue.)

What is meaningful to you? (Watching a sunset with my lover, greeting cards painted by my nieces, photos of my family.)

What are some things in your life that serve a purpose? (Pens, shredder, Tupperware, my laptop computer.)

What purpose do you serve in life? (Father, supporter, attorney, listener, friend, healer.)

What is your life's purpose? (To inspire people to feel deeply about their own lives in order to move people forward.)

the one rule. *be your authentic self.*

S o your TruthLoveMeaningPurpose is your foundation. Your solid ground. Your criteria by which you can evaluate everything in your life, including your stuff, your spaces, your relationships, the events you attend, and how you spend your time.

Use it to decide: *Should I let go or keep it?*

Use it to decide: *Shall I attend this event, or not?*

Use it to decide: *What is my next step?*

Use it to decide: *What should my career be?*

Use it to decide: *What should my life's work be?*

Use it to decide: *What clothes should I wear?*

Use it to decide: *How should I be? What should I do? What should I say?*

So how do you get to the point where you are using TruthLoveMeaningPurpose as your sole foundation and criteria?

You must first declutter the shoulds.

Oftentimes people want to be told exactly what to do to take action.

But seriously, can anyone else tell you what is in alignment with your TruthLoveMeaningPurpose?

Has anyone else lived in your body, been raised in the environment you have, and experienced the experiences you have?

I need to say this again, very clearly. This process is not about *how to* get organized. I am not going to tell you exactly what to do with every item in your life. I can't! But you can. The *how* is easy once you figure out who you truly are and what's important to you. You will naturally keep what is truly you and let the rest go!

This process is about how to get in touch with who you are, what you love, and what is truthfully you, so that you can be supremely confident that you can make the right decisions, for you, in every moment—with or without me or anyone else. The decisions that you make yourself will make you feel the happiest and allow you to say, "I LOVE MYSELF! I LOVE MY LIFE! I LOVE MY WORK! I LOVE MY PARTNER! I LOVE MY FAMILY! I LOVE MY HOME! I LOVE WHERE I AM GOING! I AM EXCITED ABOUT TODAY AND EVERY DAY!"

Can you truthfully say that in this moment?

If you cannot, that's okay.

After all, the journey of life is all about discovering who you truly are and who you were born to be. Living as the person you truly are is actually the easiest thing for you to do—when you clear your life of the clutter of others' belief systems, attitudes, and thoughts that have gotten in the way of seeing the naked truth of who you are.

They say, "Do this, do that. Act this way, be this way."

They include the rules of doing business, the rules of being on a job interview, the rules of conversation, the rules of eating, the rules of dating, and the rules of being in a relationship.

Even the rules of organizing.

The only rule you need to follow is to *be yourself*—your authentic self.

So first declutter yourself of all the rules. Release yourself from all the shoulds. Once you do, you will more easily discover your TruthLoveMeaningPurpose. You will be free to be who you truly are, have those things that honor you and your truth, and live a life where you can authentically say, "I love my life and everything about it."

You will stop worrying about what everyone else is doing or wearing compared to you. You will stop living the life others want you to live or the life you think you *should* live. You will simply check in with yourself every moment of the day and ask, "Is this where I want to be? Is this what I want to eat? Is this what I want to wear?"

The answers will come more rapidly to you.

You will just know.

Soon you won't even have to run through the checklist of TruthLoveMeaningPurpose.

In an instant, your body will speak to you.

Your gut will speak to you.

Your heart will speak to you.
You will feel no sliver of doubt.
No sliver of worry.
No sliver of wondering, *Is this right?*

You'll just know inside.

.

exercise. *get in touch with the voice within.*

Write about an experience when your mind and heart were speaking to you and you went against what you believed to be true. Why did you not listen to your heart and mind? Did you listen to somebody else and follow their advice? What happened?

Now write about an experience when you chose not to listen to somebody else's advice, you followed your heart and mind, and you experienced a positive outcome. Write down how it felt to take that action. Was it scary? Did you feel liberated listening to your inner voice?

This exercise is intended to help you get in touch with that still, small voice within you. To cultivate your intuition. To get you grounded in your TruthLoveMeaningPurpose. Only by doing so over and over and over will you become comfortable saying *Yes* or *No* based on your own inner compass. Only by exercising your TruthLoveMeaningPurpose muscles will you be able to immediately discern what to do without having to run down the list of questions. You will simply know. You will no longer need to explain, defend, or justify. You will be living and breathing your TruthLoveMeaningPurpose.

TRUTH.

truth. *the truth goes deep.*

What is the truth of who you are? What is the truth of your situation? What is the truth of your space? What is the truth of your finances? What is the truth of your relationships? What is the truth of your body? What is the truth of your work situation? What is the truth of your passions? What is the truth of your loves? What is the truth of your life?

The truth reveals itself as you dig deeper. In fact, the deeper you dig, the more truth will be revealed—if you are willing to courageously face it.

Oftentimes, however, you may stay on the surface because you're afraid to know what truth may be unveiled. I believe that your body-mind-spirit-heart knows the truth if you ask it, and if you truthfully want that answer to be revealed. So stay open to the truth as you go deeper and deeper, to mine the "real truth" behind your clutter.

You may be surprised at the truth that comes up. It may catch you off guard and not be what you thought it was going to be, and you might dismiss it as a fanciful thought. Instead, trust what comes up and explore it deeply, continuing to ask the question, "What is the truth behind this stuff?"

Do you have stuff in your life leftover from past passions and hobbies? Did you used to love playing the clarinet or trumpet, but now the truth is that it's just collecting dust in your closet? Do you have workout equipment you purchased one night while watching QVC, when you had great intentions of starting a new workout regimen, but now the truth is that it's being used as a giant clothes hanger in your bedroom?

Confront the truth about your stuff just by touching one item and asking what the truth is about this item, as deeply as you can, and you'll arrive at the truth of whether you should keep or let go of the item in question.

Okay, I'll start. I'll share a truth with you and show you how multi-layered the truth can be if you take the time to dig deep.

The truth is that I don't practice my piano every day, because when I play now, it makes me feel like I'm not very good at all, and I want to be able to play as well as I did when I was a child. The truth is that I took piano lessons from age five to seventeen, and I think I used to be very, very good.

The truth is that hitting all the wrong notes makes me confront my truth of the past, which is "I used to be very good," and makes me wish I was back there. It also makes me confront the truth of the present, which is that if I want to be good again, I must practice a lot, like I did when I was a kid. The truth is that I really didn't play piano from college until now, so what did I truly expect—that my skills would remain intact? Wishful thinking, June.

I set the goal last year of playing every day, but that never happened; I only played every few weeks. I was more realistic with myself this year and set the goal of playing once a week, and I am actually practicing for at least a half an hour every week, and that's progress. Geez, June, don't be so hard on yourself. The truth is that considering all things, I can still read music, and play spontaneously, but I would love, love, love to play Beethoven's Opus 22 again, which was the concert piece I played at my last recital when I graduated from high school. I would love to take lessons again, as humbling as that may be.

The truth is that I still love the piano, and I am willing to practice once per week—and if this practice continues, then I would love to keep the piano! If, however, after one year I am not progressing and am still not practicing more, then it might be time to re-evaluate the truth of this piano, and ascertain whether it is truly still my passion, or I am just reliving my past glory and wanting to recapture that feeling again. Is that healthy for me? For now, I am keeping the piano. It brings me joy right now playing when I do—if I let go of my ego and am at one with where I am. Where I am is perfect. I shouldn't compare myself to the June in the past. Honor the truth of the June of today who is relearning anew.

What about my clothes? Wow, this is a big one! I look into my closet—jammed, crammed, and bulging over with stuff—and yet I find myself saying, "I don't have anything to wear!" Let's look at the stuff—one thing at a time—and decide if each item is truly serving my highest good!

Looking at the suit section of my closet, I know I haven't touched some of this stuff in a while. The truth is that I no longer wear suits that are more conservative, and the truth is that I love unconventional business attire. The truth is that I only have one small closet,

I don't have space to house these old suits I no longer wear, and I only wear one dark suit to important business meetings. The truth is that I bought that suit with my mother, who thought it made me look so professional and corporate, but now it makes me feel matronly when I wear it. The truth is that I purchased it because I had this image in my mind of what I wanted to project at that time, but my image and idea of myself has shifted, and that image is no longer truthful for me. The truth is that I must invest now in a new suit for my speaking engagements that represents the new, true me and that also fits the new body that I have.

What about the jeans? Wow, I have soooo many jeans—do I really wear all of these jeans, or do I just wear my favorites that make my butt look good? Or the jeans that don't cut into my waist and make me feel fat? Or the jeans that I get the most compliments for every time I wear them? Or do I wear the jeans that are just the most comfortable? Okay, I'll share some truths with you that come up when dealing with my jeans . . .

The truth is that I no longer fit into these Seven jeans with the rhinestones, which were the most expensive jeans I ever purchased. I bought these special jeans when I was compulsively training seven days a week. The truth is that my body has transformed and I am no longer a size 24. The truth is that I was focusing on the front part of my body and building only the muscles that I could see in the mirror from the front—my stomach, arms, quadriceps—and I was neglecting my back side. The truth is that my personal trainer made me aware that I spent nearly two years building up my neglected parts, such as my hamstrings, glutes, and lats, and they have radically changed the silhouette and shape of my body, and I will *never* be able to fit into my size 24 jeans that were perfect for me when I had no butt and no developed legs. The truth is that I sucked the life force out of these jeans I once coveted, and now they've become stale. Now when I wear them, the waist is too snug and makes me feel fat—like my legs are being squeezed like sausages. Okay, they really are not flattering for my body.

The truth is that when I bought them, I spent the most I have ever spent on a pair of jeans, and that's why I kept on thinking I would lose weight or body fat to get into the jeans. The truth is that I have been working out faithfully, and I never want to go back to having a flat butt and imbalanced body shape. I must honor this new body that I am learning to love, which is more balanced, more full, and more complete, so I can use the biggest muscles of my body rather than relying on the smallest muscles. What a metaphor for my life. Use all of what I have been given, and don't use the smallest parts to drive my life. The back part that I cannot see is just as important as what I can see. I want to look great coming and going.

.

Just looking at and touching those clothes triggered an entire set of memories. It always amazes me how powerful even one item can be, flooding my memory bank with stories from the past and the times I wore those particular clothes—wow!

This stuff can be insidious. It wants to be loved, and it wants to remind you of how much you used to love it before you just toss it. It wants to be honored, not just thrown away. So go on the ride your stuff wants to take you on, like I did above. I call it fearless meandering! Rehash the stories, relive the memories, take away the lessons, and then, once you have confronted the truth of the feelings the stuff brings up, you can let all of the stuff—inside and out—go consciously, so it won't keep coming up again in your future experiences.

Why would you want to hold on to that stuff, and let those voices go on and on inside of you every time you see a glimpse of it? Why don't you today, once and for all, deal with the stuff in front of you that is screaming out for your attention? Pay proper respect to this stuff that you loved, respected, and cared for. Be a big girl or boy, stand up to your stuff, and let it go with pride and courage! True pride is not ego, but honoring your authentic self, following through on the truth that you know deep inside but may have been hiding from you in the past. Fill yourself with this authentic pride: confront that truth, shout this truth proudly to the world, and follow through with this truth in the form of action. Let go of that item here and now, and *then* tell me how you feel!

Create a ceremony where you thank the item for the purpose it served in your life at the time. Thank you, Glamorous Rhinestone Jeans, for making me feel like a million bucks. Thank you for teaching me that I can feel glamorous and sparkly, and that I can sparkle on the inside without the sparkles and glamour on the outside! Thank you, Stuffy Corporate Suit, for helping me to be more professional when I didn't feel very professional on the inside, and thank you for teaching me that I can still act professional without a traditional corporate suit, and that I can bring my professionalism with me while wearing a suit that is now more me!

I'm telling you, this stuff goes deep—if you choose to go on the ride, and if you don't stop yourself. Go on the ride! I'm not telling you to dart in and out of your closet in confusion, to-and-fro like a crazy person, but if you set a clear intention at the beginning of each session about wanting to release that which is no longer truthful to who you are today, you may be pleasantly surprised at what confronts you. If you stay in your heart, which is connected to the Higher Power, and follow it (rather than your head, which thinks it knows what to do but whose knowledge is only based on the past), your heart will never, ever lead you astray.

Here's a perfect example of how touching the jeans led to confronting and letting go of my body stuff, which led to even more stuff.

After I put the Stuffy Corporate Suit and Glamorous Rhinestone Jeans in the Giveaway Box, I spied my workout stuff in another box. I felt it calling for my attention, screaming, "What about me? Confront the truth of me!"

In the box, I found my running shorts with the special pockets for snacks, my little mini water bottles, and the elastic belt that holds the bottles. The truth is that I no longer run marathons or do triathlons, so I can let go of all the paraphernalia I collected during those times. I can let go of my Camelback and my special running pants that also have those special pockets for my running treats. I can let go of all my triathlon books. The truth is that I loved the endorphin rush I got doing LSDs (long, slow distance), plodding along at my snail-like pace for hours, and when I see runners in my neighborhood running, I wish I was running again! I also loved carb loading before races and going to breakfast after training, feeling deserving of whatever I ate!

Wow, it feels like an entire lifetime ago—it *was* a lifestyle, a way of life for me! This is huge! That's probably why I hung on to this stuff for so long, thinking maybe I would run again. But the truth is that my body is not made for running because of the numerous injuries I received every time I trained for a new marathon: my IT band, shin splints, hip flexors, and now my Achilles tendon! The truth is that now I have learned to run differently; I've learned that sprinting a few times for a short duration is better for me and my body than running for long distances for longer periods of time. The truth is that I made very special friends during my training runs, and I do miss them. The truth is that I have a lot of time now to read and write, and I enjoy working out and doing new activities that are better for my body long term. The truth is that now I'm enjoying new activities with my significant other, filling up the five to eight hours on Saturdays I used to dedicate to running. Whew! Let go of the long-distance running paraphernalia; throw it into the Giveaway Box, and don't look back. This is the healthiest act you can do for yourself, June!

Is there anything you can think of related to your health, body, or fitness that is a truth you must confront?

Did you ever have surgery, come home from the hospital, recover, and then never bothered to sort through all the stuff the hospital gave to you—and you're still holding on to it? Are you no longer in pain, but you're still holding on to the pain pills, thinking, "Just in case the pain comes back . . . " Or, if you have an ailment or disease, and you have researched all the possible cures and ailments, are you holding on to a lot of remedies and research articles? Are you truthfully going to follow through and take these pills and vitamins, and do the exercises? Are you truthfully going to call that number someone gave you or research that program on the Internet? Or are you already on a path of healing that you believe will lead you to excellent health, and you're holding on to this other stuff just in case it doesn't work out?

What are you telling your subconscious by holding on to this stuff? On one hand, you are doing what you feel is physically best for your body. On the other hand, a part of you doubts that this way is the best. You are conflicted. A part of you believes. A part of you doesn't.

Do you see what this ambivalence and lack of commitment with your stuff and your truth is costing you?

Why not let go of this stuff related to your past of being sick, injured, and in pain, and free up space for full and complete healing? Why not let go of the thought that your sickness or injury may one day return, and free up space for faith that it will never return again?

Truthfully, the health stuff that we have in our possession triggers feelings about our health. So confront the health stuff. Confront your truthful feelings about your own state of health. And let your stuff and your feelings be in alignment.

The stuff you have on the outside should align with the stuff you feel inside. When you have alignment, you will no longer experience conflict inside you or in your body about whether or not to completely commit to this new path of healing you are on.

So as you are dealing with your stuff, set the intention that you will allow the truth of your stuff, and the feelings that arise from your subconscious, to activate change in your conscious mind. As your conscious thoughts change, your feelings about your stuff will also change to align with what you truly desire in your life.

In other words, you will be able to reconcile the truth of your ideal self and the truth of your actual self. Let's say your ideal self loves the notion of sewing, particularly going to the fabric store to dream of different designs and dresses you could make with those gorgeous fabrics. You even go so far as to buy patterns. But you haven't touched those fabrics or patterns in years. Why?

Is it because you are secretly and truthfully a fashion designer who hasn't made the time to sew? Are you keeping this true self a secret from others, and even yourself? Are you so overwhelmed with living your life, your kids, and your career that you wish you had just one week to work on these projects? What if you had the time to do it—truthfully, would you?

Be brutally honest with yourself. Confront the truth of your actual self compared to the truth of your ideal self. I'm all for setting goals, going for an ideal, and visualizing that ideal so it can come to pass. But if the truth is that you are not taking any action on the physical level to match the vision of your ideal self—such as sewing in whatever free moments you have—then this ideal may be part of a fantasy version of your ideal self that you are wishing for and dreaming of, but one that will never materialize.

The truth is that we are spiritual beings in physical bodies living in a physical universe, and we must at some point take action on the physical level, no matter how many feelings and thoughts we have about that desire or dream. We must confront the truth by following through with action in the physical plane.

I believe when we withhold the truth from ourselves, or fail to take action on the truth, we create disease in our bodies, lives, and relationships. When we deny the truth of something our heart desires, we are holding ourselves back from leading an authentic life, and in fact, we are saying to the Universe that we are not deserving of that desire because we believe it is too farfetched or too grand for us to achieve.

On the other hand, perhaps your ideal isn't the truth about who you really are. If you keep putting "sewing" on your task list, but whenever you think of sewing, you instead start reading fashion magazines or go shopping or do anything else but actually sew, perhaps the truth is that you are leading yourself on and lying to yourself. If so, it is time to let go.

Or perhaps your ideal contains part of the truth. Perhaps you truly love conceiving of clothing designs, but the actual physical act of sewing and putting it all together does not thrill you or bring you joy. Then the truth is that you are not a seamstress but a fashion designer. If you come to this realization, then let go of the notions, ribbons, needles, and patterns, and give them to someone who truthfully enjoys sewing. Or, instead of letting them go, give your designs to a passionate seamstress to make those designs a reality for you.

You try it now. Think of one item that you have thought about letting go but can't decide what to do, and just start writing "The truth is . . . " and see what comes up for you. Start writing and be ruthless with yourself.

This initial list of truths will help you begin questioning what is true and what is not, and what is real and what is not. No one else needs to know the truth except you, but at the same time, only you know what truth is deep inside of you.

As you look at this list of truths, ask yourself, *Who taught me that "truth?" Who told me that was "the way it has always been done?" When did I buy into this belief system as a part of my "truth?"*

Why not start confronting your truth today? Just start by confessing your truth to yourself first. Simply acknowledge that you have accepted certain belief systems as "truth," but you can now change your idea about this belief, and thereby change the course of your life.

Then, slowly, perhaps you will gain the confidence to speak the truth out loud to yourself first, then to your loved ones, and then, perhaps, you will shout the truth out loud to the world at large. You will not care if anyone knows what your truth is, because the truth is you feel on top of the world living your truth, and that is the only thing that matters.

You can express your truth out loud to anyone who wants to hear it, as I am to you—no holds barred—because you will feel that the truth will liberate you, that the truth will be the key to receiving all that your heart desires, and you will finally believe that God/Universe brought you on to this earth to live your truth, be your truth, and speak your truth, and that your truth is what makes you special.

■

exercise. *become best friends with your truths.*

The truth goes deep. If you haven't yet done the exercise I described above, do it now. Pick one item that comes to your heart. Allow yourself to feel and write down everything that comes to your mind and heart. Be ruthless with yourself, and do not censor yourself. Remember, you are the only witness to this process and can keep it to yourself, so don't be afraid to fully and fearlessly express your truth.

Write down the truth about it, and if it is difficult to let go of it, write down the truth regarding that difficulty. Write down the truth of why you have been holding on to the item. Write down the truth of why you kept it. Write down all the reasons that come up. Write down all your emotions. Exhaust every possible angle and spin on this item you have picked. Get it all out there so you can examine it, feel it, dissect it!

Start writing like I did above and see what comes up.

The truth is . . .

align truth. *create balance.*

When you fully align the truth on the inside and the outside, you create balance. Now that you've discovered the truth about one item, aligning the truth of who you are and the truth of your stuff will become easier and easier.

As you look at the items around you, ask yourself, *What is the truth about who I am? What is the truth about my stuff? Are they in alignment?*

The truth is that I am not a "handywoman," and I must let go of the cute "handywoman toolbox" that I received as a gift. The truth is that I have never, ever used it, and always call in a handyman to take care of even the smallest tasks in the house.

It's that simple to ask these questions—the right questions—to arrive at an answer that will honor the truth so you can be set free.

What is the truth about how much you have? What is the truth about how much space you have? Are they in alignment?

The truth is that everything I still have used to fit beautifully into a 3,500-square-foot home, and now I am residing in a 1,500-square-foot apartment. That stuff was aligned perfectly with the truth about my space in the past, in that spacious home, but not now.

What is the truth about your past and your stuff honoring the past? Are they in alignment?

The truth of my past is that I was once building a career in television news. The stuff honoring that past still lives within me, with every experience, lesson, and insight etched into my consciousness.

The truth is that I do not need anything to remind me of my past experience.

101

I know it happened. I know I lived through it and achieved success. The stuff honoring that experience can be released now. It is now a part of my biography, chronology, and memories, and it does not need to be showcased as accomplishments on my walls or in my space. My past experiences are now just part of my life experience that I can draw upon for the present and future.

In order to create space for my new existence and being, I must let go of paying so much tribute to this past and living in the glory of this past success. If I hold on to the things of the past, then my life becomes a museum to my past.

If I am continually evaluating and letting go of the relics of the past, then my life becomes a living monument to what I am now creating: the ever-continuing, ever-evolving beauty of me in the present.

Yes, my past is part of my wondrous being and makes me who I am today, but I'm not allowing that past me to take up valuable space that needs to be freed up for something else that wants to grow.

Think of a container that can only hold so much. You must expand your vision of your life so that it can contain not just the past and what you have accomplished, but also ample breathing space for the new to be born. If you are constantly suffocating your life and stuffing your creative impulses with relics from the past, and constantly seeing that reflected in your environment, how can you see anew and gain a fresh perspective? It's as if your past events are fogging up your lens peering out into the world. When you are able to wipe the lens clean and peer out into the world, with a view unobstructed by the stuff of the past, you might see something new and then shift your perspective about your life, your life's work, and your relationships.

Thus, always remember the following intentions when letting go:

> *I am now letting go of [whatever stuff you are letting go of and the mental/emotional/spiritual layers attached to it] to create space for [whatever your heart desires].*
> *I am now paying tribute to the present and wonderful life I have and am creating.*
> *I am now paying respects to my divine future that Universe has in store for me by not holding on to relics from my past and allowing that to take up valuable space in my physical environment or in my mind-body-spirit-heart-consciousness.*
> *I am now creating valuable space for this new part of me that wishes to be born.*

Now, what is the truth about your desires, your heart, your mind, and your consciousness? What is the truth about your stuff? Are they in alignment?

My desire is to be healthy, fit, and energetic. My heart feels good and happy when it knows my system is flowing. My mind is clear when I am acting in accordance with what I desire and what I feel in my heart. My consciousness knows that when I am clear in my body and spirit, with all channels flowing and no clogged arteries or pathways, God is able to talk to me, and I am able to listen and hear the messages. The food I give my body is now in alignment with those desires, with my heart and mind, and with my consciousness. Everything is moving in the right direction. There is nothing sabotaging the successful achievement of that goal.

Years ago, I went on a mission to better align/balance my health. I visited Western, Chinese, and Ayurvedic doctors to find out the truth of my body. After administering tests, they gave me two lists: my food allergies, where I might have a strong reaction like breaking out in hives and/or not being able to breathe; and food intolerances, where my symptoms might be not as severe, like headache or bloating, but eating them might not be for my highest good. When I saw cheese was on my intolerance list, I decided to give it up.

Just recently, I thought I had finally found the perfect solution: goat cheese! But it didn't take long for my body and mind to start clearly telling me that goat cheese wasn't healthy for me, either. Whenever I ate goat cheese, as good as it tasted in the moment, my body would get bloated, and my mind would also tell me that it wasn't good for me. However, my heart still craved it, because I had so wanted to find a perfect solution for eating cheese. But when I fully understood the consequences, that it would make me feel crummy for the rest of the day, I let it go willingly.

If my goal is supreme health, then I don't want to waste a moment acting against my intended goal of supreme health. I am committed to eliminating anything that sabotages that goal, and I am committed to adding anything into my life that aligns with that truth of desiring supreme health. Don't confuse your consciousness with mixed messages. Don't say you want supreme health, and then take action that goes against that vision.

Here's another example: If you own a car, the experts recommend getting your tires rotated and aligned every 5,000 miles or so to make sure your vehicle can run smoothly. It's the same with our being, our health, and our stuff; they are the vehicles of your life, helping you to move forward (or not). You won't run smoothly and will eventually break down if you are out of alignment. You must consciously align yourself with your TruthLoveMeaningPurpose to live a life you love!

So if you want to be married someday, don't have stuff in your life that perpetuates being single. Act as if you truly believe you will be married. Buy two glasses, two plates, two utensil sets, two nightstands, two pillows—believing there will one day be two persons residing in your home, and you will be sharing your life with another.

Act as if you believe in your new business, and believe your life coach when she gives you homework to organize your office space as if you are expecting new clients. Stop complaining and pretending that it doesn't matter. Do whatever it is going to take to signal to your consciousness that your new business is growing, and your dream is coming true. Don't sabotage yourself now by acting against something you know to be true.

What is the truth about your dreams? Your goals? Your loves? Your passions? Are they all in alignment? And are you acting in alignment with them?

This journey of TruthLoveMeaningPurpose begins with questioning yourself, and getting down to the truth for every question you ask yourself. Then once you get down to the truth, you can begin ensuring all those truths are in alignment.

Only you know whether all the truths of your answers are in alignment.

Only you know whether you're acting in alignment with those truths.

·

exercise. *align with your truth compass.*

Write about the truth of your life today. Write about the truth of the stuff you have.

Write about truth in whatever way it comes up for you.

The point of this exercise is to get you in touch with your "truth compass" within. Inject yourself with "truth serum" daily just by saying out loud:

> *Let the truth come to the surface.*
> *I can handle the truth.*
> *I am willing to listen to my truth, confront my truth, and take action on my truth.*

LOVE.

love. *love makes the world go around.*

do I love this item with all my heart? Do I love it now, or did I love it in the past and think I still love it? Am I in love still? Was I in love then, but not anymore, and am afraid to let go of the love?

Activate your heart center and touch your heart right now. Your heart is the space I want to crack wide open for you during this journey. Without a connection to what you absolutely love, you will have a difficult time letting go of stuff. Everything and anything in your life may seem important. I'm not talking about what you *think* is important. I'm talking about how you *feel*. I'm talking about the stuff you have simply *because* you love it—and that's why it is important.

You can argue with me and say, "I don't love my tax records, but I still need to keep them!" I would refute that point by saying, "Why can't that be a love?" Love your tax records because they are a historical record of monies spent on stuff you bought, which hopefully you loved and enjoyed. Love your tax records because they will give you peace of mind, knowing you can access those records any time you please—and in case of an audit.

Do you get how you can shift toward love on the inside regarding the stuff in your life? All you need to do is activate your heart center, and shift your perspective to see your stuff in a different light. Even the purposeful stuff can be stuff you love.

Try to be vigilant about not bringing anything into your life that you "kinda sorta" like, and try instead only to surround yourself with what you absolutely love. Why can't everything in your life be something you absolutely love? Notice how difficult it is to make a decision based on kinda sorta, or when somebody is prodding you to hurry up and decide, or when you are pressuring yourself to choose *now*. Why not wait, even for a day or two, to allow that kinda-sorta feeling to subside? If you are accustomed to following the crowd or checking in with somebody else, your default may be kinda sorta. You may not even be aware that you continually operate from this low-grade, kinda-sorta mode: you feel kinda-sorta good about what you're doing, about the relationship you're in, or about the clothes you are wearing.

Wait until something hits you from deep inside that makes you want to jump up and down with joy—or get excited in your own special way—about what you are wearing, eating, going, and doing.

Pens. They are writing tools. You may sigh and say, "Who cares about pens? I don't care about pens!" But I can't begin to tell you how many times in my workshops—with even the most cynical, sarcastic audience—I have passed around different kinds of pens and have asked people to choose one, and *everyone* had an opinion about which pen they chose and why.

Do you get it? You do have an opinion. You do have a choice. Perhaps you think you don't, and you just pick whatever is given to you. You settle. But how deep have you really settled? Does this kind of thinking permeate other areas of your life, where you have settled because you thought it didn't really, truly matter? I'm saying to you, here and now, that it does matter.

Your choices matter. Your preferences matter. Your feelings matter. Your thoughts matter. It all matters.

Do you want a life that is full of love and infused with love? Do you want to be giddy in love with your life every single day? Do you want to love your stuff—the stuff that you use every day, the stuff in your closets, the stuff in your kitchen, the stuff in every single space of your house—so your space and life is filled and permeated with this love that is pouring out and oozing into every single part of your life?

When you have this kind of love permeating your space, you will walk outside the door every single day filled with this love! You will carry this love with you into other spaces! You will bring love to every encounter and experience—to work, to the grocery store, to every space you visit and inhabit—whether it's for a minute or hours!

Are you getting how deep this goes?

The happiness and love you feel starts first with you—inside of you. How is it activated inside of you? When you choose to have stuff that you love. Even something as innocuous or seemingly trivial as a pen makes a difference. Making a conscious decision about using that pen you love helps you to be more discerning and vigilant about other stuff in your life that you love.

Start with the small stuff in your life, such as pens. Use the fine discernment skills you are acquiring with your heart center to be supremely aware of every detail. Then apply that vigilance to other areas of your life.

I can go on and on about the kind of stuff you can use these discernment skills to evaluate. Just look at what is sitting in front of you and what you are wearing. Your underwear. Do you love it for its functionality, price, or comfort? How about the knives you use to slice and dice your foods? I know some of you have strong opinions about what the best knives are! How about baby stuff? I know many mothers are opinionated about the pacifiers, cups, and baby food containers! What about linens? Many consider themselves "thread-count connoisseurs," who only like to use 500-plus thread-count sheets for sleeping.

If you can get on a roll with the stuff you love about your life, big and small, it will get you in the spirit of love and get you into that "love space," where things that are not of love will stand out like a neon light and scream to you, "I don't belong in your life because you do not love me like the other stuff you just went on and on about!" The best way to do this is with an I LOVE list!

I'll start with my stuff so you can see how love flows.

I love my life! I love my life when I am being of service to my clients, and they feel a perceptible shift in their space or life after we have worked together! I love my life when I am in "love magic" with my significant other. I love my life when my house is in order when I arrive home. I love my life when everything flows easily and effortlessly. I love my life after I have gotten a colonic because I feel like I have let go of the old stuff. I love my life when my family is happy and healthy. I love my life when I am staying true to my heart. I love my life when I am treating my mom like the incredible mother she is—the best mother in the world. I love my life when I am not having regrets and living in the moment. I love my life when I have reconciled my past and taken the lessons from it. I love my life when I am writing, and the writing flows. I love my life when I feel there is nowhere I would rather be than here with you now. I love my life when I wake up in the morning excited to start the new day and excited about what the day will bring. I love my life when I'm seeing the miracles in every moment. I love my life when coincidences happen, because that means I'm on the right path. I love my life when I get the messages that the Universe is sending to me. I love my life when I've just had an incredibly deep, profound connection with my best friend, and we are inspired by our journeys. I love my life when I make somebody else happy. I love my life when I feel like I don't have a care in the world, even if I have a pimple on my face. I love my life when I don't have as much stuff to deal with. I love my life when my stuff fulfills me. I love my life when things are in their homes and paths so I'm not wasting valuable time looking for stuff. I love my life when I appreciate the beauty of people and appreciate my own beauty. I love my life when I follow my intuition and don't care so much what others think. I love my life!

Now, I'll do an I LOVE MY STUFF list:

I love, love, love where I live! I love, love, love the furniture I carefully selected to furnish my space! I love my furry collared clothes. I love my furry pens. I love my sparkly pens. I love my sparkly tops! I love my twenty-four pound super-duper white paper. I love organic foods! I love raw chocolate and Bulletproof ice cream! I love matcha green tea! I love my mother! I love my family! I love my iPad and its sleek red cover! I love my colorful bags that I've turned into laptop cases! I love my different makeup bags that I've turned into organizing tools! I love Ziplocs that hold my snacks! I love my P-Touch label maker! I love my comfy All Saints boots! I love my Jane Iredale makeup that covers up my rosacea! I love my Juice Beauty lip gloss! I love my Shu Uemura eyelash curler! I love my sunglass collection! I love my closet and how it's organized! I love my housekeepers! I love my Vivo Barefoot shoes! I love my cords that charge up all my tech stuff! I love technology! I love the Internet! I love Outlook! I love Whole Foods! I love money! I love my Midori journal! I love the weekend edition of the *Financial Times*! I love *Elle Décor* magazine, *InStyle* magazine, WhoWhatWear.com and NoMoreDirtyLooks.com! I love browsing through Net-A-Porter and creating fashion treasure maps! I love hats, caps, and berets!

Okay, so you get the idea. I could go on and on. The point is that your love list can include anything and everything. You don't have to say why (at first)—just get on a roll, because I want you to connect to your heart and your loves so that you can easily discern from there what is definitely not a love. Once you start doing this with everything you have, you will no longer buy sunglasses that are kinda sorta like the ones you love, or jeans that kinda sorta fit.

You will start honoring your loves, and you'll be hyper-vigilant about having stuff in your life that you absolutely *love*! You will be able to easily and effortlessly let go of the stuff you don't love, knowing that even having a little of that "loveless" feeling in your life can be contagious and infect everything else you do love.

Do you get how deep this goes?

If you have a lot of stuff, and it's all mixed up and jumbled up in a giant heap of love and love-less, your conscious mind will be confused. You will be confused every time you walk into that space with the confused stuff. The confused stuff is screaming to you that you are confused, and you'd better decide what you love and what you don't—and you just leave the room because you can't decide. That's why you feel overwhelmed when you look at that giant pile, not knowing what to do.

Remember, one thing at a time. Yes, this process may take longer than just throwing everything out, but don't you want to deal with this issue once and for all? Don't you want to learn something from the stuff you have accumulated over time so you don't make the same mistake again?

You may have thought you were saving yourself money by getting something you really didn't love because it was on sale or lower priced than the item you really, truly wanted. But really you caused yourself confusion and heartache, because you loved that other item, but decided to settle and purchase this item instead, thinking that it would suffice.

Get it?

Do you really feel settled? Did it really suffice? Do you really want to live a life of mediocrity, an "I kinda sorta like it" life?

Or do you want to live a life where you scream to the world, "I love my life!"

It's not really about the money. In addition to those who settle for what's on sale, some of you think that paying more money makes it better and more attractive. But are you buying it because it's a designer "this and that," or are you buying it because you truly love it?

So yes, yes, yes—this delving within for the truth of your heart and what you truly love, love, love can be the most challenging journey you take. But I guarantee that if you continue on this journey, you will be liberated and feel a sense of freedom you have never felt before.

For the first time in your life, you will "own" what you have, own who you are, and own your heart. You will honor your heart and the beautiful stuff in your own heart, as you love something just because it sings to you. You will love it because you think it is beautiful. You will love it because it makes you want to cry. You will love it . . . just because . . . with no need to explain it to anybody else. You will just know inside that you love it.

Whoa! I am crying as I'm thinking about how awesome you will feel when you do this!

I urge you *now* to start examining every single item in your life, and asking yourself, *Is it a true love or not?*

If it is not, have the heart and courage to let go—and let somebody else love it and honor it for the purpose it was intended. Yes, for function, but also for love.

And as you ruthlessly evaluate your stuff with the criteria of love, making conscious choices to only have stuff we absolutely love, you will see how this love spreads freely and makes your world a happier place. When you are in true love with your stuff and your life and the people in your life, your entire life is infused with love. This "love magic" transcends spaces and boundaries and spreads like wildfire, wherever you go.

Why not, then, have more of this love in your life? Why not seek out more love? Why settle? Why not only get things that are infused with love? Why not keep things that shout out love? Why not only wear stuff you love and that loves your body? What happened to the love in your life? Did you forget that love is what life is all about?

When people are at the end of their lives, no one wishes they would have worked more or acquired more stuff, or fondly remembers the stuff they possessed. Everyone wishes they could have spent more time with their loved ones, or reminisces about the good times with loved ones!

So if love is truly the most important thing in life, how did you end up forgetting to love yourself first and foremost? It sounds so cliché to say love conquers all, but it's true. It's the only nutrient, tool, weapon, system, gauge, and metric you'll ever need. When you love yourself and your TruthLoveMeaningPurpose, you can give love freely because you will be filled with love that will constantly feed you and nourish you.

Imagine a world where everybody is co-existing and living harmoniously side by side . . . where everybody is in love with their being and their own lives and their own stuff . . . where no one judges anyone else's stuff. Imagine a world where this amazing love we create in our own world connects us to other people's worlds, and we experience a mutual love that permeates the consciousness of everybody in this world in that same love space. Wouldn't you love to be a part of that vision? You can do your part by going through your stuff using the criteria of love and making a conscious effort to only have stuff you love in your life.

I can't wait for you to see what you discover about yourself. I can't wait for your heart to crack open. I think I hear your heart beating faster and faster, louder and louder. No more murmurs. I think I hear your heart singing a tune that no one can sing because it is your own song, with your own notes and own rhythm!

Claim your loves now! Seize the love! Shout out your love to the world so everybody else can feel it and know it!

.

exercise. *become intimate with your true loves.*

Write "What I love is . . . " and see what comes to mind. You may be pleasantly surprised at the stuff that you love.

Don't get overwhelmed by this process. Discovering your loves may be a lifelong journey for you. Remember, the goal is to honor and love the stuff you have now. The goal is not to hold on to every single item you loved in the past. The goal is to be aware of how much stuff you have in your life that is not filled with love, and to start keeping and buying only stuff that you absolutely love. Even if you cannot explain why you love something, you will know that you do love it.

Maybe your eyes twinkle. Your being sparkles. You smile for no reason. You feel all giddy inside. You have a pep in your step. You have a bounce in your spirit. Your heart feels soooo good and just right when you are connected to love. Love permeates your being and you don't have to explain it to anyone.

exercise. *your love muscle.*

Journal every day about what you love. As you keep adding to the list, you'll start cultivating this all-important "love muscle," so you can immediately sniff out the stuff you love and let go of the stuff you don't. It doesn't matter what you love. You may love big things or small items. Your loves can be silly, or not.

Begin to exercise your "love muscle" so that you actually start noticing the stuff, spaces, and people you love the most. And guess what—more stuff, people, and experiences you love will start becoming magnetized to you. When you start connecting to love and vibrating love, this is what all your experiences will be. Full of love, love, love! Notice your environment. Notice the people around you. Notice colors. Notice nature. Notice your home. Look in the mirror. Notice yourself.

Focus on what you absolutely love, love, love about it all. Don't leave anything out.

Keep adding to the love list every single day.

If your heart has been closed to this kind of love, this exercise may be incredibly eye-opening for you. Allow your heart to crack open a bit and let the light in. Allow yourself to peek into the truth of your love.

MEANING.

meaning. *it all means so much.*

What do you mean by that? Is it truly meaningful to you? Or is it meaningful to somebody else? What meaning are you giving that? Do you really, really mean that? How much does that mean to you? Does it still mean so much to you? What does your life mean?

Just like truth and love, the meaning of a person, place, or thing goes deep.

When we decide to keep something, we may decide that it is meaningful to us based on the role it played in our lives in the past. We often call it *memorabilia*. The memories attached to the stuff make us feel that this stuff is meaningful and important, and thus we should keep it.

The process of examining the meaning behind our stuff is also partly about looking at whether something truly holds meaning for us, or whether the stuff is actually meaningful to someone else. Oftentimes we hold on to stuff based on the meaning it had to other important people in our lives.

For instance, one of my clients had decided to hold on to the chess books of her husband, who had passed away several years ago. But really, the chess books were meaningful to him and not to her. Her husband was meaningful, and chess was a meaningful part of his life. But does she need to keep every single chess book from his collection to hold on to the memory of him and how much he meant to her? Or are her memories of him playing chess every day—along with other memories built over nearly fifty years of marriage, including annual vacations overseas—enough to hold on to how much he meant to her?

The meaning we assign to our stuff is a huge factor in our decision of why we decide to hold on to something or not. However, we can always redefine the meaning by shifting our perspective. For instance, after I explained this to my client, she decided to donate all the chess books to a local high school's chess club and just hold on to his favorite chess piece. After realizing that the stuff simply represented her deep love for him, and that her meaningful memories of him were etched in her heart forever, she was able to make peace with the other stuff she had been holding on to and let it go.

Personally, I am such a nostalgic person and feel so deeply about everything that I could literally hold on to it all. But if I kept everything from my past, I would be a jumbled mess. On one hand, I'd be full of memories from the past and full of gratitude, which wouldn't be a bad thing in and of itself, but finding meaning in every single thing would eventually weigh me down.

When I realized that certain relics from my past represented success in a certain arena, I consciously chose to let go of them. As I mentioned earlier, for years acting was my passion, and it was the only thing I lived, breathed, and thought of. Everything that I did was for the positive progression of my acting career. I kept every acting book I purchased, every journal in which I took notes from every single class I ever attended, every piece of fan mail, every accolade of how great my acting was, every call sheet and contract from every acting gig, my acceptance letter into the famed Sandy Meisner training program, and even the Kleenex he gave to me to comfort me during a vulnerable moment!

When my organizing career started taking on a life of its own, with more demands for my being and talent in this arena, I still acted, but not with as much passion as before. I finally let go of all the books and plays I collected for a few years that I hadn't touched, and I gave them away to a client who owned an acting studio so her students could enjoy them. I gave her my journals, and she said it was a godsend being able to read them and use them as a new resource and tool. I threw away the contracts and call sheets, realizing that they were symbols of my past successes. Those successes now live within me, and I do not need to hold on to those contracts to validate my roles of the past.

But at the same time, I still held on to the acting tapes of every single project I was hired for, thinking that I would one day show them to my kids, even though I had already compiled the "Best of June Acting" in my acting highlights DVD. I still held on to the acting memorabilia as reminders of who I used to be, and I think a part of me wanted to hold on to my dream of being a thriving actress—would I ever revive that career?

Then, after starring in a season of the *Home Made Simple* show on the TLC network, I found myself holding on to the paraphernalia, the accolades, and the fan mail connected to that show.

Finally, one day, while going through all my stuff, I decided to let go of all of these relics of the past, except for my one acting highlights DVD and the highlights from my season on *Home Made Simple*. I decided to let go of all of this because I had made a conscious decision to declare to the Universe that I would once again star in my own television show. I was letting go of the past and of past successes, and creating space for my dreams and the desires of my heart.

It's funny, because my assistant was present the day I did this in one fell swoop. He had wanted to break into the film industry and was unaware of my acting career and television work. While witnessing my "purging," he was amazed at my past successes. He tried to convince me to keep the stuff, asking me repeatedly if I really wanted to let go of the stuff. "Yes!" I confidently exclaimed. "I am creating space for a new starring role in television, grander, greater, and more divine than these past roles."

Less than twenty-four hours later, seemingly out of the blue (but of course, not in the spiritual universe), I received a call from Harpo Studios, Oprah's production company, asking for footage from my past television work.

The message was loud and clear: I was allowing these items representing past successes to be tentacles holding me in bondage to my past, and they were, in fact, barriers to my next steps. Subconsciously, I was holding on to these items because I wanted that success to happen again, but I obviously didn't really believe it would happen again. Holding on to the memorabilia of my past successes actually meant I was afraid I wouldn't be successful again, and the stuff would be all I had.

But when I let go of the memorabilia, I didn't let go of my dream. I didn't dishonor those experiences. I still hold those experiences within my heart, soul, and spirit, and am grateful to every single person I met and every lesson I learned. I just let go of the stuff that represented success, and the fear that I would never be successful in that arena again. And it created the space I needed for success to reenter my life!

Truth and meaning are very closely related. Confront the true meaning of something in your life, and speak the truth out loud! It feels so liberating to release the stuff that has been holding you in bondage based on your false perception of its meaning in your life. The meaning of stuff changes with time. The meaning of stuff is redefined with time based on your ever-shifting perspective on your life: who you are inside, where you are, and where you are going.

In my case, the stuff was "energetically charged current" during the years I was actively pursuing acting. But it eventually was no longer meaningful to me in that way, because my perspective had changed, and my dreams and goals had evolved.

So continue to go through your stuff and ask yourself, *Does this stuff still hold meaning for me? Did it have meaning for me at one point, which is why I kept it, but now that meaning has changed and I am ready to let go? Or does this stuff hold meaning for someone else in my life, but not me?*

See what smells and feels like it needs to be awakened or touched. Once you start touching your stuff, you will feel it calling to you, urging you to touch it and evaluate it. You will know if you are supposed to put it into a box until you are ready to deal with it. And you will know if you are supposed to fearlessly let it go because it no longer holds meaning for you in your life.

Also, remember that memorabilia is dense with emotion, because every single photo or item can trigger an entire range of feelings attached to that place, person, or time. Be gentle with yourself during this process, and allow yourself to feel the emotions that come to the surface as you examine the stuff. Allow yourself to cleanse your soul and spirit by crying, screaming, or getting pissed off. Let it all out! This emotional work is the real work with your stuff that no one else can do but you.

Do you get it?

Once you touch an item, you will know why you chose to keep it and why it exists in your life. Once you get to the source of pain or frustration or resentment or nostalgia or meaning in your life, you will be able to release it once and for all. You will think twice about collecting something or holding on to something because you now know that you will have to deal with it someday—so why not deal with it today? Perhaps you will be so discerning about something as soon as it enters your life that you will be able to let it go immediately, knowing its meaning in your life.

While in college, I wanted to study abroad in Japan. But I was seeing this boyfriend who was upset that I would be gone for the entire summer, so I nixed my desire to travel and live abroad to please him. But at that time, I didn't know that I was succumbing to his desires and living out his desires instead of my own. I had allowed somebody else to dictate to me what was important and I had not followed my heart.

Finally, when we broke up, I still held on to that brochure for the trip to Japan. To somebody else, it was just another travel brochure. To me, it was heavily loaded with meaning—it represented my promise to myself that I would never let somebody else dictate to me how I should live my life.

I finally let go of the brochure, knowing that by letting it go, I was most importantly letting go of the built-up resentment and the blaming of somebody else for a conscious choice I had made. I had to let go of the anger and take personal responsibility for my choice. And so when I chose to forgive myself and forgive him, I was able to let go of all the emotional clutter that was deeply connected to the physical stuff.

So often we hold on to stuff that has meaning we are not even aware of, until we question ourselves deeply. Why we are holding on to this stuff? Why is it difficult to let go?

Delve deep for the true meaning behind the stuff.

What about my cards from friends? I need to explore the meaning behind the cards: they remind me that I was popular then and stayed connected to so many friends. But what is their true meaning now, June? What is meaningful is that you opened up your heart to these people, they opened up their hearts to you, and the memories remain in your heart forever. Do you need the cards to remind you of the meaning of their love for you?

Or what about the custom-made diamond ring my ex-boyfriend had made for me? Do I need to keep it to remind me how special it was that somebody would take the time to make something especially for me? Would I ever receive such a unique and special gift again?

So the meaning of stuff goes deep, and that may be the reason you are stuck and have been stuck. Because you have so much stuff with so much meaning, you have kept every single meaningful item, but you have not chosen to examine that stuff *in the present moment*, to ask yourself, *Does this item still have meaning for me? Do I need to keep every item that has this meaning for me?*

I think of the only thing from my childhood that I have held on to—a hot pink furry jacket for my Barbie. Why did I choose to hold on to this and nothing else? I let go of my special stuffed animal from Japan. I let go of the light blue jumpsuit my Mom made for my Barbie. But I chose to keep the furry jacket. Do I have to know exactly why this was a huge love? I had an exact jacket like it while growing up. My Barbie and I matched. I guess it represents my mom's love for me and how much she "got" me, and the core of who I was, even when I was five. This Barbie jacket represents glamour, and I have always envisioned leading a glamorous life filled with furs and diamonds. It represents the fact that I was surrounded with glamour and sparkles even at the young age of five.

I truly hope you will liberate yourself and remove the stuff that holds you in bondage to the past. Release the stuff with bad memories. Who says you need to keep the stuff? Keep the stuff with good memories. Keep the lessons learned, and let go of the rest of the stuff.

Why hold on to anything that doesn't make you feel great? Why not assign new meaning to your stuff, and keep only the stuff that makes you feel like a million bucks? You can redefine who you are and your life story by touching your stuff and letting go of whatever is no longer a part of your new story. You can release yourself from the shackles you have put on yourself when you gave your stuff ill-defined meaning. You can create a new life for yourself and new energy in your space just by evaluating your stuff with the criteria of meaning and giving your stuff new meaning!

Touch your stuff and realize that you are holding the key to your future. You are holding the key to feeling good about you and your life, here and now.

I am excited for you! You will have a new relationship with your stuff that will lead you to a life filled with joy, happiness, and freedom. I know that the journey thus far, for some of you, has been tough, and that maybe you couldn't see your way out of this part of the path. How are you going to let go of all this stuff that holds so much meaning for you?

I did it, and that's why I know you can do it. I've been there, and I know you can do this. I have taken a long, hard look at my stuff, touched it not just once but many times, and finally had the courage to let go. And guess what? I have never looked back.

Letting go of some of this stuff means you have faith in yourself and your future. And you are creating your future by living in the present now. You are giving your life meaning in the here and now. You no longer need to live in the glory of the past, because the glory is here for you today.

So assign meaning to your life now. Love the stuff you have now and give it a new meaning. Or choose to hold on to the past meaning. Just ask yourself honestly: *How much stuff do I need that only has past meaning?*

If you truly want to remember, why not have a museum of your stuff, proudly displayed, that represents your journey and the relics from this journey? Why not spend the time to chronicle your journey, if that is why you are keeping this stuff? But to hold on to all this stuff with past meaning, combined with all the stuff that has present meaning, confuses and overwhelms you, and it will not allow you to live fully in the here and now, enjoying what you presently have.

Meaning. What do *you* mean by that? What meaning does your stuff have for you? Don't ask anybody else. Only you know inside. Only you can decide what meaning the stuff has based on the past, the present, and the future. Only you can decide what your stuff means to you based on what the lesson represented by the stuff meant to you.

Don't let the stuff give meaning to your life. You give meaning to your stuff! Let your life be defined by you. Give meaning to your life. It's your life, so choose to love everything about your life, including the meaning you give to it!

∎

exercise. *meaningful stuff.*

Start journaling about what life means to you and what your stuff means to you. Begin with the following words, thinking of the stuff you see around you right now, and see what comes up. Then keep writing.

This means so much to me because . . .

This is meaningful because . . .

What is meaningful to me is . . .

My life has meaning because . . .

Life means so much to me because . . .

PURPOSE.

purpose. *being on purpose.*

everything can potentially fulfill a purpose. Why do you have that item? Is that stuff serving a greater purpose? What does it help you to do? What is your intention for possessing that item? Going deeper . . . what purpose are *you* serving? Are you staying on purpose? Are you fulfilling your life purpose?

The purpose is what defines the item's home, or where it belongs.

Let's start with scissors. You can buy scissors at an office supply store, kitchen store, building store, arts and crafts store, or toy store. There are also different kinds of scissors. To know where to keep your scissors (or even if you should keep them at all), you must ask yourself, *What purpose do these scissors serve?* What if you have ten pairs of scissors—do you need all of them? Yes, they all *could* serve a purpose, but do you truthfully need ten to perform the same task or fulfill the same purpose? Let's say you identified at least three purposes for your scissors: arts and crafts, utility, and cooking. So you can put the pair used for arts and crafts into the Arts & Crafts home. Put the tough scissors that cut wires in the garage with the other Tools & Hardware. And put the cooking scissors into the Kitchen Utensils drawer.

How about rubber bands? Everybody seems to have them, in assorted sizes, widths, and colors. Everybody seems to have a different purpose for them. Mothers keep them to do special projects with their kids. That means rubber bands kept for that purpose should be in the Arts & Crafts home with the other Arts & Crafts tools. Dog lovers keep rubber bands to tie up the plastic bag they put the dog poop into. Then those rubber bands should be kept with the Dog Walking tools. Still others seem to keep them just in case, with a variety of reasons: "My mother told me to keep them . . . We've always had them . . . You could use them for . . . "

Do you know what's strange? I also have rubber bands in my office supply drawer, and now I'm thinking, *When is the last time I used any of those rubber bands?* But, then, as I was editing this book, the rubber bands played a cosmic joke on me, reminding me of how purposeful they are—as I found myself using rubber bands to organize my index cards of book chapters! Funny, huh?

So, even if an item could potentially serve a purpose, still examine it carefully and take the time to ask yourself, *What purpose is this item serving in my life?* If you can't think of a good purpose, let it go. Otherwise, your life will be filled with stuff with potential purpose, but no real purpose. Get it?

A life filled with stuff that is full of potential, but not being used to its full potential, is a life that is merely a theory. A concept. It means you are living in your mind. Living in an idea. Living in fantasy. Not rooted in the here and now, honoring your life purpose.

It means your life is not fully actualized.

Where else am I doing this in my life? What else do I keep for an intended purpose, but never get around to using it for that purpose? Does this represent clutter? Yes, it does, because the stuff that was created with attention, love, and care is now just sitting in a dark place, not being cared for or loved or used for its intended purpose.

My yoga mat cleaner. When was the last time I used it? Once in a blue moon, I do use that special cleaner I purchased just for that purpose. However, I more often find myself using the Method cleaner to wipe down my yoga mat. Or I use the convenient wipes I keep in my yoga bag. But the truth is that I don't use that super-duper special cleaner. I'm cringing because I know I purchased it for this particular purpose—why don't I use it? The why doesn't matter. The point is that I'm not using it for that purpose. So I will give it away to somebody who cleans their mat at home and will use it as intended.

My wok. When was the last time I stir-fried veggies in that giant wok? The truth is that I always use the ceramic pot to make my veggies. I will give away the wok to somebody who would love, love, love to use it for its intended purpose.

The cute little index cards in a ring that I found at a Japanese stationery store. It conjures up memories of school, when I created index cards to test myself with vocabulary words or Japanese characters. I had thought, *What an easy way to carry affirmations around in my car, or learn new vocabulary words! How fun would that be? And, it's all ready to go!* Well, I never actualized that plan for those index cards, and the cards sat in my Office Tools home, dying by the day, wanting to desperately breathe life into somebody else's life. So I finally gave them away to my nieces who are currently in school, and who told me, "Yes!"—they could definitely use them. I hope they're using them, and they're not sitting lifeless in a box. No matter; I will let them go and free them for the next part of their journey to serve some purpose.

My bicycle. My Gary Fisher city bicycle serves a purpose in getting me from point A to point B. But so does my car. I bike to run errands, thinking that I might be cutting down on my carbon footprint. But the truth is I love biking around the city, because it's fun and I love getting dressed up to ride my bike. The bike serves a definite purpose in my life, and it brings me joy every time I use it for its intended purpose. I last used my bicycle today to bike to a coffee shop to write. I love, love, love my lime green and ivory bike with the coolest matching basket ever, adorned with a hot pink flower and a horn that toots and declares, "I love my bike!" The bike has special meaning for me because it was a surprise gift from my boyfriend who has a matching bike in ivory. It serves a purpose if I choose to use it to get a breath of fresh air and take a leisurely ride around the neighborhood. It's a definite keeper!

Are you asking yourself about the purpose of your stuff in this way?

Everything *could* serve a purpose. You can come up with any reason you want to justify keeping something this way. But the real question is, Does it *truthfully* serve a purpose? Once again, this kind of questioning begins with the truth only you know deep inside. Only you know the truth of an item's purpose in your life. Only you know whether you will truthfully use it or not, based on love.

So that's why I always say that even those items with meaning and purpose can be "loves." And how cool would that be, if you loved everything in your life that serves a purpose from the bottom of your heart? You would love cutting with those purposeful scissors because they were so easy to use and cut so well. You would absolutely love the pens you use because they write so fluidly, they in fact help your writing flow, and you feel like a better writer writing with them. Why not have things of purpose that ring true for you? Why not have scissors that are turquoise because you love the color turquoise? Why not have pens that write fluidly and are also silver and bejeweled because you love the color silver and jewels? Why not incorporate beauty and fun into your life, which are themselves full of purpose, by having stuff of purpose that resonates with your truth, love, and meaning as well?

Why not live a life on purpose with a sense of purpose, full of purpose, purposely choosing stuff that serves a purpose but purposefully selected with love and truth in mind?

The amazing truth is that your life purpose is connected to the stuff you choose to serve you and fulfill a purpose. It is all intricately connected.

Live your life on purpose: with the stuff that is truthfully you, that you absolutely love, that is meaningful to you, and that authentically and truthfully serves a purpose!

.

exercise. *a life and world of purpose.*

Let's begin with a broad focus. Look at the stuff in your life. Start journaling about the purpose just one particular item serves. Then go on to the other items in your life. Journal about the people in your life and what purpose they serve. Journal about your home and what purpose it serves. Think about your car and what purpose it serves to you. Journal about your job and what purpose it serves to you, your company, and your family.

Lastly, journal about your life and what purpose you believe it serves to others, to yourself, and to the world at large. This exercise isn't about getting the right answers. It is all about helping you engage fully in the world of *purpose* and showing you how powerful it can be to understand the purpose of all the stuff in your life.

exercise. *a life and world of TruthLoveMeaningPurpose.*

Now let's narrow our focus. Choose one item from the exercise above that serves a purpose in your life, and journal about the following:

Truthfully, when is the last time this item served its purpose?

Do you truly love this item?

Does it have meaning?

As I said before, you can come up with a purpose for almost anything. But the purpose means something only if it is purposeful to *you*, and only you know in your heart whether you are making something up to defend that item's purpose just so you can keep it. To check yourself, think about whether this purpose is truthfully the reason why you have this item. Think about whether it is something you love, love, love! And finally, is this purpose meaningful to you?

So as you continue on this journey of self-reflection, decluttering, and vigilantly evaluating your stuff, remember your foundation of TruthLoveMeaningPurpose. When you are examining an item, a person, a thought, or a belief system in your life, use the following criteria to fearlessly examine your stuff and decide whether to hold on or let go:

Truth. What is the truth of my situation now? What is the truth of my stuff? Is it truthfully me?

Love. Do I absolutely love my stuff—not just kinda sorta like it?

Meaning. Does my stuff have meaning for me in my life here and now? Or did it have meaning in the past, or have meaning for someone else but not me?

Purpose. Is my stuff fulfilling the purpose for which it is intended, and is it helping me to fulfill my life's purpose?

PART TWO.
THE JOURNEY.

SHIFT
MINDSET.

your defining moment. *embrace it and move forward.*

Your defining moment is that moment in your life when you feel like you've hit rock bottom. Perhaps you just went shopping for flour for your Thanksgiving dinner, and now you can't find the flour in your garage or kitchen. Perhaps you forgot to pay the utility bill again—not because you didn't have money to pay for it, but you just plain forgot—and now all the lights are out. Perhaps you misplaced the keys (again), and you are now running thirty minutes late to your meeting (again). Or perhaps you just walked into your house and saw your stuff all over the place, and you became so depressed and it just kept getting worse! You're frustrated, anxious, tense, worried, and stressed. You know this can't be good for your health or your family's health, but you don't know where to begin.

Suddenly, a light bulb goes off in your mind. You have a moment of lucidity, and you scream, "Something needs to change! I don't want to live like this anymore. There must be a better way!"

What if I told you that all you need to do to start is to *take physical action?*

Can it be that simple? Yes.

You tell me, "There needs to be some radical change in my life, or I won't survive. I can't breathe."

Today, just take one action.

Tackle only one drawer, one space, one box, or one area that makes you feel crummy, that has been bugging you. Start in your underwear drawer or your toiletries drawer or your pantry. Don't worry about completing the area. Just start tackling it, one item at a time.

Trust that whatever stuff is calling for your attention right now is exactly what you are supposed to be working on, that it is exactly what you are supposed to be touching to move forward. Don't get into your head. Don't logically think it through. Trust what the Universe has brought into your life to evaluate right now. Your intuition and gut will lead you to the right stuff to declutter right this moment, as we're talking about defining moments. Don't feel that you must have a grand master plan in order to make positive progress.

Begin small—take baby steps—and practice going through a small manageable area to build your confidence before tackling a big project like an overstuffed garage or patio. In this section called The Journey, you're not going to find a logical, step-by-step, master plan to go through all your stuff in thirty days. Ultimately plans like this set you up for failure, as everybody will need to follow a different rhythm and pace to go through their stuff using the foundation and criteria of TruthLoveMeaningPurpose. Some might take a bit longer to process and give a proper eulogy to their stuff, while others might just throw everything away without dwelling on the why.

The most important thing to remember is that there is no right or wrong way to deal with your stuff. The only way is your way, honoring your TruthLoveMeaningPurpose. That is the journey. That is what I mean by fearless meandering.

See how that feels, and don't worry about anything else.

Because whether or not you are fully aware of all the internal stuff, once you start letting go of external stuff that makes you feel crummy, you will immediately feel better.

Just going through your stuff will make a tremendous difference. You don't have to go anywhere to analyze it or talk about it. You'll just feel a difference.

Time and time again, I've seen it! Moving stuff around and out of your life will move you forward in some way.

Yes, I am the kind of person who will always seek out the deeper meaning behind why we have all this stuff, and why is it hard to let go of that stuff, and I love the journey of delving within for the truth behind the stuff.

But the truth is that you don't have to psychoanalyze anything right now. You don't even have to talk about it if you don't want to. You will still immediately feel a shift in your consciousness, mind, and heart.

Touching your stuff, moving it around, and hopefully moving it out is the best therapy I know of—and I hope you become addicted to it!

Interestingly enough, your stuff will start talking to *you!* By going through the stuff which has significance and meaning, you'll begin to see where you're blocked because that stuff will be a stubborn source of inertia, and then one day you'll know that's exactly where you need to begin to get over the inertia, the sluggishness! Trust me. You will feel clearer in your living space, office, and life so you can actually feel where there is positive life force emanating, and where there is stagnant dead energy.

C'mon, just begin now. Touch that ratty underwear and let it go!

.

exercise. *stuck energy, spaces, and stuff.*

Without thinking, what is the first thing that comes to mind when I ask you: Where in your life do you feel stuck? (Don't judge the answer that comes through. It doesn't have to make logical sense.)

In the same way, answer these questions in your journal: What area of your home is stuck? Do the two correlate? Are the two connected?

It's okay if the answer doesn't come to you right away, or if you don't see the connection. Ultimately I believe the two stuck places are connected, and that if you were to move forward and do something differently in one area, you would be freeing up stuck energy in the other.

Embrace where you are stuck. Acknowledge the stuckness. Express your anger and frustration out loud! Let it all out! Declutter the emotions attached to the stuff.

Now, take action in that stuck area in your home you identified above. Begin by touching just one item, evaluating it, and deciding whether to keep it or let it go. Continue going through the area until you touch something to let go of. Repeat this process until you have let go of five items.

Congratulations! You finally took action on the stuck energy and stuff. Vow that you are moving forward, trusting that this defining moment—here and now, where you unglued and dismantled the stuck energy—is the starting point for new beginnings.

With this baby step, seemingly so small and insignificant, you are finally doing something differently, and this is a huge step in the right direction! Just touching and letting go of five items in this stuck area will unleash a power within that space. It may be subtle, but notice the shift in you and your space as a result of this simple action.

courage. *it takes courage to begin, be vulnerable, face your stuff.*

i t takes courage to begin the journey.

It takes courage to be vulnerable. To admit you are wrong. To admit that you don't have all the answers. To admit that you cannot do this all by yourself. To admit that you need help.

I know you are smart, but for some reason, you are stuck. Or perhaps what you have been doing all these years is no longer working. Or perhaps something inside of you thinks there is a better way, a faster way, of getting through your stuff.

Change and transformation requires courage. It takes a leap of faith.

Thank you for having the courage to be on this journey, for delving deeper inside yourself for the answers that lie within.

As you are reading this book, this journey is going to bring up stuff you didn't even know was there and don't really want to deal with, and you are likely to get stuck. When that happens, ask for help. When you feel you are lacking courage and want to crawl up into a ball, ask for help.

Help is everywhere! Help will appear. Help is here.

Just keep reading and know that by simply admitting you need help, something is shifting within. In that admission, you are calling out to the Universe for help, and don't worry— the Universe will conspire to bring you help.

Don't resist the help, though, when it comes along.

Continue confessing that you are open to a new way of doing and being, and that you are ready for change. And see what feelings and thoughts come up. See what events, people, emotions, and feelings show up in your life.

The great thing about this process is that even when you feel stuck, you can continue working through your physical stuff, with the conscious intention of getting unstuck and changing for the highest good. Inevitably something inside will shift, and you will feel something open up inside of you that will shift you for good. Trust the process you are on for now. Trust that by touching what you are touching and paying attention to what is before you, you are moving your life forward.

Courage is taking action in the face of fear. Acknowledge the fear, and say out loud, "I don't know why I am afraid, but this next step feels right and good, and I will continue moving forward with what my attention is being drawn to . . ."

For me, when I looked at all the boxes in storage from the time I spent with my ex-husband, it was daunting. I did what I could do on my first pass. Then I attempted a second pass one year later when I was ready to deal with it again. I made several passes at the stuff over the course of two years, and did not deal with it or let go of all of it in one fell swoop. The wedding dress. The wedding memory book. The wedding cards from family and friends. The photos of our twenty years together. What do I do with it all?

I decided to give the wedding dress to my housekeeper's sister in Brazil, whose number-one dream is to be married. A wedding dress in her life will be a tangible symbol that represents her active faith that one day soon, her dream of being a bride and being married will come true. That dress to me contains immense gratitude that my mother and father spent lots of money on not only the dress of my dreams, but also the wedding of my dreams and my hopes for a lifelong marriage. But now that the marriage is over, and that dream of being married forever to that person is no longer a truth, it seems unfair to punish the dress, leaving it lifelessly sitting in my Memorabilia Box. The truth is that it served a wonderful purpose, and I fully sucked the life force out of the dress on my wedding day. Now it's time for somebody else to inject it with their own life force, hopes, and dreams.

Even if you go through a little bit of your stuff and let go of just one thing today, pat yourself on the back and congratulate yourself for having the courage to move forward and deal with the stuff in the best way you can. Even evaluating and letting go of a few items is progress. Don't start judging the process now. Begin your journey now.

Courage is taking one step at a time. Courage is facing what's right in front of you, and doing what you can do today based on your current energy and resources. Courage is telling yourself that you are important and the stuff you are dealing with is important.

Today, do only one thing: touch one item, let go of one item, evaluate one item in your mind and heart. And know you have been courageous in dealing with your stuff, one item at a time.

·

exercise. *confront the hardest item first. let go with courage.*

Today, think of one item you have been meaning to let go of but never had the courage to, and touch it.

Touch that one item, and let this item affect your entire being. Let the item bring memories and thoughts to your mind, and emotions to your heart.

Say thank you to this item for the purpose it served. Say thank you for the love it gave to you. Say thank you for the meaning it had in your life. Say thank you, and goodbye. Today let go. Take it all the way outside the house and into your car. Drive it to your local charity store. Don't think about it too much. You know what this item is.

Then physically pat yourself on the shoulder, and say out loud,

> *I am so proud of myself for taking this one step.*
> *I am so proud of myself for letting go of this one item.*
> *I am moving forward today with courage, love, and light.*
> *Every day it is getting easier and easier to let go of more and more items that are not in alignment with the truth of who I am.*

embrace change. *change is the only constant.*

t his journey with your stuff is all about change.

It's about changing the way you see your stuff and your life. Changing the way you see people and relationships. Changing your ways. Changing your habits. Changing your stuff. Changing not for the sake of changing, but changing for the highest good. Changing because it feels better. Changing because it will better serve you. And, of course, letting go of what is no longer serving you anymore.

Change one thing. Change your life.

If what you are doing is working for you, continue doing it, and don't fix it unless it's broken.

But if you are looking for another way, then stay open to an "answer" that may be better than whatever you're doing. Obviously you have made it to this point in the book because you think there may be a better way to do what you're doing, and you want to take your life to the next level. Perhaps you think I have an answer for you.

What should you change? Should you do this, or do that?

The change I'm talking about is not necessarily a giant, monumental change—although that of course can radically shift your life, too.

More often I have seen that *baby steps make the difference*. When you start doing more of the little things you realize are important, and doing more little things differently, that's what changes your life.

When I was little, I would spend money immediately upon receiving it. When I got gift cards, I would immediately use them. In my family, I was known as the spender, not the saver. "With June, money runs through her fingers." I listened to that mantra, and without even being aware of how destructive it could be to myself and my mastery of finances, I took on that belief that I was not a very good manager of my finances.

Through the years, I have committed to changing that mindset, and I confess to myself that "I am a sound steward of my monies." The changes have happened with every little baby step.

When I was audited by the IRS in my first year of being an actress, I was shocked! I had spent more money on my education and marketing than I had earned in income, so how could this possibly be? But rather than playing the victim, I looked at this experience as a blessing from God, so I could become a better steward of monies before I started making a lot of money. Fortunately I learned then from my mother, a bookkeeper, and my brother, a CPA, to keep every single receipt, no matter how small the expenditure. I learned that every penny I spend does count and adds up when you are writing off your expenses. I learned how to use Quicken to keep track of every single expenditure. What an incredible experience! Since then, I have set up financial systems for clients, helping them know exactly where they are with their finances, preparing them for audits, and reassuring them that there is nothing to fear. So empowering!

The truth is that I've been in and out of debt . . . paid stuff off . . . incurred some more debt . . . and finally thought, *Wow, something must change!* What baby step can I take to do this? I created charts that documented the interest rates, from highest to lowest, with running totals of my debts. That was enlightening. Seeing the numbers staring at me every week was a wake-up call, and a call for change. Then, paying off the bare minimum each month, I got a credit card where I was forced to pay everything off every month. Now there was no turning back. There were no ifs, ands, or buts. There was no more incurring debt. I was forced to look at every expenditure to see if I was spending my money on *truthful* needs and desires. I started downloading my expenses electronically every single month to get a grasp of my financial picture, which was also very eye-opening and empowering.

The truth is that I have always believed that money would flow in no matter what. When I got divorced, I was petrified, thinking, *How am I going to support myself?*—even though I was making a decent income. I was missing that safety net of knowing that if something should happen, we could fall back on each other and support each other. Without that safety net or support system, I was forced to believe that I could do this. Rather than buying into the fear, I decided to change my mindset and confessed every day,

> *I am a powerful creator, passionate about my business, and infinite riches are pouring into my life every single day.*

And guess what? I made more money than I ever had. I nearly doubled my income, trusting in myself and my ability to generate revenues, believing that I was a powerful creator and that I was unstoppable.

So change begins with a shift of perspective. In order to change the reality of my finances, first I had to shift my perspective about my finances. My reality didn't change all of a sudden. I had to think differently and then act differently, one step at a time.

And I changed with every single step I took. I still confess to myself daily that I am a powerful, prosperous creator, and I continue to prosper day and night. On the other hand, I find myself falling off the "faith wagon" when surrounded by other fearful beings who buy into the tribal mentality that these times are difficult times to make money and prosper.

I'm still learning and changing every single day. To me, if you're not growing and learning every single day, you're dying. Being alive is welcoming the change and leaping off the cliff, trusting that the safety net will appear. The best safety net is faith in a Higher Power and faith in yourself. Believe that it will happen. Believe and see yourself as successful. Believe and see yourself as prosperous. Shifting your perspective doesn't mean being lazy and letting your mind get lazy.

Change from within is a day-by-day endeavor. Changing the mindset you have worn for years won't happen overnight, but it can happen if *you truly believe you can change.* Believe that the miracles will happen, and they will.

The monumental change is shifting your perspective and opening your mind to a new way of seeing things. Suddenly you will find yourself doing different things, and then acting and feeling differently, which then triggers other new behaviors, actions, and thought patterns.

With this shift in thinking comes a fresh, exciting hope that change can happen—in small ways and even big ways—and that perhaps it won't require giving up everything you know, but it can be as simple as letting go of one fear at a time. Change happens as you let go of the dead energy, the old attitudes and belief systems that are no longer working for you, and incorporate new energy, new thought forms, new belief systems, new behaviors, and new ways of being! In the end, you have to follow what feels right in your spirit. If something feels fresh, exciting, and a bit scary, and you feel a rush inside of you—go for it!

When you stay in your comfort zone, you won't experience fear. Doing something you've never done before, on the other hand, will trigger all kinds of fears! That scary, on-the-edge feeling means you're on the right path! So use it as a sign to keep going and keep working through your fears.

Remember, change is the only constant in life. Change is the one thing you can count on that is dynamic. So why not flow with the change rather than fight it? Why not activate change from within? Why not go on the change ride with joy?

Today, take a risk and do something that turns you on! See what change happens within you that will activate change all around you!

.

exercise. *one baby step towards change.*

What is something you have always wanted to change about your life?

Write about the change you are desperately seeking, and write down three action steps you can take that will activate some kind of change in this area.

Today, take one baby step by taking action on those action steps!

exercise. *change your mindset, change your life.*

If you want something in your life to change, you must first change your thinking about it. You must first get to the source of the dysfunction and declutter the belief system that's not working.

What one belief system would you like to change, regarding the change you listed above? Where did this belief system come from? Why do you want to change it? What belief do you want to create in its place? Journal about this.

For one month, start confessing the opposite of what you have been telling yourself about the issue you want to change. For instance, if you have believed all your life that you are terrible with money (like I had), then start confessing the opposite: *I am a winner with money!* If you are always saying to yourself, *I cannot save money*, then say the opposite: *I am great at saving money!* See what happens inside you, and what action steps you start taking to match this new belief system.

Be aware of the feelings and thoughts that come up when you start affirming this new belief system. A part of you may rebel and say, "Liar!" but trust that change will happen whenever you change your thinking. It just takes conscious work, step-by-step and day-by-day, to shift your mindset in order for that change to be activated within—and for that change to become visible in your life.

enjoy the journey. *it's all about the journey.*

listen to your intuition! Stop when you feel burned out. Stop when you feel stuck.

When becoming clutter free, the journey is just as important as the destination. Take the journey seriously, knowing that what you learn along the way will keep you from accumulating more clutter in the future. Take the lessons all the way through, so you don't find yourself on the same path again, needing to learn the same lessons again. Stop pretending that something keeps happening and or keeps showing up in your life for no reason. Stop cursing and getting pissed at yourself with where you are.

Where you are is the perfect starting point. Where you are is exactly where you are supposed to be to get to your destination.

If you are feeling overwhelmed and don't know where to start, ask for help, and ask for the message behind the overwhelm. Identify any deep-rooted feelings of unworthiness: *I feel like an idiot. Why can't I do this? I keep shuffling the same papers over and over and can't move forward.*

First of all, stop being so hard on yourself. Forgive yourself. Give yourself grace and compassion. Beating yourself up is counterproductive and is preventing you from moving forward and seeing the grand lessons of your amazing life.

Don't keep pushing past the overwhelm, pretending it will go away. If you do, I guarantee that you will keep recreating the stuff, lessons, body clutter, and cluttered relationships. Don't you want to deal with it once and for all? Don't you want to see the clutter of your life as presents—with priceless gifts within?

Remember to think of this journey as a treasure hunt. Embrace the gifts of your stuff—past and present. Have fun going through your stuff, and allow the stuff to teach you.

And, if you get tired, take a break. No one is forcing you to do it all at once.

Don't lament about how long it is taking. How long did it take you to get here, anyway?

C'mon, how many years did it take you to accumulate your stuff? Yes, you could be chosen to be on an extreme makeover television show where—poof—all your stuff is magically gone, and you have a brand new living space filled with new stuff. Lucky you! But should that happen to you, you may one day find your life and living spaces filled with stuff again, because you didn't get to the root cause of why you accumulated the stuff in the first place and allowed it to get into this state of disarray.

In fact, I have gotten several calls from people who were on those shows who experienced exactly that. They said it felt good at first, having their place decluttered and beautified for the "wow" factor and for entertainment sake, but then stuff slowly started creeping back into their spaces again because they hadn't learned anything about why the clutter got there in the first place.

So when I created a surprise makeover for *The Nate Berkus Show*, I told the family about TruthLoveMeaningPurpose both before and after the makeover (although this never made it to air). I explained how to set clear boundaries, and create homes and paths. I even explained the importance of being vigilant in maintaining their stuff. It was very important to me that the family learned something from this experience and could apply those lessons to the other areas of their life.

But if the family had to declutter their home themselves, I would tell them the same thing I'm telling you. If you're on a roll and are consistently vigilant about organizing and decluttering your stuff, terrific! But if you suddenly feel tired and overwhelmed after going, going, going—stop.

Take a break.

If you start hitting the wall of inertia when you think about your stuff and want to take a nap—good! Take a nap, and imagine your space as you desire it to be. Then after your nap, wake up to your stuff, and vow to yourself that you will learn once and for all to deal with it consciously, so you will never have to deal with it in this way again.

Let's say you don't know even know where to begin. Just get started on one tiny area of your space, and feel good about the fact that you have begun dealing with your stuff.

What if you don't even feel like you've made a dent in your stuff after you've dealt with that tiny area? Then dedicate an entire day to one area. Take it all out, and bring back into that space only that which meets the criteria of TruthLoveMeaningPurpose, while committing to a goal (i.e., I am letting go of 95 percent of the stuff in this space, because the truth is I haven't touched it, looked at, or needed it for all these years).

Or ask for help. Perhaps you do need professional help to help you move forward with momentum, so you can continue from there. It's okay to admit you need help. Get help, if that is what your intuition is calling you to do!

Only you know what the truth is inside you.

Another tool you might employ is writing. Write about your journey. Even if you are not a writer, I encourage you to write down the answers and questions you have. Start a dialogue with yourself, your inner voice, and God, whomever your God may be. Write down your prayers for help: *God, help me to complete this task. God, show me how to complete it.*

Based on my own experience, my best advice on this journey is to just show up. Just show up one day at a time. Just show up with your fears, doubts, and uncertainties. Write them down, and keep at it. See what else comes up.

Even if you feel like you are walking through molasses, continue moving forward, touching your stuff. Keep asking why you are clogged up. Keep asking why you cannot let go.

Allow your feelings to express themselves out loud or on paper.

If you receive the answer "just move forward," heed that sign. Continue moving forward, one step at a time.

Yes, you may feel like it is fruitless. You may feel disappointed with how long it is taking. But guess what? You created it. Did you expect it to instantly disappear the moment you decided you didn't want it anymore? Don't you want to be responsible from this point forward with what you bring into your life? Don't you want to use the stuff in your life to teach you on the deepest levels?

Accept where you are. Where you are is perfect.

You know this is what you are supposed to do. You feel it in your heart. You may not have all the answers, but something feels like you're on the right path. You feel a bit lighter.

Suddenly, you may start gaining confidence. You may even hear a booming, loving, internal voice say to you, *Trust that by taking this action step, the next step will be revealed to you.*

Step by step, item by item, space by space, you will tackle one thing at a time, and in doing so, you will be transformed. Let the process flow easily and effortlessly. Let this process be completed for the highest good. With clarity. Certainty. Assuredness. Power. In turn, you will be empowered. Confident.

Trust that help is everywhere. Trust that your unique journey will teach you everything you need to know.

Let the journey unfold and reveal to you the truth of who you are. Let the stuff come to the surface of your consciousness so you can deal with it once and for all.

You asked for help because what you were doing was no longer working. You knew there was a better way, and that's why you are here. Don't quit now.

Embrace the unknown day by day and item by item, and only focus on one task at a time: this one item in front of you.

Enjoy the journey, and know you are exactly where you are supposed to be for now, to fully suck out all the life lessons from this stuff.

That's all you need to know for now.

·

exercise. *this journey is worth it. remember why.*

As you continue on this journey, you will inevitably feel overwhelmed, stuck, and defeated, and you may even feel like giving up. When you do, I encourage you to remind yourself why you have embarked on this journey. So let's revisit the *why* behind your stuff. Reminding yourself of the why will create the mindset shift you need in order to continue moving forward on the journey.

Write down your answers to the following questions, now that you have reached this point in your journey:

Why are you getting simplified, organized, and decluttered?

How do you feel having a cluttered life and cluttered spaces?

How would you feel if the clutter were gone and you were organized?

Write down the goals and dreams you want to accomplish once the clutter is out of your life.

Embrace the journey, and embrace each step you take. Don't worry about ten steps from now. Say to yourself,

> *I trust that every action step I am taking is moving me forward with love and light.*
> *I trust that I am being guided with every step I take, and the only step I need to be concerned about is the step to take now.*
> *Taking this one action step will inform me of what to do next.*

Bookmark this section to reread whenever you feel overwhelmed or discouraged. It will allow you to get back in touch with the reasons why you are on this decluttering journey, your most positive intended outcome, and allow you to keep moving forward.

messages. *pay attention.*

W hat message are you receiving?

What insight have you gained for your next step?

What have you learned from your stuff so far?

What lesson are you taking from this experience?

What are you letting go of?

Speak the truth of your heart.

TruthLoveMeaningPurpose.

Why do you keep repeating the same mistakes? Here's one mistake I kept making in my early twenties: I kept getting speeding tickets and getting into accidents. I realized I needed to pay attention to how fast I was going in my own life and to slow down. At the time, I was so concerned about my charity activities that I forgot about my own needs. Racing from need to need, or charity to charity, I was forgetting about myself—the biggest charity case of all. Finally, when I got my drivers' license suspended, I was forced to slow down and take care of myself. When I forget this lesson, I get speeding tickets to remind me not to race through life—to pay attention to the signs in my life—to take care of myself. The last time I got a ticket was when I was driving downhill, thinking I was late for a client meeting—where I was to teach about time management, of all things. Of course, the Universe was prompting me to take care of myself first and foremost; otherwise, how can I be there for others and teach anything to them?

Why do you keep recreating the same experiences? When I was younger, I kept recreating the same types of friendships, in which I was always the counselor rescuing others. When I had a problem, I realized that my friends were too busy with their own problems to deal with mine and be there for me. At first, I got angry, thinking, *I'm always there for them. Why are they not there for me?* Then I realized that I had created these friendships myself, and I needed to take full responsibility for them.

What messages were in these relationships for me? Did I enjoy being the rescuer? Did it feed my ego, thinking I knew more than someone else? Did it keep me from confronting my own issues and thus rescuing myself? Understanding the truth of this unhealthy pattern helped me to do something differently: I began holding all my friends capable of managing their own lives and solving their own problems, and creating new types of friendships where my needs, desires, and dreams were just as important to my friends as their own.

So—why do you keep dating the same kinds of people?

Why do you keep encountering the same situations?

It all begins with you.

Yes, you.

Unless you accept personal responsibility for your part, get to the root cause, and understand why you created this situation, person, place, or thing, you will continue to recreate the same experiences, encounter the same situations, and meet the same types of people (just with different names), and make the same mistakes. Your soul has created each experience to help you grow, evolve, learn, and transform—not to torture you. The reason "this" keeps happening is that your soul is trying to get your attention, to get you to look at the root cause so that you can create different results.

How do you get to the root cause and create different results? Fully embrace the lesson of every lesson, experience, place, and thing, and do something differently when you are faced again with the same situation, experience, or person. It can be as simple as saying no to a request for your help, instead of saying yes like you usually do. By saying no, you are holding that person capable of handling and solving their problem. Every situation and person is different; the more you clear the clutter within, and go deeper within for the truth of the situation, the more the "take-away" message will reveal itself to you.

What is on the forefront of your mind and heart in this situation that keeps repeating itself? What goal are you trying to achieve?

You must believe that the Universe is conspiring to get you to that goal. You must believe that the Universe is giving you powerful messages about which way to go, how to be, or how not to be. With every single encounter and experience, the Universe is conspiring to give you a tool you can add to your toolbox, so you can create a different kind of relationship or experience.

Open up your eyes and believe that everything happening right here and now is a message to you on your journey.

If every single thing that happened today, every single person you encountered, and every item you have acquired, were perceived as messengers for you, what would their message be to you?

While you're reading this book, I would love for you to see everything as a message. View every item you touch as a powerful messenger for you. Dig deeper for the message so you can be propelled forward, so that day by day you will begin to see how everything is woven together and connected. And believe the Universe is conspiring to get you to wherever you want to be.

Then see what miracles come into your life.

∙

exercise. *what's your message?*

Exercise your "message" muscle by writing down one recent experience or encounter with your stuff. It could have happened while you were going through your stuff. It could have happened during a talk with somebody. It could be an interaction you had. It could be anything.

As you begin to see that there is a higher purpose and reason for your stuff, encounters, and experiences, you'll be more likely to embrace your journey and your stuff, and love it all, rather than lamenting or regretting or blaming.

First write down only the facts of the story. Then write down your answers to the following questions to find the message:

This happened to me because I am learning to . . .

This happened to me to remind me that . . .

This happened to me to show me that I am . . .

This happened to me to show me not to do this anymore—what is "this"?

This happened to me to show me to do this more often—what is "this"?

This happened to me to help me love myself more because . . .

This happened to me to help me accept myself for who I am because . . .

Now write the following:

>*I love my stuff and what it is teaching me!*
>
>*I love my life and who I am!*
>
>*I am now letting go of the items that have served me in the past but are no longer serving me now, and that are contradicting the powerful lessons I have learned and the powerful messages for my journey.*
>
>*I love the messages I am getting for my journey, which are moving me forward in my life!*

time is precious. *the clock is ticking.*

all of us are given 24 hours to spend in a day. That's 86,400 seconds. Let's say your bank deposited $86,400 a day in your bank account. If they said to you, "We will deposit this much in your account every day, but you must use it all each day—you can't roll any over into the next day," what would you do? You would use it all, right?

Wouldn't you invest it in making your life more fulfilling? Easier? More fun? You would spend it on the things that you love, that have meaning, that have purpose, and that are truthfully you—perhaps on causes you feel passionately about or charities you believe in that bring you joy. You would use it to build a secure, happy future. You wouldn't hoard it, deny it, or pretend it doesn't exist.

Think of time in this way. We all start with 24 hours of time every single day. We are rich with time!

Do you have a time prosperity consciousness, or a time scarcity consciousness? Do you get how powerful this perspective is?

Are you one of those who lament, "I don't have enough time . . . I wish I had more time . . . I wish there were more hours in a day . . . I wish, I wish, I wish I could turn back the clock of time . . ."

Wait! We *can* use all of it, but we can't carry anything forward. Like some phone plans, we don't have any rollover minutes! We must use every precious second.

Don't fight the truth of time! Don't complain and whine because you, like everybody else, have been equally and fairly and squarely given the same amount of time every single day. The truth of time is that you are the king or queen of your Universe. You can slice and dice it however you like: the Source has abundantly gifted you with 365 days or 52 weeks every year, 7 days or 168 hours in every week, and 24 hours or 1440 minutes or 86,400 seconds in every day.

Stop right now to be grateful and thank God for all the time you have been given in the past, all the time you are getting right now, and all the time you will be receiving in the future.

Right now, at this very moment in time, everything in your life is a result of what you have created, allowed, or promoted at some point in time.

Accept responsibility for what is in your schedule. If you don't like what you see, change it. What don't you like? How does it make you feel? How would you like to feel?

Something has to give; something has to go. What is it?

Learn to say NO to the time robber, to whatever de-energizes you and robs you of your time. NO without apology. NO without guilt.

As you begin saying NO with ease and effortlessness, you will begin to say YES to those things that give you more time, more happiness, and more joy.

Watch your horizons expand; watch your time expand. It's true: you will feel as if you have more time, that you have expanded time.

•

exercise. *the truth of time.*

For one week, stop complaining about not having enough time.

For one week, start saying:

> *I have plenty of time to do everything my heart desires.*

Notice how you feel as a result, as you are going about your days, and journal regarding your journey with time. For example, see if you feel more grateful for the time you have. See if you start making different choices based on this declaration.

exercise. *let go of time robbers.*

Is there something in your schedule that brings your energy down, that makes you feel de-energized? For one week, decide that you will remove this "time robber" from your schedule, and notice how you feel without this time robber stealing your vitality.

Say no to a request for your time. How does that make you feel? Write down the truth about your feelings. Acknowledge that saying no may feel uncomfortable at first, but in doing so, you are also acknowledging that saying yes is okay and is the gateway to a new way of life honoring you and your happiness.

Say yes to everything that brings you joy, and no to anything that makes you feel yucky. Journal about your revelations regarding these "time robbers."

SHIFT
STUFF.

listen to your stuff. *your stuff speaks.*

Listen!

What is your stuff saying to you?

If your stuff *could* talk, what would it say to you?

> *Stop buying more stuff.*
> *Take care of me, the stuff you neglect.*
> *C'mon—if you can't take care of me properly, please give me to someone who will.*
> *I have feelings, and I am hurt because you have neglected me.*
> *You let me rust.*
> *You let me get dusty.*
> *You let me be broken.*
> *You don't wear me.*
> *You don't use me.*
> *You don't let me see sunshine.*
> *You keep me in the dark.*
> *Please take me out of the darkness and let me shine.*
> *Let me be born anew and feel new again.*
> *Let me play with someone else.*
> *Let me be something new in someone's life so they can see me with a fresh pair of eyes.*
> *Let me feel the warm embrace of love.*
> *I don't feel loved by you.*
> *You don't care about me.*

Well, if you did, why are you treating me so badly?
Why do you keep buying more of me when you already have me?
Let me serve you first.
When you keep buying "better and newer," you keep pushing me to the back of your house and closet and fridge, and then you cannot see me anymore.
Please release me from your jail.
You are keeping me in prison, and I am so unhappy, too.
This unhappiness is all over the house, permeating your environment.
I've talked to the other stuff in your space, and they feel unhappy too.
Let us go now. Let the unhappy stuff go. Let the unused stuff go.
Let us be born anew elsewhere.
Let the space be created for stuff that truly makes you happy.
C'mon, brace yourself and be courageous.
You made the choice to bring us together, and now you are just neglecting us.
Take charge. Let go of us once and for all!

exercise. *dialogue with your stuff.*

Pretend that your stuff is speaking to you. Pick one item and start a dialogue with it. What is the stuff saying to you? What are you saying to it?

If your stuff is reminding you that you haven't used it for years and is asking you to let it go, be ruthless and let it go. And don't forget to write down these subtle but powerful conversations.

question your stuff. *face the truth behind your stuff.*

I t takes courage to face your stuff and hear it speak. It means admitting that you have an overflow of stuff in your life, and there are things in your possession that you truly don't need, want, or haven't used for days . . . okay, months . . . maybe even years. It means you haven't been conscious of what you were bringing into the house, allowing more and more to come in without paying attention to what was already there. You've been neglecting these precious beings in your home.

I know I talk about these things as if they have feelings.

But here's what I hear my paper lantern lamp saying to me: *Hey, you already have a lamp in the corner that lights up the room. Why do you have me? You used to have me in the bedroom where I helped you to read in bed, but then you replaced me with a beautiful lamp from Cost Plus—and that's okay, because the other matching lamp got crushed during your renovations. So now I'm all alone, no longer part of a matching pair. What are you going to do with me? I feel a bit crowded sitting next to your desk when there's a perfectly good lamp in the corner.*

So, what am I to do? Throw away the lamp? Give it away to someone who might find it beautiful, a piece of artwork for their space? Yes, give it away.

So this constant questioning, listening to your stuff, and truthful answering takes courage. Courage to confront the truth of why you have something. Courage to do it all the time since we are constantly shifting, evolving beings. Last year I loved the lamp when it had a matching lamp on the other side. This year, it doesn't quite fit the room with the new paint. It doesn't belong.

Ooh, I feel badly.

Don't feel badly. The lamp doesn't. The lamp wants to serve a distinct purpose in this world, just like you do. It has a life purpose, and it certainly isn't serving it being with you, so let it go with love and faith.

See, it takes courage. Courage to face your stuff. Courage to confront the TruthLoveMeaningPurpose behind your stuff. Courage to confront my insecurities, my guilt, my self-doubt, and my uncertainty. Courage to confront the truth of what I really, truthfully think, and saying it out loud, and taking action upon that truthful thought (if no one would judge me, of course).

Again, the journey begins with you.
You are you.
I am me.
I will take responsibility for me and my stuff.
You take responsibility for you and your stuff.
No pointing fingers. No blame.

I created my life and stuff.
I will now start taking responsibility for my stuff and release blame.
I will stop berating myself.
I will stop whining and feeling sorry for myself after all I've gone through and endured.

You might be feeling that no one else can understand what you've been through.

Well, you're right. Only you can understand what you've been through, and only you need to know the why and the truth behind your stuff. But you do need to understand. Understand the reasons why you created this stuff. Understand why you have all this stuff.

Then, most of all, believe you are a powerful creator. Thank God that you created all this stuff so you could learn from it.

Start confessing:

> *I am a powerful creator. I can envision a new future, a new life, and new stuff.*
> *I realize that this moment is the starting point for my delving within to gain self-awareness and become self-actualized.*
> *I can honor all of it: my past, my present, and my future.*
> *I can examine my past experiences and past stuff, suck out all the life lessons from it, and let go of the rest.*
> *I can let go of the past and move forward, bringing my past lessons into the here and now.*
> *I can create a new future by bringing forward only the new, positive, life-affirming lessons I have learned into the here and now.*

So, moment to moment, as you constantly question the stuff in your life to make sure it belongs in the here and now, you will be creating a new present and a new future.

If you begin looking at your stuff, dealing with it differently, and taking just one action step that is out of the ordinary, then you are charting a new course for yourself.

So as you become familiar with the story behind your stuff and what is fighting you or holding you prisoner, you can release yourself from the cell of your stuff. You will be free to experience and create new futures with new stuff.

You can finally examine how you got here so you can learn from it, end this chapter of your life with stuff that is no longer serving your highest good, and create a new chapter in your life.

Can it be that simple?

> *My past is who I was. My heart carries it. My mind carries it. My past made me who I am today.*
> *My present is who I am now. What do I want and need to carry with me from my past into my present?*
> *My future is who I want to be and what I want to do. What do I need from my past and present to create a future of TruthLoveMeaningPurpose? What stuff will make a difference in the future?*

Yes, it can be that simple.

Once you are willing to truthfully and courageously confront who you are today, trusting the present to give you everything you need, and trusting the future holds many promises of what can be, you may surrender to the journey of letting go of all this stuff.

Lay it to rest. Let go of your past stuff. Let go of your past painful memories. Honor the past. Weep about the past. Keep the lessons of the past.

Then, in the present, be at one with who you are today. No more lamenting. No more blaming. Take responsibility for your stuff, and believe you created everything to make you who you are today.

If you don't like what you see or what you are creating, start collecting different stuff. Create different ideas, thoughts, and beliefs, and hold different feelings in your heart, to become a different person today and to chart a different course for your future. Redefine the past. Tell a different story about your past and how it has served you to get to where you are today.

Be ruthless with yourself. Ruthlessly confront your truth. Ruthlessly deal with your heart, and what your stuff does to your heart. Ruthlessly cut out the stuff that brings you pain.

Ruthlessly decide to paste new pictures on your mind, imagination, and heart to create a new collage of the life you desire and are creating right now.

Can it be that simple? Yes.

You just need the courage to confront your TruthLoveMeaningPurpose.

.

exercise. *confront the truth behind your stuff.*

Pick one item that you feel bad letting go of. Why do you feel guilty? Why do you feel badly? Why can't you let go of this item? Dig deeper. What is the truth behind this item? Does this item represent success, wealth, hurt, or anger to you? What is the feeling behind this item? How does it make you feel when you are around it now?

Are you willing to let go of that feeling?

Are you willing to change and heal?

This exercise is intended to help you find the courage to confront the TruthLoveMeaningPurpose behind your stuff, and to make you aware that you are truly free to let go of what no longer serves you and recreate another future with new stuff *or* old stuff.

It is your *perspective* about your stuff that must shift. It is your perspective about your stuff that is causing the grief and heartache in your mind and heart. Once you let go of your negative perceptions about your stuff and make peace with why you have it in your life, you will easily take responsibility for your stuff. You will stop blaming others, and you will stop being hard on yourself. Free yourself today. Take this exercise all the way through to its end, no matter how much resistance you face. Keep digging until you feel a shift, or a "click," in your consciousness. The click means, "I know this is the truth!"

exercise. *pay homage and have a funeral for your stuff.*

Create a ceremony to say goodbye to those items you have decided to let go of. Write a eulogy. Hold a funeral for your stuff.

After holding the ceremony, how do you feel? Do you feel better having acknowledged the service the stuff provided to you, rather than letting it go unconsciously? Let yourself feel what comes up. Cry! Scream! Shout! Laugh!

The intention of this exercise is to help you give yourself permission to feel your feelings, rather than judging or critiquing what you have done in the past. Merely allow yourself to feel your feelings, and let them drift in and out. Only once you have fully allowed yourself to experience the feelings attached to your stuff will you be able to let go fully without guilt. Love your stuff. Love your journey. Love your process. All is unique to you and only you.

fighting with your stuff. *get over it and let go of the guilt.*

hat's screaming to me?

What is wreaking havoc in my life and consciousness?

Unused stuff.

Neglected stuff.

Unloved stuff.

Stop fighting with your stuff.

Get over it.

Your stuff is there, so deal with it and stop battling the stuff.

Stop having to climb over your stuff to get to the stuff you really need.

Listen to the stuff. Confront the stuff. Then finally let go of fighting the stuff.

Stop fighting me already.

Stop creating a battlefield.

You are a powerful creator.

What do you want to truly create?

What kind of stuff do you truly want?

Listen.

Face the truth.

And let go of fighting me, as that has been the landscape of your life for a long time.

Let go of the drama.

Let go of the lies.

Let go of the guilt.

You're too busy to take care of me.

168

So why did you bring me into your life?
You're too busy to use me.
So why did you think I was useful in the first place?
Can't I be useful to someone else?
So why don't you love me anymore?
It's okay.
Stop fighting the truth of me and your other stuff.
You used to wear me.
You used to cook with me.
You used to love me so much and use me over and over and over again.
Use me again then, if you feel so guilty.
But do you feel more guilty using me just because you're feeling guilty?
Or are you using me because I sing to your heart and soul?
Use me then . . .

I can't use you, because I don't feel like it anymore.
I know the truth.
I'm tired of using you.
I'm sorry.
I spent so much money on you.
I fantasized about you, and then I finally had the courage to buy you.
But you were so expensive that I thought I'd better save you for a special occasion.
I thought I'd better not use you now, or else I would wear you out.
I need to save you, just in case, for that very special time. If I use you every day, then you will be worn out when that special time comes.

But what if that special time never comes?
Can't every day be a special occasion?
Why can't you treat me like everything else in your life?
If you loved me so much, then why don't you use me more often and play with me more often?

I'm afraid to use you because you cost so much.
I can't ruin you.
I bought you for that special time.

But I see you using your old stuff that looks so worn out to me.
I see your tired stuff on you, and your stuff is saying, "I'm all worn out, and I'm not energetic anymore because you have worn me out." You even look tired with this stuff you're wearing. I'm feeling tired just looking at you with that tired look on your face.

I love you, stuff. I am letting you go now. You have served me so well. Thank you for being in my life. I am grateful for you. I am moving forward and embracing new stuff with new energy and new experiences.

I am only holding on to the old stuff that still feels energetic to me.

I am now letting go of the stuff that feels like dead energy to me.

Thank you, stuff.

I love you, stuff.

·

exercise. *stop battling dead stuff.*

What stuff feels like it's a battlefield?

Why are you fighting the stuff?

What stuff feels like dead energy to you?

Where are the dead spaces in your life?

Are you fighting the truth of your stuff?

What is your dead stuff saying to you?

Write about it.

exercise. *let go of dead stuff—now!*

Or, if you don't feel like writing about it, try walking around your house, start taking the stuff that no longer resonates with your TruthLoveMeaningPurpose, and form a pile. Speak to the stuff. Eulogize it. Then, let go. Put it in a box and take it to your local charity and/or to the trash. Now.

exercise. *let go of the false illusion of expensive stuff and instead fill yourself up with love stuff.*

Think about an item that you spent a lot of money on.

How often do you use it?

Are you truthfully holding on to it because of the money you spent on it, rather than the love you have for it?

Say out loud what the truth of the stuff is. Talk to the stuff and apologize if you have to. And let go of the stuff now.

exercise. *express gratitude for the stuff you love.*

Now think about something you use often.

How much money did you spend on it?

Do you use it every day with love and gratitude? Why are you so grateful for these items?

Notice the correlation between the money you spent on something and the love that you have for it.

Recognize when there is dead energy around the stuff you no longer use, appreciate, or love, and recognize that no matter how much money it cost, having it sitting around your space is not for your highest good. Let it go with love.

The intent of these exercises is to help you get in touch with your feelings of love and gratitude. Cultivate your appreciation of the stuff in your life that gives you energy, and gives back to you every single day.

seduction of stuff. *don't buy into lies.*

b *uy me!*
I'm new and shiny!
You need me!
If you don't buy me, you're a failure.
If you don't buy me, you're not "in."
If you don't buy me, you're not a success.
If you don't buy me, you aren't "with it."
C'mon, get with it!
C'mon, get with the newness of now!
More is better.
Fill up your empty heart with me.
I can help you feel a high . . . temporarily.
Buy me so you can feel that high you crave.
That feeling of newness for the moment will make you feel so good . . . for now.
Yes, browse the aisles and sparkle when you put me in your cart!
Bright, shiny, and new— and I can make you feel dizzyingly happy for a little while.
Buy me so I can turn off your pain for a little while.
Buy me so you can feel "more than."
Buy me so you can feel important.
Buy me so you can feel rich.
Buy me so you can feel something.
Buy me so you don't have to feel so much.
Just feel me, and you don't have to feel your life and what's really going on.

Buy me because you think you need me.
Buy me so you don't have to go shopping as often.
You can buy me in bulk, and then you will have a lot of me and feel secure that you won't run
out of me.
Buy a lot of me to fill up your space so you don't have to feel empty inside.
Buy me so you can see me—a lot of me—and you'll feel safe knowing I'm there.
Wait . . . don't leave just yet! There's a better me out there. Have you seen the latest and greatest?
You need me to make your life better . . .

Next time you go to the store, be aware of how the stuff seductively speaks to you. As you recognize how powerfully stuff pulls you in like magnets, you may think twice about going into the store unless it's absolutely necessary.

You will brace yourself for battle and protect yourself with your TruthLoveMeaningPurpose armor, thereby shielding yourself from any unwanted voices coaxing you to buy this or that. You will then be truly empowered next time you are shopping, knowing that your decision to buy or not to buy is coming from a place of true intention within you. You will understand why you say yes when you could be saying no. Your shopping experience will not be driven by forces outside of you, but instead will come from that still small voice within. Once you become acutely aware of the seductive interplay that happens between you and the stuff on the shelves, you will start making different choices.

Keep cultivating this keen sense of awareness every time you go shopping. Don't walk into a store in a daze or haze. Instead, walk in with a sense of purpose and clarity.

.

exercise. *understand the power of stuff and how it affects you.*

Journal after every single time you shop and see what feelings arise. I believe that with a shift in feelings and perceptions comes a change in behavior. Self-correction comes from knowing what is driving your actions from within. Check into what this stuff is saying to you—in your home, in the store, or wherever you are!

Have fun listening to the stuff, and enjoy the conversation!

SHIFT
PERSPECTIVE.

confront your feelings. *feel the inside stuff.*

hat is the truth behind my stuff?

Ooh . . . if I got rid of the stuff, what would I be left with?

My truth.

The truth of my life.

What do I really have in my life besides my stuff?

What is my purpose?

Why am I here?

I have my family. I have my life purpose. I have my career.

I have lots of stuff, and yet I keep going out and buying even more stuff.

And, if I get rid of the stuff I'm not really using, as this book is recommending, then what?

Getting rid of my stuff means I will have to deal with my feelings.

As long as I have the stuff, I don't have to look at empty spaces on the shelf. I don't have to look within.

Because I feel emptiness when I see an empty space.

I feel like there must be more to life than this emptiness I feel inside.

I feel like if I get rid of everything from my past, then I will have nothing in the present and the future. My past represents all my hard work and past successes. It represents me. I can't bank on now.

Ooh, this is hard.

Emptiness.

Loneliness.

I have all these friends, but I still feel empty inside.

I have all this new stuff, but I feel empty inside.

I feel like eating ice cream. I feel like grabbing that chocolate bar in the freezer.

Why?

What am I searching for?

I am seeking a feeling of excitement, adventure, love.

Can I get that every day? Without getting new stuff?

I tried love, and it didn't work out.

I tried organizing somewhat, and it didn't work out.

I tried putting my heart out there, and it didn't work out.

I can count on my new clothes to make me feel better in a split second.

I can count on my new lipstick to give me a boost.

I can count on going down the aisles at Target to give me a boost, seeing all the colorful new stuff I could buy. It's not that much. A few things here and there—it won't make that much of a dent. I'm a bargain shopper, and hey, I work hard. I deserve it.

Sometimes I feel like I'm in a time warp when I'm shopping—time passes so quickly. What am I searching for that I can't get without the stuff?

What am I replacing? The stuff is replacing something deep inside—what is it?

I feel like it is right there. If only I could see it.

Feel it. It's there.

Love.

I feel loved when I put on something new that makes me feel loved and brand new.

Am I addicted to the feelings I get when I get something new? Do I want to keep getting newer stuff so I can feel new and better inside? So I can feel love?

Am I addicted to that feeling of love?

I am addicted to that high. I crave that excitement—that sense of adventure—from a person. From a drink. From smoking. From buying. From spending. From drinking an espresso. That jolt of adrenaline.

Why manufacture the feelings from the outside?

Why not feel the feelings on the inside?

Be, do, and then have.

I need to be that person and feel those feelings. Then I will start acting differently and doing different things because of the feelings I have and the person I am *without* all that stuff. Strangely enough, that's when the stuff I do truly want becomes magnetized to me.

So, my addiction to stuff, buying stuff, filling myself up with stuff, and surrounding myself with that stuff is a temporary high.

The only lasting high I have found comes from within. From having that deep sense of satisfaction, joy, and fulfillment based in knowing myself and being proud of myself. I don't need that stuff to feel complete or important. I don't need that stuff to show off and say "this is me" to the world. Otherwise I feel empty even after I have the stuff. I realize that the high feeling quickly subsides, and I am still left with me.

So the stuff is temporary. The stuff is a false measure of me. The stuff is a false symbol of me.

The items I have are merely companions on the journey to help, serve, elevate, and inform—but not to make me who I am.

I am everything I am without all that stuff.

Learn to feel like you're on top of the world without the millions in the bank.
Learn to feel a high without taking stuff.
Learn to feel like royalty without the tiara.
Learn to feel full of love without physical love.

Feel your heart.
Feel your passion.
Feel your desire to be of purpose in this world.
Feel your desire to serve.

Let go of the vain imagining that it's all about you and your stuff.
You created that reality.
You thought you were addicted to the stuff.
Stop that line of thinking that says you really need your stuff.
Let go now and be fearless. Decide to be different, starting today.

You are in charge of your life.
Take command now.

■

exercise. *feel the emptiness.*

Do you ever feel empty inside? What do you do when you are feeling that way? Journal about it.

Do you ever feel like something is missing? What do you do when you are feeling that way? Journal about it.

Do you ever feel a restlessness in your spirit? What do you do when you are feeling that way? Journal about it.

Allow the emptiness to communicate to you what you truly need and desire. Is it self-love? Do you need to take better care of yourself? Is it silence and stillness? Do you not need to take any action at all for now?

Journal about what you feel like doing out of habit. Journal about what your soul/heart is truly longing for. Dig deep and allow the truth to reveal itself to you.

exercise. *infuse just one item with a million-dollar feeling.*

Pick one item in your closet that makes you feel like a million bucks!

Put it on, and write down how you feel when wearing this item.

Now, take off that item.

Just imagine you are wearing it and feel those same feelings.

This exercise demonstrates the power of your stuff and the feelings it evokes. I want you to realize that you can induce those same feelings without the stuff, and attract the same reality you would create with the stuff.

When you realize how powerful your imagination is, you can manifest and attract anything to you by acting *as if* you have the stuff or are wearing the stuff—by simply being who you are without it.

You don't need that stuff to make you feel a certain way. All you need is your powerful imagination.

So which came first, the stuff or the feeling? You may have thought the stuff had to come before the feeling. But this exercise demonstrates that you can create the feeling without the stuff—which causes you to attract the stuff you want! And this feeling—with or without the stuff—can create even more "feel good" sensations and "feel good" experiences.

Expect miracles to keep happening wherever you go once you learn to cultivate this powerful manifestation tool! You'll learn it's not about the stuff at all—it's about the powerful stuff we are made of!

embrace your feelings. *even sadness is good stuff.*

is sadness truly bad? Is sadness truly the opposite of happiness? I don't believe so.

Remember when our teachers at school would give us a happy face if we achieved success, and a sad face if our work was imperfect or incomplete, or we did something wrong?

I believe that you must acknowledge your sadness before you can move to happiness. But you cannot let go of sadness with the snap of a finger. You cannot let go of sadness simply by telling yourself that sadness is a bad thing.

I have seen so many incidences where true feelings are never acknowledged, and this suppression of true feelings leads to more clutter in people's lives.

How do you let go of sadness? Embrace the sadness, and let it inform you, teach you, and connect you with what is making you sad.

If you are extremely exhausted after a decluttering session—not just physically, but mentally, emotionally, and spiritually—remember that the physical stuff is connected to all those layers. So it would make perfect sense that sometimes we feel lighter when we're letting go, and sometimes we feel angry, sad, or guilty.

Why? The stuff brings up the feelings that we need to deal with, get in touch with, and let go of to move forward. And that's awesome!

Allow yourself to feel *everything*. This is how you will finally, once and for all, let go of the clutter of the emotions pent up inside, and truly be able to release it once and for all— paving the way for miracles in your mind and heart.

What stuff have you been letting go? What does it symbolize to you? Uncovering and unveiling this truth is the key to your sadness.

What's the truth of the situation? Is it still truthfully you?

Perhaps the stuff is connected to who you were in the past, and that's no longer you. Perhaps you are lamenting about how long it took for you to deal with this, and you're getting down on yourself. Perhaps you are getting angry at yourself, beating yourself up because you let it get this bad—how could you? Perhaps you are sad, thinking about how this stuff has affected you and led you to make decisions that were not for your highest good.

Have you been letting go of the stuff—things/papers/activities—that are associated with your past careers? Past relationships? Are you letting go of a way of being in this particular career, or in this relationship? Are you sad that you were once there, and you are here now, and you wish you were back there? Are you sad that time has passed, that you yearn for yesteryears?

Mourn. Feel it all. Then, realize you are exactly where you are supposed to be today, here and now. Remember all the love, lessons, and experiences with fondness, love, appreciation, and gratitude. And let them go, trusting that you will once again experience the joy and exuberance that you felt, albeit in a different form, if you truly believe.

It is beautiful to get in touch with your emotions so you can consciously let them go—the stuff along with the feelings. Now is a time to be brutally honest with yourself.

Are you not sure about the truth behind your sadness? I'd prefer you sit there and pray about it, rather than forcing the answers to come to you.

Trust me. The answers will come to you if you want to know the truth.

For now, be at one with your sadness, as it will cease to be that soon enough; it will undoubtedly turn into something else. Let the sadness inform you of what you have been holding on to, what has been buried in you for so long, and what you are now letting go of. Let the sadness bring the tears and cleanse your soul and heart. Let the sadness talk to you so you can honor it, and then move forward with the lessons and insights gained.

Believe this will be a huge opening for you—on every level—and that the deluge of miracles will start pouring in. Perhaps you're letting go with faith those things you thought you needed, and you're now living on a different plane with faith and trust. Operating on that level tends to bring feelings of sadness, because we're letting go of a way of living with stuff, and this other path seems so foreign.

Only when you start judging sadness as bad do you not want to deal with it, push it away, and shove it down. When you become at one with your beautiful array of emotions, from sadness to excitement, you will feel alive, expressing whatever comes up inside and honoring it. You will own the sadness, feel it, evaluate it, and then finally let it go, creating space for something other than sadness—perhaps joy and exuberance at this amazing life you have created or are in the process of creating!

Today is all you have. Let go of judging sadness, and celebrate the beautiful you that feels everything!

.

exercise. *the miracle of sadness.*

Write about something that made you sad or makes you sad presently. Exhaust this subject and write about everything connected to this sadness and story. What is it that you truly need to let go of? What truth is this sadness connected to? What is this sadness teaching you? What is this sadness connected to that you must let go of?

Confront it head on. Don't stop writing. Let the tears pour over you. Let the feelings wash over you. Release completely.

Thank the sadness for living within you, protecting you, and being your friend. Forgive yourself for judging the sadness, forgive others, and forgive the experience that brought on that sadness.

Honor the sadness. Remember the blessing and miracle behind the sadness. Let go of the rest.

Vow now to be happy that you have dealt with the sadness. Be happy that you were courageous enough to face it fearlessly.

Be gentle. Don't force. Allow your feelings to keep coming to the surface and don't push them down. As you continue to practice seeing the miracle in the sadness, the miracle becomes the happiness behind the sadness.

The next time you get sad thinking about this incident, event, person, or item, remind yourself of the miracle. You may have gotten so accustomed to thinking about it as sad that you need to build new pathways in your brain to think about it as "happy," to fit your new perspective.

stuffed feelings. *don't stuff yourself with food or more stuff.*

S *tuffed feelings.*
    feeling stuffed.
    filling up with stuff.
when is enough stuff enough?
stuffed up.
full of stuff.
stuffing.
the journey of stuff.

what does your stuff tell you?
what is the story of your stuff?
what is your stuff made of?
is your stuff dead?
is your stuff alive?
is your stuff bringing you down?
is your stuff uplifting you?

TruthLoveMeaningPurpose.
c'mon, what is the truth of your stuff?
do you love your stuff?
does your stuff truly have meaning?
does your stuff serve a purpose?

The bottom line is that no matter how much beautiful stuff you have and no matter how often you Feng Shui your stuff, go through your stuff, give away stuff, and acquire stuff, you will always feel empty as if something is missing inside until you examine your true intentions behind the stuff and get clear about the purpose of the stuff in your life.

So, you've accomplished everything in your life you have set out to do: you've met all your financial goals and career goals, you have a beautiful home, a great family, and great friends. You have millions in the bank, and you're climbing up the ladder to success.

But why still do you feel something is amiss? Why do you continue eating fatty snacks late at night when you just hired a nutritionist and a trainer to get you into shape, and promised yourself this would be a new beginning? Why do you continue to sabotage yourself?

Dig deep within for the answers. See if the stuff you have surrounded yourself with brings you true joy. See if the stuff you are doing every single day brings you joy. See if the stuff of yesterday still belongs in your space as you are making this transition to the different life you envision for yourself.

You can hire all the experts in the world, including the best therapist. But I believe that unless you actually work on yourself from the inside out, your change won't last.

You will continue to do the same things—thinking the same thoughts, repeating the same behavior, and yielding the same results.

You, then, must examine the thoughts that are repeated in your consciousness. What mindset do you have when you're reaching for those fatty snacks? Is there a battle being waged inside you? Guilt about having so much. Guilt about wanting more. Guilt about wanting to just relax and not work anymore.

So you squash those feelings. They're too painful to deal with. It's much easier to stuff them down and soothe the scratchy feelings with a scoop of vanilla ice cream.

When you leave your spaces in the beautiful way they have always been, all you will get is status quo. Why not turn everything upside down and create a bit of chaos by going through your stuff now? Question the stuff that has been there for so long and is now the general landscape of your life, and ask if it truly belongs now.

As you slowly touch every single item, you will begin to peel away the layers of deceit and untruths you have been living and unveil the truths you want to honor, so that the feelings, thoughts, food, space, and stuff are all in alignment with the true beauty of you!

TruthLoveMeaningPurpose.

Yes, you are someone who cares deeply about others and has given your life to everyone. Now it is time to give to yourself. Now it is the time to be selfish and think about you and only you. No more depending on advisors to determine your next step.

You have been so accustomed to checking in with them that you forgot to check in with yourself.

Turning to a book or your usual resting pursuits is not the answer. The book is a getaway of sorts, an escape from the feelings you feel so deeply.

Delve deep within your heart. Your heart is what makes you who you are—uniquely you. You have built an empire by speaking the truth of your heart.

Now it is time to speak the truth of your heart to the child within. Let the truth resonate deeply within, and let the truth rock your spirit to the core. Let the truth of who you are and what you desire now—not tomorrow, but now—rise to the surface. Acknowledge the surprise eruptions of truth that you did not even know were there. As you slowly peel away the layers of untruths by touching your stuff and examining why it's in your life and why it's important, you will uncover some surprisingly monumental truths you were afraid to express because they seemed silly or selfish. They are not.

Live the truth of your heart. Crack your heart wide open! And trust that your journey will continue to be just as magnificent this time around, opening an even wider pathway into your heart for everyone to experience.

Trust that since we are in a physical universe, working on the physical stuff might help you uncover the mental, emotional, and spiritual stuff contained in your physical stuff. This process might be just what you need to touch those places deep within that were hiding from you!

I love you with all my heart and soul. You can do this. You are amazing. You are magnificent.

You are divine!

•

exercise. *touch the stuff deep within your soul.*

Without thinking too much, write down your answers to the following questions:

Is there something you are hiding from your true self?

Is there something you want to share with another soul?

What are you running away from every time you reach for food?

What is your heart trying to say to you? Pretend as if you have the answers and start writing about them, and don't worry if they're right or wrong. And don't analyze them.

The point of this exercise is to break through the inertia, or non-activity, or non-feeling, and do something to move yourself in a different way. Shed light into the dark places of your heart and mind, and slowly let those feelings and thoughts be heard. Now is not the time to criticize, judge, belittle, or doubt. Trust that whatever comes up is an issue you are supposed to deal with in order to move beyond the inertia, to take action, or to make amends with this issue. Perhaps once and for all, the truth will be unleashed, and you will start taking different kinds of action, because you will no longer be hiding the truth from yourself.

Just start today by answering the questions above, and don't be scared by what comes up. Trust that you can handle whatever comes your way. Trust that it is now coming up so you can heal yourself.

make friends with fear. *let it be your greatest teacher.*

in a personal growth workshop I attended, the seminar leader—who was a millionaire—said that he thought when he became a millionaire, the fears inside him would go away. But the truth was that the closer he got to his goal, and even when he reached his goal and went beyond that goal, the fears exacerbated and changed. They never really went away.

I also love Susan Jeffers' book, *Feel the Fear . . . and Do It Anyway*, because it acknowledges what I believe to be true and what I have witnessed while coaching and in my own life. The fear will always be there, so you might as well get used to it and do it anyway!

Whenever I have a speaking engagement, I overprepare and rehearse, yet I still can't wrap my head and heart around an audience or a venue I'm not familiar with. There are so many unknown factors that it doesn't really do me any good to worry and be scared of what I don't know. So I have learned to let go of all that I can't control, such as how people will respond, and whether people will like me or not. The only thing I have control over is my speech, how much I prepare, and my heartfelt intention to be a blessing. So I do whatever it takes to "ground," or center myself, so I can let my fears stay on the sidelines and focus on my intentions on why I am here. I redefine my fear as excitement, or anxiety, or not knowing about the unknown. I'm no longer buying into the fears and letting them dictate how I feel or what I do, but seizing the fear by its bullish horns and making friends with it.

I'm no longer pushing it away or shoving it under a rug and denying it's there.

I am letting go of that "clutter of fear" and replacing it with love and faith, trusting that although I am leaping into the unknown and don't know what to expect, I am loving the journey I'm on and trusting that I will be okay. I am making friends with my fears and allowing them to live on the sidelines while I befriend excitement about the unknown and focus on my purest of intentions of being a blessing with my speech, words, and presence.

Oftentimes I have found that the thing you fear most suddenly disappears when you walk up to it. Although I have been speaking in front of audiences from a very young age, I still am challenged to stay out of my fear thoughts and be in my love thoughts about being of service. I even tried to allay my fears of speaking by joining Toastmasters.

But in the end, I found out that my greatest weapon for this fear was being myself, and not trying to be a great speaker or some speaker that I was not. Having studied speakers for a long time, I learned that the best speakers are those who speak from their heart, who love the messages they deliver and love being there for their audiences. They are not worried about being good or right. They are not worried about being Martin Luther King Jr. or being a great orator. They simply focus on being their best self and offering their gifts to the audience.

So I have decluttered and let go of my fears by talking to them and becoming friends with them.

"It's okay. No one is going to hurt you. You are going to be fine. You are going to be more than fine. You're going to feel great."

Focus on the service. Let go of the fears. They are nothing more than scared little kids wanting love and attention, and they don't know you can handle it. You can handle whatever comes your way; you have God by your side.

This is how I have stepped up to face my fears time and time again.

The same has been true with writing this book. I am presenting my stuff to the world, finally, with fear. But I am friends with this faithful companion, whose presence lets me know that I have meaningful work before me, I have some clutter to deal with, and I can be a blessing while sharing my stories and innermost fears, thoughts, and feelings.

Forge ahead. Move ahead despite the fear.

Unless you take that next step, unless you go for it, fears and all, you will never know how far you can go.

Why not be at one with the fear, once and for all?

Acknowledge that it's there to challenge you to go for it and do it anyway.

Perhaps there's a new way of doing something you are unaware of because you are caught up in your own fears and a view of reality that is only a figment of your imagination.

It's okay for you to acknowledge your fears. When you are no longer denying them, they are no longer controlling your next steps. Fear prevents us from taking that next step, as we're afraid we will fall.

Why not believe in a new way of life?

When you put your fears into the light, you can identify the truth behind this "clutter of fear," and finally let it go or redefine it. The light of the truth will blind your fear!

You are now moving forward, fears and all, letting go of the past fears, and encountering new stuff (including fears!) that might challenge you to keep moving forward.

Trust that as you let go of old ways of being, new ways of being will take their place. Trust that as you let go of your fear of interacting with strangers at a party, you are creating space for making new friends.

Trust that as you let go of your fear of what will you say or do in a particular situation, you are creating space for a new way of being that exudes confidence that you are enough.

Love yourself enough to trust and have faith that you will be okay, no matter what.

Have enough faith in God and the Universe to believe that when taking that first step, you will be led to the next, best step for your journey.

For now, all you must remember is that although you might feel fear, acknowledge it, let it go, take a deep breath, and take that next step, whatever will move you forward.

Remember, you are a powerful magnet attracting new experiences and new stuff to your journey, so if you keep focusing on the fear that this bad stuff might happen, that is exactly what will happen.

Believe you are attracting only the good stuff now.

Believe you are creating your new reality now by letting go of those fears.

Make friends with your fear.

.

exercise. *three ways to befriend fear.*

Write about one fear you would like to release from your life. When was this fear born? Where did this fear come from? Did somebody else plant this fear inside of you? If this fear were gone, how would it alter your life?

Are you willing to let go of this fear now? Write to this fear, acting as if it is a being inside of you. Thank this fear for living within you, trying to protect you. Write about what this fear was protecting you from, and how it helped you to get to where you are today. Write about how this fear prevented you from taking action in other areas of your life and stopped you from moving forward. Forgive this fear for living inside of you, and tell it gently that you are now letting it go so you can create space for fearlessness regarding this area of your life.

Now, list three actions you can take right now that will signal to you that you are releasing this fear.

For instance, if the "fear of not being good enough" prevents you from going online to date, then three actions you can take are: Sign up for online dating. Say out loud to yourself, "I am good enough now to get married." Go out and buy *Bride* magazine, signaling to yourself that you are ready to get married and believe this will really happen.

Or if your fear is of public speaking, three actions you can take are: Sign up for Toastmasters. Speak up at your next company meeting. Sign up for a speech class, or buy a book on overcoming the fear of public speaking.

memorabilia. *your heart is the best memory book.*

do you need to display or keep everything you've ever gotten in your life? Every memento? Every award? Every photo? Every card you've ever received?

How much stuff do you need to remind yourself of the love you have? The recognition you've received? The places you've been? How loved you are?

Don't we carry the memories, the thoughts, and the feelings with us in our hearts and minds?

Let's go deeper.

Can we just say "thank you" to the memories, the people, and the times?

And be okay with that?

Do we have to keep that relic from the past to remind us of how meaningful our lives are, to say, "Yes, it really happened, and we exist. It meant something to me. I meant something to them."

Does putting your memories into some box labeled "Memorabilia" truly do them justice? I guess if someone were to unearth the Memorabilia Box of yours one hundred years from now, they would know that you lead a significant life, that you meant something to people, that you were loved, that these were the places you went, and that these are the things you accomplished.

Putting your memorabilia into a memory book for your loved ones to cherish now is better, because then you can flip through this special book, appreciate and honor your life now, in the present, and those who know you can know who you truly are.

Or instead of keeping it to share with others, do you keep the memorabilia—whether in a box, in a book, in files, or underneath your bed—just for yourself and only for your viewing pleasure? No one needs to know about it or see it; it's your special secret stash and private treasure box containing the meaningful stuff of your life that you take out every once in a while to visit, and going down memory lane in this way brings you joy.

Even so, how much stuff do you really need to remind others or to remind yourself of your important moments in life?

Yes, it's great that your child painted his first masterpiece and wrote his first letters in kindergarten. Indeed, these are "firsts" and accomplishments in and of themselves. But do you need to keep every single memento of every single accomplishment in kindergarten? How about just keeping the highlights of the year? How about keeping the elements that tell a story? What does your stuff tell you about yourself, and what story do you want to tell to others?

That's all that matters.

You don't need to capture everything and worry that something is missing.

Is there?

If there was, wouldn't you have thought of it in your heart and mind—then or now?

Cherish the depth and richness of the memories in your heart, soul, and spirit, which will stay with you forever.

Your heart is the best and truest memory book.

.

exercise. *three landmark mementos.*

Write about an important event in your life. Write about what it meant to you. Write about what you remember from the event. For example, what are your fondest memories from your high school reunion? What are your fondest memories of your child's first year in school? What are your fondest memories of your wedding? What are your fondest memories from the last party you attended?

Now, gather all the mementos from this occasion. Look at each one and pick one item that is the most significant reminder or symbol of this occasion. If you have several, that's okay. Ask yourself if you really need every single memento to remind you of this event. If you had to select only three items that were the best representations of this occasion, what would they be?

Keep only those photos and mementos that tell a story from your heart.

Don't include anything you don't want to remember, or a photo you don't love.

If you have felt burdened with the enormous number of souvenirs or photos from this event, now is the time to let go, trusting that your heart remembers every subtle nuance of this event, and that you don't need all this stuff to remember its significance in your life.

promises. *let go of broken promises.*

Y ou are not following through with your promise.

What promise?

That you would repair me. That you would take care of me.

What promises have you made to yourself that you are not keeping?

That you would go after that job opportunity or follow up on that referral.

What promises did you make to someone else?

That you would fix the leaky faucet. That you would take that person out for a cup of coffee.

Look around at your stuff.
What represents broken promises?
Broken stuff?
Stuff you promised to repair?
Stuff you promised to give away?
Stuff you promised to give to someone?
Thank-you letters you meant to write?

Today, do one thing you promised you would do.

Take that first step.

Because we are in a physical universe, we can think and dream of things we want to do, but unless we take action on the physical level, we are not moving forward.

Just thinking something and promising to do that thing will not get you there.

Today, promise yourself that you will follow through with one promise you made to yourself.

A baby step is all you need to take in that direction—and take that baby step all the way through, even though it might not be perfect.

Don't berate yourself for how long it took you to write a thank-you note, to write a letter to someone to say "I'm thinking of you," or to follow up on a referral, or to call somebody.

Be completely truthful.

Speaking directly from the heart will free up the guilt inside your mind and heart. The truthful communication between your heart, who yearns to do something and be somebody who follows through on their promises, needs to be aligned with your mind, who is convincing you that you really don't have to do it. Yes, the truth is that you don't have to do anything you don't want to do. But what do you have to lose if you take this action, even if the outcome is not something you intended and you feel rejected as a result? No matter what the result, when you follow through on a promise to yourself, the only thing you have to lose is your ego, while you gain pure liberation. Now there is nothing to hide, or to hide from. You have exposed your true self; you have put yourself out there no holds barred, without apology for who you are. What can your consciousness say to your mind and heart then? What can anyone else say?

Again, don't beat yourself up if the outcome is not what you intended. Be open to happy, unexpected results and surprises. Be open to the messages from this action and what you might learn.

Right now, you have the perfect opportunity to make a difference today that can affect your entire life!

Take one action step to fulfill a promise you made to yourself, and see what is freed up on the inside.

Or perhaps the action you need to take is let go of the promise. Perhaps you need to confront the truth of the situation and the importance of this promise within the greater context of your life, and decide it is okay to break that promise you made to yourself a long time ago.

If so, release the guilt. Now.

Okay, when I read this again, I remembered visiting my chiropractor yesterday and feeling guilty when he mentioned that I never forwarded him some health information that I "promised I would." I could have sworn I did it earlier, but rather than dwelling on it, defending myself, or feeling badly, I immediately went home and sent him that e-mail I promised to send him weeks ago. Sometimes, rather than proving you're right, it's just best to take action. I felt great doing it. Plus, that action triggered another action for me: I had the opportunity to say thank you for the free body-fat composition test I had received at his office weeks earlier.

As for letting go, I promised myself that I would let go of my list of "old acting contacts," since acting was no longer a truth in my life. Why did it take me literally years to fulfill my promise to let go of the contacts I had carefully built up in my rolodex while building my acting career? I had let go of the memorabilia, with just that one DVD of "The Best of June's Acting" remaining. For some reason, letting go of those contacts meant that I really meant what I said I was going to do—cut the cord once and for all. And, it also meant that I had to trust in the Universe/God that should this passion be somehow reignited in the future, new contacts would be born at that time. Once I finally let go of the old contacts, I felt so liberated. I was creating space for the possibility of another career in television and more contacts to truthfully engage with, cultivate, and nurture.

See what miraculous lessons and insights come your way that will free you up for your next steps—and the next, and the next.

·

exercise. *fulfill one promise.*

Acknowledge a promise you have not kept to yourself or another.

Today, take action on that promise. Fulfill that broken promise and fully complete it this time.

Write down how you felt while taking the action, your feelings about that action now that it's completed, and why it has taken you so long to take action.

Restore your faith in yourself to follow through on your word.

Forgive yourself for not fulfilling your promise.

Acknowledge your courage in confronting the truth and taking action to do something differently today.

From this point forward, write down every promise you make to yourself on your task list, and commit to take action in a timely fashion, so you don't accumulate a backlog of guilt about broken promises. If you've changed your mind and decide it's a promise that's okay to break, take it off your task list. If not, take action today. Remember, it's better to take action imperfectly than to expect yourself to do something perfectly and never take action at all.

symbols. *search for metaphors behind your stuff.*

t his morning while I was meditating, I had an epiphany.

I was still holding on to two things from my far distant past that for some reason I could never let go of.

I could let go of my Hello Kitty stuffed animal—the one that saw me through college, in which I sniffled away a lot of tears after my heart was broken in a very intense, first love relationship. Just the other day, my old college roomie wrote to me and told me that she loved that "great Hello Kitty" I had on my bed, whose body faced sideways and whose beautiful head faced front! I still have Hello Kitty pens that my mom's neighbor gave to me in all shapes and sizes, with sparkle, fur, and dangly stars, as well as a pen and pencil holder and a contact lens case that my assistant bought me as a gift! But, sorry Kitty, I had to let go of you after graduation because you only reminded me of heartbreak and heartache!

I could let go of the Miss Friendship trophy I received from a beauty pageant I was in when I was seventeen. I have many photos of me and the trophy, and I don't truly feel that title is me anymore. I also could let go of the necklace that a friend found on the street with my birthdate on it. At the time, I thought it was a sign that we were supposed to be friends. That's trippy—how she could just find a necklace with my birthday on it? Yes, my birthdate will never change, but do I need a necklace with my birthday on it? No.

So . . . getting back to the two things I haven't been able to let go of. One is a doll I had received from a relative in Japan. She sits prim and proper in a black wicker chair, with a beautifully sculpted face and blond hair, perfectly coiffed. The other is the Barbie from my childhood. She's leggy and voluptuous with a very, very tiny waist and blond hair nicely flipped out. After my meditation this morning, I realized that she represented someone I wanted to be a long, long time ago. She was an image of a beautiful girl I was trying to emulate. She obviously did not look like me. I mean, I have almond shaped eyes. She has wide doe eyes. She has blond hair. I have brown hair—even if it is lighter than most Asians.

I then realized that I need to let go of my clique—precious dolls—whom I had befriended many years ago. I need to let go of seeing them in my closet every time I open it as a reminder of someone who I am not, and who I no longer crave to be like.

I also remembered the connection with a memory I shared earlier in the book—the time when I tried out for the play *Cinderella* when I was seven, and one girl told me, "Cinderella is blond. She's not Asian." Just like that, I had allowed this girl's idea of what was possible for me squash my desire to be an actress and put it into a dark box! In that same box, I also stuffed my belief that I, like Cinderella, could have my fairy tale dream of being an actress come true!

My desire and my memory of that experience went into repressed memory for twenty years, until I studied with Sandy Meisner, and I shared that experience with him. I sincerely believe I went through that experience when I was seven so I could nurture other talents and pursue other desires until it was time for that dream to be reborn.

The point is that out of all the dolls I had held on to into my adulthood, the only two that remained were that blond doll from Japan and my blond Barbie. *Was it true,* I had thought often, *that blondes have more fun?* Is that why I had dyed my hair nearly blond during my teen years?

Yes, I had to get rid of both of them. Both blond dolls represented someone I was not, and these dolls were no longer going to rule my perceptions of what I could or what I couldn't get, achieve, or be in my life. As an adult, I now know that even though I'm not blond and Caucasian, I can act. I can act with my almond-shaped eyes and my brown hair. I can be Cinderella still.

Okay, truth—perhaps I haven't fully let go. I still have blond highlights in my hair.

But just the other day, I realized the other day that I no longer wanted yellow in my hair. I wanted more brown or more orange in my hair, but no more yellow.

I'm getting it corrected on Tuesday. I'm excited!

Perhaps I should fully let go of that doll and Barbie that day, too. They're just sitting in my closet, waiting to find a home.

Let's see what happens when I try to let them go.

Will they scream out, "Don't! I want to be with you! Don't you still long to be like me, look like me?"

Or do I want to keep them as reminders of this important lesson I've learned? Embrace fully who I am and what I look like . . . the inside is what counts. The outside body is the body I've been given this time around to learn particular lessons. My brunette hair color I was born with is thick and gorgeous, and my life has always been filled with fun.

I would love to create a line of Barbie dolls that look like me!

Come to think about it, I think someone already has. I remember buying an American Girl doll for my niece one Christmas that had almond-shaped eyes!

Anyway, does it have to be this complicated, this evaluation of stuff? For me, I realize it goes deep, and it is complicated.

Okay, I put the Barbie and other doll into a paper bag! Immediately, I felt badly, as if they're suffocating. My parents worked hard to buy me that Barbie doll. A relative brought that doll all the way from Japan. I remember seeing it on my shelf while growing up. It reminds me of my cheery yellow room with the rainbows from childhood. Whoa, there's so much attached to these dolls.

Should I go rescue them from the paper bag I was going to give away?

No, I feel this yearning to just let go.

Let go, and give them to a little girl who will cherish them and love them forever. Okay, maybe not forever, but for a long time.

I was going to give them to my nieces, but I don't want to perpetuate this idea of Barbie being the "ideal." I once asked my niece if she ever wanted to be someone else, and she said, "Sometimes." I very consciously told her then, "That's okay—but you're unique, and there's only one of you. Enjoy being who you are."

Okay, Blonde Barbie and Blonde Doll, I'm going to give you a nice home where some little girl can enjoy you and play with you, okay? I'm no longer punishing you just because you have blond hair. I'll let you have some fun, too.

Goodbye, Blonde Barbie and Blonde Doll. I release you with love.

•

exercise. *symbols behind stuff.*

Pick one item from your past that you would consider memorabilia. In other words, it has meaning because it represents a memory from the past. Start journaling and complete the following sentences:

This item represents a time in my life when . . .

This item makes me feel that . . .

This item makes me want to . . .

This item is something I love because it . . .

What does this item symbolize to you? What does it represent? Go as deep as you can. But don't worry if your answers are right or not, or if you've gone deep enough or not. The point is to start uncovering the reasons behind your stuff. Just start writing about it and see what comes up. Whatever comes up is perfect. It may not be apparent right away, but you may discover a pattern in the stuff you have collected over the years.

Eventually, I believe the answer will be revealed to you, when you are ready to deal with it.

Come back to this exercise anytime you want to explore the deeper meaning behind why you have something and what it represents to you, beyond its superficial function and purpose.

choices. *choose to see your stuff in a different light.*

g et clear.
What is it you want?
What kind of life do you want to lead?
In the end, what kind of person would you want others to say you were?
What would your stuff say about you?

There are so many choices you can make in life.
There are so many choices you are faced with every single day in your life.

From the minute you wake up in the morning (actually, before that), you get to decide whether you want to wake up to a blaring alarm clock, to the sun streaming in and waking you up gently, or to a clock radio playing your favorite song. Then, you get to decide what to wear in the morning. Then, you get to decide whether to eat breakfast or not, and if you eat, what to eat. Every single day, you are faced with a million choices. And, whether or not you believe it, you are making a million choices.

Even where you are living is a choice.
Who you are living with is a choice.
Where you are working is a choice.
What thoughts you are thinking is a choice.

All life is a choice.
The choice to love.
The choice to hate.
The choice to live.

The choice to die.
The choice to live life on the surface.
The choice to live life deeply.
The choice to feel.
You can think, *I love my life!*
Or you can think, *I hate my life!*

Just today, I forgot to turn off the engine to the Prius, and I had to call AAA to jumpstart my car—again! I could have gotten all stressed out that the battery was dead, but instead, I chose to enjoy the parking lot and city in which I was "stuck" for a while. Then, after my car was jumped and running again, I chose to roll down all my windows and take a drive along Pacific Coast Highway to enjoy the ocean breeze and the beautiful Indian summer weather in early November, to give my car the thirty minutes it needed to energize the car battery again. It definitely energized me in a different way as well, giving me a boost of gratitude in my heart for the amazing place I live!

What a marked contrast to this morning, when I walked out of the elevator and jubilantly said, "Good morning!" And this man at the laundry machine said, "Terrible morning! This machine is giving me a hard time!" *Wow!* I thought. *This man is allowing himself to have a bad time, giving his choice of feeling over to this machine.* The truth was that he lived in a grand place and life could be worse. If his only problem in life was that the laundry card machine wasn't working, he had it pretty good! No judgment, but still, it reminded me of how we make choices about what happens to us every moment.

On my birthday last year, I went to work out at a gym, and while the class was in progress, the trainer spotted a meter maid giving me a parking ticket. I thought, *Why is she giving me a parking ticket when I thought I had obeyed all the signs?* It turns out that I was in a "one hour zone"—and because I had arrived a few minutes prior to class, I was over the hour limit. *Oh, well,* I thought. But interestingly enough, when everybody found out that it was my birthday, they exclaimed, "What a bummer that you got a parking ticket on your birthday!" And I immediately rebounded with, "Actually, thank God I have a car that can be ticketed, and what a great thing that I'm celebrating my birthday exercising my God-given body! So actually the parking ticket is a minor hiccup to my day in the big scheme of things, and I'm so lucky for all I have!" To that, no one said a word, and I bounced out of the gym energetically, didn't take a look at the "price" I had to pay for parking in that space, and instead chose to focus on the amazing life I had, and how lucky I was to celebrate my birthday doing what I chose to do that day!

Choice. That's what it all comes down to.

You can choose to be jaded and shut down your heart due to your mishaps, mistakes, misunderstandings, and being misunderstood. Or you can choose to shut down your heart for fear of being hurt again.

Or you can choose to crack your heart wide open, even though you have been hurt, betrayed, and misunderstood, trusting that lessons live in every experience, and it may not even be about you at all. The choices you make about what happens to you makes all the difference in life.

I can choose to step in doo-doo, and exclaim, "Oh gosh, I stepped in doo-doo. I can't believe it. I can't believe I did that. Stupid June, you stepped in doo-doo—didn't you see it coming?" I could examine it and dissect all the different shapes, sizes, and smells of the doo-doo, and choose to hold on to the doo-doo. I could show everyone the doo-doo over and over and over, sharing the story wherever I went. I could even choose to throw the shoe with the doo-doo into a closet, without even bothering to wipe it off, so I could hold on to that shoe full of the painful memories of stepping in doo-doo.

Or I could choose to wipe off the doo-doo, laugh, and let it go, keeping only the lesson—to remember to look where I step next time, so I don't step into doo-doo again! Ha ha ha ha!

So, today, why not take a risk and make a different choice from the choices you have made in the past? Why not choose to look at your stuff and the stuff that happens to you in a different light?

Start with the little stuff, and make choices that bring you joy. Make choices that make you feel giddy inside. Make choices that make you feel like you are putting yourself out there in a way you have never done. Yes, yes, yes! It might feel scary at first, but more than that, I bet you will feel so alive! You will feel like you are living life to its fullest, and perhaps living life on the edge. Make those choices that make you scream like you are on a roller-coaster ride! Why not just make choices that thrill your heart, not knowing what will happen next?

Your heart knows all things and is the direct link to Source. Remember, your mind only can process stuff based on your past, like a computer. Your mind is filled up with what has happened in the past, and knows only what it knows based on the past, whereas the heart is linked to intuition and infinite intelligence, and knows and feels way more than what is contained in your mind and past experiences.

Today, make choices that make your heart smile, laugh, and beat faster! Make choices based on how you feel in your heart today!

·

exercise. *find the blessing in the annoyance.*

Write about something that annoyed you recently. Why were you annoyed?

Choose to see the event in a different light.

If any miracles came from the annoyance, what would they be?

What was the blessing or lesson learned from that event?

exercise. *make it a great day, no matter what happens.*

For one week, decide to have a great time every single day, no matter what happens. If something happens that would usually irritate you, this time laugh it off! Pretend as if you actually created this "irritation" to test or teach yourself. What would the test or teaching be?

See how you feel living life this way by framing your events and stuff that happens from this perspective. Do grander, greater, and better things happen to you because you're in this state of bliss, expecting every day to be great? Most importantly, how you do you feel about your life? I guarantee you that you will, at the very least, feel better and better every single day.

decisions. *prioritize your top three choices.*

L et the right choices and decisions come easily to you. How? By letting life flow. Let it ebb and flow.

I'm at the Fran & Ray Stark Sculpture Gardens at the Getty Museum. I notice there are only three sculptures.

Only three.
Not four.
Not five.
Not two.
Three.

Someone made a decision: three sculptures.

Serving as the backdrop for the sculptures are lines of identical trees, low grass, and the mountaintops in the distance. Simple, because assortments of trees or grass don't clutter up the background.

The beauty and simplicity of the sculptures stand out.

Think about one thing in your house.
Do you love it?
Does it stand out on its own?

Group your items into threes and arrange them against a plain backdrop.
Put only three items on a shelf.
Put only three plates on a shelf.

Put only three books on a bookcase.

See how it feels.

Do those three items stand out?

Are they special?

What is the message you are giving to yourself that you picked those three items?

Do they resonate with your TruthLoveMeaningPurpose?

I once taught a little girls' class on organizing, and I asked every girl to bring her favorite three items. It was revelatory when they described to me why they brought these three favorite items. At their tender young age of seven, eight, and nine years old, they were clearly able to decide, discern, and express why these three items were important. They were able to choose only three items. When I asked the TruthLoveMeaningPurpose of the items, they talked about their feelings. The stuff was not necessarily the stuff they had displayed.

One of the little girls talked about one of her favorite stuffed animals. I asked her where it lived. She said, "Underneath the bed." I asked her why it lived there in the dark. She shared, "My father was killed, and this is the last thing he gave to me." I asked her how she felt about that, and of course she missed him and was very sad. I suggested that she let this special animal live in the light, and to love it and cherish it with all the love she had for her father. Her decision to share her favorite item with the other girls was the child within crying to be expressed and dealt with. I encouraged every girl to remove all the other stuff from their shelves and rooms, and pay proper respect to these three favorite things they had picked.

You can do this exercise as well: Pick your three favorite items and display them in a place of honor. Then, a month or two or even a year later, do this same exercise, and if you pick three other things, then you can retire the items you had displayed, either by letting them go because they had already played their part to remind you of the love, beauty, and other gifts behind the stuff, or by stashing them in a Memorabilia box to remind you of the memories.

Why as adults do we get so confused when making a decision? Why do we sometimes fear we are not making the right decision? Why do we second guess our choices? Why do we look back and relive the past and think, *If I had made this choice, what would have happened?*

I teach people that every choice they make is divine and perfect in that moment, so why not evaluate each decision and choice based on the brilliant lessons you gain? Sure, we wish we could go back in space and time and "coulda woulda shoulda" done things differently, but rather than lament, why not be compassionate with yourself, and say instead, "I did the best I could with the information I had, and obviously I had an important lesson to learn in making that decision at that time."

Decide now that whatever you decide in this moment is for the highest good. You can only make a decision based on who you are today, what you have gone through, and what you have. So don't lament about or regret the decisions you've made. And don't be afraid you'll make a mistake now.

Liberate yourself today: pick your "top three," and see how that feels. Just expressing out loud your preferences and decisions will free you and help you to soar. Once again, we're trying to get you to shift your perspective in order to move you forward. That shift can happen without vacillating, by making clear decisions about what's in front of you.

.

exercise. *three special items.*

Pick three items that are special to you. Don't overthink this one. Just pick the first three items that come to your mind.

Clear one shelf in your house and display only those three items for one week. See how you feel when you look at that bookshelf filled only with three items that you love. Look at it every day.

Write down your feelings. How does it make you feel? Do you see these three items differently when displayed prominently on your shelf?

At the end of the week, do you deem these items just as important as the day you picked them to display? Were they worthy of being displayed for one week? If not, replace them with the three items that you most love at that moment at the end of the week. And, if you are feeling no more "love" for the three items that you displayed, let go of them.

exercise. *three favorite books.*

Pick your three favorite books that you are reading and/or want to read. Take out all the other books in your nightstand or next to your bed. Now put these three favorite books there.

Write about how you felt doing this. Did you feel badly putting the other books aside? Why was it difficult to make these choices? Notice your propensity to want to justify your choices and not make firm choices. Notice how you feel everything is important.

Write about how your inability to choose is, in fact, choosing to make everything important, and how this choice can be contributing to your clutter. Write about this, and see if this realization activates you to start making different choices from this point forward.

tell a new story. *own your stuff.*

i n his book *Four Agreements*, Don Miguel Ruiz says that we have been making agreements with ourselves since we were little through the belief systems fed to us.

What agreements have you made with yourself? What truths do you stand for?

Start writing down those agreements and truths—anything that rings true for you. Just keep writing and see what comes up. Once you have a list, start numbering them in order of priority. You'll realize which ones are the most important for you and this list can then become your personalized commandment list.

This commandment list is about honoring the truth of your priorities. It is about honoring the truths that ring true in your heart. It is about the way you would love to live your life in your ideal world. Now, by encouraging you to list as many agreements and truths and ideals as you can, I don't mean to encourage you not to take your rules seriously or to violate them. Including them on the list will remind you of what you are striving for.

Every single time you go through an experience, don't just slough it off. Don't just lament or bemoan what happened. Look deeper for that golden nugget, that amazing lesson you learned by going through this struggle or situation.

Think, *Thank God I went through that, or else I would not have learned this important lesson.*

Think, *Thank God I went through that again to remind me of something I had forgotten a long time ago.*

Think, *Thank God I went through that again. I thought I had learned that lesson and thought I knew better, but I think this time, it will be with me forever. I am over having to go through this—again. I get it now, God. Thank you so much, God!*

209

If you do this with every single encounter, experience, relationship, and event that occurs from now on, the result will be a lifestyle and a state of being that will emanate "thank you" wherever you go. You are thanking every single person on your path for being a powerful messenger, conspiring to help make your dreams come true. Everyone and everything is here to teach you how to get to happiness and joy and love more quickly and easily.

Can it be that easy?

Yes.

The opposite way is also just as easy. When we shove aside the experience, chalking it up to ignorance or blaming somebody else or something else, and fail to look within, we start building up a wall of resentment, anger, and unforgiveness.

We start looking at the world as if it is conspiring against us and doing something to us. And the more we begin thinking like this, the more we create this exact experience. Why not stop that right now?

Take responsibility for what has happened, what you have created, what you are doing and being and living now.

There is no blame.

There are only questions that can be asked to get to the truth of the answers that live within your spirit. You will know if you choose to shed light on it.

And, don't say, "I don't know."

Don't cop out and pretend that you don't know.

You do know. Wait for the answer. It will reveal itself.

You are a powerful creator.

If you created what you have—the relationships you are in, the messes, the mistakes— you can create their exact opposites. You must first believe, however, that you are a powerful creator. Then, take responsibility, and start asking why you created what you see before you.

Start at the beginning of your life. Even if it seems like a stretch, ask why each event happened and what you were supposed to learn. Then, write the lesson down. Do this for every single experience you have ever had in your life. Write the story of your life as it happened from your perspective.

Now, write the story of your life from a different perspective, from the perspective that everyone and everything is here to teach you how to to learn, grow, evolve, and transform.

See what happens when you look at your past from this shift in perspective. Then, write your commandments from what you have learned.

I have used this powerful tool and exercise with many clients to help them declutter their past, and shift their warped perspective on their lives. Some have thought, *I had a f***ed-up past. I was born into this f***ing family. I grew up with f***ed-up parents. I f***ed up.*

To shift that f***ed-up attitude and perspective, I first ask them to relay their story to me in their own words.

Then I ask them, "If everything happened for a reason, and everything that happened to you was beautiful and blessed and intended as a gift to get you to where you are today, then tell me about every single person and experience in your life, believing there was a million-dollar lesson in that experience."

I have been able to shift the perspective of many by taking them on a different ride. The only requirement for going on this ride is to take personal responsibility for your life, and to stop playing the victim and "poor me." If you continue to think things are being done to you, and—poor you—you had to suffer so much, all the therapy and tools in the world will not help you. You can have all the money and all the stuff in the world, but as long as you choose to live this story from this perspective, you will continue to create and perpetuate more experiences, people, and events that are "being done" to you.

You will never have true power, because you are always giving away your power through your belief that you are not empowered.

Today, take your power back. Rewrite your stuff. Write the commandments that you adhere to and abide by what you have learned is the most important, based on your unique life experiences.

Own your experiences. Own your stuff. Own your life. Own your lessons. Own your insights. Own the blessings, miracles, and messages.

·

exercise. *commandments, core beliefs, and values.*

Write your own personalized list core beliefs and values that will become your Ten Commandments for Living. Don't think too much about it. Just start writing and see what comes up. And if you come up with more than ten, great! Continue writing. This exercise will help you own everything about the stuff of your life, inside and out. If your inner stuff and outer stuff are not in alignment with your own commandments, you will recognize it and make a decision to let go or keep whatever stuff is standing in the way of living your ideal life.

exercise. *million-dollar lessons.*

Start a new journal. Call it Million-Dollar Lessons Learned.

Now, on each page, write down every lesson you have learned and write the story behind the lesson. The heading of each chapter is the name of the lesson.

Your life is the culmination of the experiences and lessons learned, so what better way to look at your life than as if you have millions of dollars of experiences in the bank? Why not carry that forward with you, to create a beautiful existence where you feel like a million bucks wherever you go?

The point of these exercises is to get you engaged in your unique perspective and stories of your life. The stories of your life are actually your unique lessons learned from your life experiences. In writing about the lessons learned, you are radically shifting your perspective of your life, and rewriting the stories you tell yourself.

true age. *it's all in your heart and mind.*

People have always thought that I'm much younger than I really am.

My brothers make fun of me when we're together, because I still swing my hair to-and-fro, like a little girl bouncing down the street, singing a silly song, like I used to do when I was little. They always say to me, "How *old* are you?"

I retort, "How *young* am I?"

Who says that we have to stop acting a certain way when we reach a certain age? Who says that we have to start doing things when we reach a certain age? Who made up those rules?

I attended a party yesterday where I was talking to someone who said, "I better get into shape now, before it gets harder and harder to get my body into shape. If I do it now, it'll be easier to maintain that shape for years to come." This person was in their early thirties! I disagreed and said, "Your body can get into shape no matter what age you are, whenever you decide you want to. Your body will listen to whatever you tell it. Your body will believe whatever you tell it. If you tell your body that it is old, and that you are old, you and your body will behave as if you are old. If you tell your body that you are young and that your body will get younger and younger with each passing day, your body and your subconscious mind will carry out these orders as if you are young."

I did this experiment and started confessing to myself that every day I'm getting younger and younger. That same week, I visited a Chinese doctor who performed acupuncture on me, who remarked, "Whatever you are doing, you must keep doing it. The insides of your body are as if you are a teenager." I was forty-eight at the time.

When I turned nineteen, I thought, "Wow, I don't feel like it!" That's when I started saying on my birthday, every year, "I am getting younger and younger every year." I know it sounds crazy now, but it actually has worked for me, I think, because people always think I'm much younger than I really am.

I had another conversation with a woman who said that she had always wanted to rock climb since she was little, but now she was getting too old, and her body would not be able to handle it. I asked, "Who told you that?"

Who told you that you cannot do something now because you are a certain age? The other day I read the most inspiring article about an eighty-three-year-old fearless super grandma who kayaks, parasails, skydives, and go-karts! Who said that you cannot learn a new language when you are in your sixties? Who said that you cannot fall in love when you are eighty or eight? Who said that you cannot learn the piano at age fifty-eight?

I skied at least once a year from age eighteen to twenty-five for seven years, sometimes twice a year, usually for one week at a time. I thought I was quite good, but actually I was just fearless. I skied diamond slopes and challenged myself to keep up with the "risk takers," and I didn't care if I looked like a fool, falling all over the place. I didn't think twice about not doing it because of how I looked or how old I was.

Then I took a nearly twenty-year hiatus, and when I went skiing again, when I was forty-five, I remember how frustrating it was because in my mind's eye, I thought I could just pick it up again. While my nieces came zipping down the hill a few times, I was still on my first run, struggling to get down the intermediate slope. Perhaps I should have tried the beginner slope the first time around. My ego got in the way, and I kept cursing to myself, "You were good. What happened?"

In retrospect, I realized that my ego prevented me from improving more quickly because I was so caught up in the past of "how good I was" and comparing myself to "how I was then," which kept me from just being at one with where my body was in the moment, so that I could not even embrace what I was doing in the moment.

When I finally let go of my past and embraced the present, guess what happened?

My body remembered how to ski.

Aha. Rather than beat myself up, I was gentle to my body, and my body loved being loved and talked to nicely, and responded quickly. Suddenly, it was as if I was eighteen again, going up and down the hill without being in my head. I was in the moment, paying attention to each of the moguls and navigating around them just like a pro again.

I learned an important lesson. Let go of the past, and stay in the present. Lamenting the past only holds me back from moving forward. Honor the present for what it is. Embrace the past and all its glory. The glory of the present is a gift itself. The lessons of the present are what are important for me to move forward.

How often do we get stuck in our heads, thinking about how great we used to be at something and how good we used to be at something, and stop attempting to even try something we used to do for fear of not being "that good" again? And how often do we stop ourselves from even trying something for fear of what will happen or what it would look like at our age?

Next time you say, "I'm too old to do/be/wear/have . . . ," remember that you're never too old or too young. You're the perfect age, whatever age you are.

Age is a number we are assigned when we are born. But that doesn't mean you need to keep that chronological number forever.

And next time you catch yourself saying, "I used to do this . . . I used to have this . . . I remember how good I used to be when I was that age . . . ," stop yourself.

Today decide the age you are in your head and heart, and be that age. Do, be, have, wear stuff as if you were that age, and see how that makes you feel. Do you feel more alive? Do you feel more energized?

If you do, great—continue on with that wave of thinking, and see what else you want to do/be/have today with this new age you've assigned yourself.

Infinite possibilities arise when you begin to think like this, outside the box.

.

exercise. *anything is possible at any age.*

Write down your feelings about your age.

Write down a few things you have not done because of your age.

Now, pick one thing on that list, and do it.

Now, write down how you felt doing that activity, and your feelings about your age again. Even tackling the activity can be enough to change your mind about your age.

dig deeper. *get to the truth behind the stuff.*

Photos are one of the most difficult items to sift through and let go of, because every single photo brings up so many memories. All of a sudden, five hours later, you've spent all your time going down memory lane, triggered by perhaps just one photo!

Oh, I remember that '50s backward dance when I borrowed my aunt's circle skirt, put my hair up, and looked like I was straight out of a scene from *Happy Days* and won an award for Best Costume!

Oh, no! What was I thinking when I tried to bleach my own hair? It turned blond, and then orange, and then, when I finally went to the expert, it turned pitch black and I looked like helmet head! I'm throwing that photo away—I hated the way I looked!

I remember when we all went to Santa Barbara's wine country and stayed at the Charlie Chaplin Montecito Inn to celebrate Mom and Dad's fortieth anniversary. Wow, my nieces were so tiny, and now they're all grown up. Mom and Dad looked so happy. We all looked so happy together. That was *so* special spending time together—I wish we could do that again. Oh, right, we won't be able to . . . Dad is now gone. I miss Dad.

The act of going through photos is so emotionally charged, with so many layers, that it's not as easy as perhaps organizing and decluttering office supplies or kitchen utensils.

While in the midst of helping my brother move and get his house organized, my mom suddenly showed up with a box of photos from my past. She was letting go of the shed that contained the overflow from the garage. *OMG,* I thought. I had gone through everything from my past and thought I hadn't left anything at her house, but somehow this box had escaped me.

I knew this was no accident. I welcomed this unexpected gift! As I've learned from my past, there are no such things as mere coincidences, and everything happens to propel me forward. I just need to look at the deeper meaning behind the seemingly trivial stuff.

I smiled, knowing that the Universe conspired to bring me this particular box of stuff to go through so I could confront something I had been holding on to mentally, spiritually, and emotionally. Until that moment I didn't even know that box existed. But according to divine order and timing, my consciousness somehow signaled to the Universe that I was ready to confront more stuff, and this physical stuff would trigger more "letting go" of on other levels to free me in my life!

I encourage you to deal with the box or stuff that presents itself while you are on the journey. The paperwork that slips out of your hand, calling for you to read it. The box that your attention is drawn to. A nagging feeling you are supposed to go into the garage to deal with the memorabilia. Instead of denying those feelings or promptings from the Universe, look at them as opportunities to do work on yourself, let go, confront an issue, or even forgive a person from your past that may have betrayed you or hurt you.

Don't shove that stuff, box, or feelings underneath more clutter. "Deal with it now!" is what the Universe is asking you to do, especially when it seems as if the stuff came out of the blue! Confront the feelings that the stuff triggers. Deal with the feelings, attitudes, and belief systems that come up, one at a time, and trust that the stuff is there to help you shift your life for the highest good.

All of the stuff, whether it's photos, paperwork, letters, clothes, or pots are symbolic metaphors for your life and where you are today, and you can use all of this stuff as powerful tools in your personal growth and evolution.

So while in the midst of setting up systems for my brother's new house, I took a break to go through this mystery box of photos my mom had found! As I soon as I saw the first picture, I knew this box was laden with memories and stuff that I needed to release. I felt an invisible stream of heavy energy pour out of the box as soon as I took off the lid, and I took a deep breath. This subtle but powerful energy was telling me, *Slow down. Take your time. Notice. Be aware. This is extremely significant.*

I saw stacks of these mini three-by-three-inch photos of different girls and boys. I noticed that on the back of these photos, there was a recurring theme. Everyone had written on the back of their photos, "Dearest June, Stay Sweet and Don't Change." These were photos from when I was about twelve to when I was in high school. I started remembering what a good friend this person was, what they did for me, and the happy times we shared. And I got very emotional and nostalgic, and I started pondering, *Where is this person today? What is she doing?*

At first, I enjoyed going down memory lane and recalling these friendships, but then after a while, I became exhausted. It's as if all the buoyant energy that I started the day with was sucked out of me. I started feeling badly and punishing myself for not remembering anything about these photos that I had in my possession. Then, my mind went into a mad frenzy: *What should I do with these photos? I should throw them out. Just do it! No, I can't. Oh, I know—I'll send it to this other friend who knows that person and that . . .*

The truth was that these people were friends I had exchanged pictures with in grade school, and not really close friends anymore, but it didn't matter. It didn't make logical sense in my head. I felt confused, overwhelmed, and ripped up inside my heart. I didn't know what to do with the photos. I was torn.

So I told myself: Go deeper, June. You are the client. Confront the TruthLoveMeaningPurpose of the here and now. Okay, what is holding you back from letting go of these photos, when the truth is you are not close to these friends anymore? Do you want to create a memory book? C'mon, when was the last time you did that? Oh, right—you never have. Great idea in theory. That's not truthful, June. Okay, will you ever look at these photos again if you keep them in the box? Probably not. Will you go through photos and reminisce again— will that bring you joy? Probably not. You kinda sorta did that, and look at how you're feeling now. Okay, do you still want these memories? What memories? You don't have too many memories of those times, so what is the truth? Are the class pictures you still have of every grade enough? What is your intention in keeping these photos?

So many feelings stirred up. So many thoughts running rampant in my mind. I could feel myself getting resistant and defensive—a part of me didn't want to deal with it and just wanted to throw the box away. But I knew I could never do that, because in the back of my mind I would know I cheated myself out of the lesson of whatever this box was trying to teach me. A part of me wanted to throw the photos back into the box and do it later. But then I would have to carry that box with me wherever I went, knowing I would have to deal with it someday. Still, it would be much easier to push whatever it was to the side— would I be able to handle it if I dug even deeper for the truth behind this stuff?

Go for it, June! You can handle whatever comes your way.

Whoa! OMG! It was fear! Fear of what? Fear of change. Fear of what they would think of me. What would they really think of me if they knew I was throwing away their picture?

So then, realizing this, I started imagining "them" saying to me, "Wow . . . you have changed. That's not what a sweet person would do. That's not very nice, June, to just throw away my picture . . . " So was I holding on to the pictures because of what they supposedly might think, and carrying their opinions with me inside my consciousness? That's deep. That is a huge insight. Go deeper, June.

So was I holding on to this image of myself as the "good friend to everyone, the sweet one," and that I liked that idea of who I used to be. But is the truth that I'm no longer that "sweet friend," and I have let go of trying to be good friends with everyone and being there for everyone, and that these photos, this physical stuff, are making me confront again what I had already done mentally, emotionally, and spiritually? Is the physical stuff taunting me, questioning me, making me stand up for myself about the decision I have made: "Are you sure this is the path for you? Are you sure this is who you are?"

Then it struck me—I was allowing these photos to become tentacles to my past. On one hand, I want to honor my past and love my past, because it is what makes me who I am today. But on the other hand, I want to let go of my past and release others' perceptions of me, so they do not constrict who I am today and/or get in the way of who I am still becoming. "Don't change" is a huge burden to thrust on me. Why would they say that? Not just one person, but many people said this to me. Interesting, huh?

Was I still carrying this "don't change" directive around with me? Was I not changing because of this subconscious belief locked deep inside that I needed to "not change" and always be there for others—and that if I changed, I would not be sweet or be a good friend anymore. I thought I had gotten over this "people pleasing" and "seeking approval" a long time ago. Why is it coming up again? So I could, once and for all, let it go.

So do you see how deep going through your stuff can be? This box of photos brought up an entire can of worms for me that I did not know existed in my subconscious mind. I could have just kept each photo and put them into a memory book to honor the memories of those in my past. I could have kept the photos for a while and sent them to friends who knew these friends and written a note. But neither of these actions felt right in my spirit and gut.

In fact, it was perfectly synchronistic for me to go through these photos on the day I was going to my twentieth high school reunion—just before I was going to reconnect with friends from my past!

As I was confronting my stuff, I was honoring who I am today. Letting go of others' ideas about me and what they may want me to be or do. Letting go of what seem like tentacles to my past. Because really there are no tentacles. No one is holding me back or moving me forward. This confrontation was a confrontation of myself, of my perceptions about who I am or was or could be. It was an opportunity to remember the goodwill, kindness, and friendship of others and that everyone is doing their very best at all times.

I cried as I realized that saying "Don't change" was also their way of saying, "We love you just the way you are." That's a beautiful thing, and I am *so* lucky to have so many friends who loved me and cared for me.

So, with this shift in perspective, I consciously chose to do a ritual and pay homage to each and every single person who had been in my life. I sat at the dining table with my stacks of photos, and I looked at each photo, thanking each person for being a friend in my life, for our good times together, and for their kind words. And one by one, I started throwing the pictures into the trash.

Guess what? I don't even need the photos to bring up emotions. I am getting very emotional and shedding tears even now, just thinking about how lucky I have been my entire life and how grateful I am for every friend that I have ever had. Simply recalling these memories triggers other memories of other friends whose photos I don't even have, because their presence, being, and spirit are etched in my memory bank forever.

The truth is I am such a sentimental person that I don't need the photos to remember the memories. I don't need the physical photos to remind me of how lucky, how blessed I am. When I consciously think of somebody, I bring up a photo memory book in my mind's eye, rifle through the pages of my memories, and arrive at exactly the right image in my mind to honor that person or experience. Thinking of someone in this way may lead me to take action by writing them an e-mail or letter, or just sending them love, or whatever feels right in my gut.

Now, I don't recommend that everyone should throw away all their pictures. The issue was that I was keeping the pictures for the wrong reason. The truth was that I hadn't looked at those photos for twenty years, and the truth was that I didn't have that many photo albums anymore, so I had to let go of them. And I had to trust that the memories, and everybody's kind words, deeds, and actions, will always be a part of me.

This journey of going through your stuff can go deeper than you could have ever imagined, as you honor what is true and let go of what is no longer true. But if your intention is to go through your stuff to allow it to inform you about your authentic self, and let go of the stuff that is no longer you and is therefore holding you back from being all you are now, then I guarantee that you will get huge messages about your journey. Just by putting your intentions out into the Universe in this way, insights and truths you need to remember will be brought to the surface, allowing you to release any feelings or thoughts that are keeping you from moving forward.

You will then realize how valuable it is to go through your stuff consciously. That there is no such thing as "wasting time or energy" when going through your stuff. That every single item you touch, process, and evaluate is an opportunity for you to touch yourself deeply inside, and witness the rebirth of this beautiful miracle called your true authentic self!

•

exercise. *three pictures. three profound lessons.*

Take out a box of photos. Close your eyes and pick three pictures. Believe that these three pictures were "selected" by your soul to teach you something. Look at each picture and ask yourself, *What does this photo represent and mean to me?* Depending on the meaning and symbol, decide whether to keep it or hold on to it.

The point of this exercise is to remind you how deep this process goes. If you are willing to delve deep and stay open, everything that comes to the surface will be powerful messengers on your journey, propelling you forward. These three photos are communicating to you a deeper message that your life is deep, wide, and expansive, and that the only way to move forward with love and light is to touch what you have, become acutely aware of why you are holding on to it, and choose to let it go or keep it based on those deeper, meaningful reasons.

exercise. *one talisman to exemplify one quality of your authentic self.*

Think about a quality that you want to add to your life.

Now go and seek out one item, photo, object, or even a piece of paper you possess that exemplifies this quality you would like to embody. Place it in a visible place where you can see it every day.

It can be a photo of yourself as a child, happy and giddy, without a care in the world, reminding you that this carefree child still lives within you. It can be a special rock you kicked all the way to school and deemed as your lucky charm, reminding you that you still believe in magic and miracles. It can be a poem you wrote when you were little, reminding you of the wonderful writer you were then and are still now.

exercise. *let go of the symbols of the old you.*

Now think about qualities in your life that you want to delete, edit, and let go of. Go and seek out items, photos, objects, and papers that represent this quality or essence that you no longer want in your life. Let them go with love, and thank the objects for serving you.

the deeper meaning. *what am i saying to myself with my stuff?*

g et to the deeply rooted meaning behind your stuff. Get to the deep purpose behind your stuff. Get to the truth of your stuff. Love yourself and all your stuff for now, because it is where you are right now.

Believe that by looking at your stuff in a different light, you are assigning a different meaning to it, which will radically shift your perspective about how you deal with your stuff, and you will start doing things differently. And you will feel a measurable shift in your life!

What does all this stuff mean? When I see someone's stuff, or can feel someone's stuff when I talk to them, I get a sense that the stuff is talking to the person. Your stuff is talking to you, whether you think it is or not. The stuff is robbing you of your vitality, energy, and life force whenever you stuff it somewhere—in a closet, your body, your mind, or your heart—and pretend it is not there. Deal with it.

Let's start now by going through your underwear to see what the deeper meaning is behind it all!

Go to your underwear drawer now.

Dump the entire drawer out.

Now, sort through the underwear by type. *Boxers, thongs, boy shorts, jockeys.*

Now, that the underwear is sorted by type (or in like-item piles), look at each pair. And ask yourself these four questions:

What is the truth of this underwear? When was the last time you wore this? *Once. Last week.*

Do you love this underwear? *No, I bought it because I ran out of underwear because I didn't do laundry. Yes, I love it because it is comfortable and fits perfectly.*

Do you have this underwear because it has meaning? *I bought it for my first date with my husband. I bought it for our wedding.*

Now go deeper. Examine another pair closely.
How would you describe it? *Tattered, worn, stained.*
Does it feel like it is "tired"? *Yes.*
Does it have positive life force? *No.*
Do you get excited at the thought of wearing this underwear? *No.*
Would you wear this underwear if you knew your lover was going to see it? *Of course not.*
Would you wear this underwear on your wedding night? *Never.*

What does all this mean?

I'm trying to get you to go deeper with your stuff. I'm trying to get you to have in your life only those things that truly bring you joy and elation. That make you feel so alive that you feel like singing and you're on top of the world.

Can you do that with your *underwear*? Yes.

Your underwear is what you wear underneath your clothes. When you go to work, no one will see your underwear. So many people choose to wear tattered, torn underwear that is merely functional because "no one can see it." What does that say about you? You are wearing your Armani power suit—and "tired underwear" beneath that power suit?

Are you in alignment from the inside out? Do your values, belief systems, and attitudes align with what your heart desires?

Go even deeper.

What do you care about?

You only care about outside appearances.

You focus all your energy on the outside and what people can see.

What does your higher self, who is always watching, think about this?

What does your child self, who is always so truthful, think about this?

Are you pretending you don't care about your underwear?

Do you not even know if you are wearing underwear that reflects your consciousness?

Prosperity consciousness thinks, "I don't want to spend even one day wearing ratty underwear."

Poverty consciousness thinks, "I don't want to spend extra money on fresh underwear that will make me feel brand new, because no one can see it and it doesn't matter anyway." Or it may think, "I want to save my prettiest underwear for when I may be going out, or for a special occasion."

Why aren't you honoring the beautiful nature of each day and the gift of today, and why are you waiting to reward yourself with wearing your special and prettiest underwear at a later date? Why are you saving your best for later?

Do you know that tomorrow may never come, and today is all you have? I know it sounds harsh, but it is the truth. We can't predict what tomorrow may look like, but we do have control over our thoughts today, and even what kind of underwear we choose to wear today. Our thoughts and attitudes—even those attached to our underwear—will be a magnet for what we will manifest tomorrow, and in the future.

Are you still trying to be "reasonable" and pretending it doesn't really matter?

What are you telling your consciousness when you do this?

You know deep inside that you have ratty underwear on, but you're telling your consciousness that it doesn't matter because no one will see it—unless, of course, you are at the gym, or you get into an accident where they have to take off your clothes, or you have a torrid love affair at work where your underwear is exposed.

You are telling your consciousness, "It doesn't matter."

But does it matter, truly? What is the truth?

If your authentic "brand" is wearing tattered, worn-out clothes, then so be it.

But I'm talking to everybody else.

If you want to make a radical shift in your consciousness that will make you feel liberated and alive, where you can breathe in your life again, then start with your underwear drawer.

If you care, and it really does matter to you, stop pretending that it doesn't.

Get rid of your ratty underwear, now that you know the truth that what you're wearing does not resonate with the truth of your consciousness.

Believe that you are worth it, and that you deserve to wear stuff that makes you feel like a million bucks from the deepest layers to the outermost layers.

Believe that when you know inside that you are dressed like a million bucks from head to toe—whatever that looks like for you—you will radiate the confidence and magnetic energy that will draw million-dollar experiences to you—and a million dollars in the bank!

How you perceive your underwear is a metaphor for how you perceive your life. Confronting the truth of your underwear will give you a sense of freedom and liberation, leading you to self-awareness. Delve within for the answers. Only you know the truth. I cannot come into your house and tell you what is important to you.

I use this illustration to demonstrate how powerful our stuff is. The reason we have so much stuff is because we don't realize all of our stuff has a consciousness. We don't really think our stuff has a life force, positive or negative. But it does.

We create a consciousness, a life force, for our stuff when we assign truth, love, meaning, and purpose to it, even if it is just our underwear.

That is why when we infuse our stuff with a positive life force and positive energy—our TruthLoveMeaningPurpose—this stuff elevates our lives!

That is why dealing with your underwear today may elevate your consciousness, shift your perspective, and change your life!

▪

exercise. *deal with your "under-wear" now.*

Do not turn to the next section. Go immediately to your underwear drawer, and throw away the ratty, torn, and beat-up underwear into the trash *now!*

The point is to *move* your body and do something differently *now*, which will signal to your mind, heart, and body that you are changing, shifting, and growing. It will also signal to the Universe that you are willing to let go of the stuff that is no longer you, and create space for miracles to flow in!

exercise. *find the deeper meaning behind one item.*

If you were completely disgusted with the idea of going through your underwear, pick another item, like your car. Ask yourself why you have this kind of car. What meaning does your car have to you? Does it elevate your consciousness? Do you love your car? Does it represent beauty to you? Or is it merely functional? State the truth internally to yourself, and then out loud. Confronting the truth about the deeper meaning behind your stuff will help you to make choices in the future that honor the TruthLoveMeaningPurpose of who you are and what is important to you, thereby allowing yourself to live an authentic life.

exercise. *create more space for a more authentic you and new future.*

Pick another type of item that you know you are keeping just because you don't want to spend the money on something better, such as raggedy socks with holes.

As you let go of whatever it is, always remember to say out loud:

> *I am letting go of this [name the item or stuff—i.e., ratty underwear], which represents [name the self-limiting belief behind the stuff—i.e., scarcity consciousness, unworthiness].*
>
> *I am creating space for miracles and [name the belief that represents the new you—i.e., prosperity consciousness, deservability!].*
>
> *I am letting go of these holey socks, which represent the beliefs, "I only care about what people can see," and "I don't want to spend money on what people can't see."*
>
> *I am making space to create beauty in my life that I know, see, and feel.*
>
> *I am making space for what I deserve, which is beauty and love in all parts of my life, seen and unseen.*

is it really worth it? *how much are you really saving?*

When I first started shopping at the local discount warehouse, I rejoiced at how much money I saved when I purchased the 24-roll package of paper towels. But I soon discovered that I had nowhere to store that many paper towels in my condo, so I would shove them into the living room closet where my bike lived! OMG, it didn't look pretty at all! You would all be mortified!

The mantra that I advocate now—your life is a work of art, so even behind closed doors, you want everything to look like artwork—had not yet been born in my consciousness.

Every time I wanted to go biking, I would open the closet door and then shut it immediately! I felt drained just walking by the closet, knowing what was waiting inside—chaos, mess, and avoidance! Biking and my bicycle were no longer joys in the cacophony of the closet, where they were sharing space with the paper towels. Every time I would muster up energy to get out my bike and exercise, I would have to muster up another reserve of energy just to get the bike out of the cluttered space, as it required a climb over the paper towels! The whole experience zapped my joie de vivre. I just wanted to go upstairs, veg out in front of the TV, and eat nachos!

So, I realized that even though I thought I was saving money by buying the paper towels in bulk, I was actually paying a huge price. I was not exercising, and I was getting fat and depressed. The clutter in the closet became such a powerful energy drain that I was not motivated to do much else. Wow, I had created this! What was this really about?

I realized that this fine, noble act of "saving a few dollars" was actually robbing me of my peace of mind, my emotional and mental health, and my physical health, and it was costing me stress. I was losing my vitality, life force, and energy every time I looked into that chaotic closet!

I finally realized I had enough and moved the paper towels to another closet. I vowed only to buy six paper towels at the local grocery store instead of going to the discount warehouse, and let my bicycle live in peace by itself, unencumbered with any other stuff.

I swear I heard my bike scream with joy when I did this! It didn't like sharing its space with anything else—just like a child who has outgrown sharing the same room with a sibling. Freed from the cave of darkness and clutter, my bike glowed and sparkled, and seemed to ride faster and more easily! The closet space felt even more spacious than it did before! The space and the door were beaming with white light!

Now, with no clutter standing in its pathways, the bike was vibrating its positive mojo all the way from the inside of the closet, to the living room, to wherever I was in the Universe—urging me to bike!

Wow! I even felt the shift of energy when I left the house! I felt the expansive energy when I walked into my house and every single time I walked into the room! The space just felt different! Even though no one else could see the clutter behind the closet door when the bike was fighting with the paper towels, I felt and knew the difference when the space became clutter free.

Revelation! In the past, I thought I was saving two dollars, which contributed to my financial well-being, but the resulting clutter was costing way more than two dollars in stress! Now I was building a wealth of peace, empowerment, confidence, joy, ease, and effortless living that was priceless. It was worth a *million* dollars to me. I seriously felt like a million bucks! So the two dollars I thought I was saving physically was costing me millions of dollars mentally, emotionally, and spiritually.

Where are you doing this in your life? Where in your life do you think you're saving money by overstocking on toilet paper, light bulbs, canned goods, water, or cleaning supplies, but the truth is that you squeeze it into whatever space you have in your garage or home. You don't have the stuff organized, and you will never organize it. Sometimes you can't even find some of the stuff you bought, so you just go out and buy more. You just keep on overbuying so you don't run out, but the truth is you don't even know how much stuff you have!

What if you confronted the truth that if you spent the time to organize the stuff in the first place, you would know exactly what you had, how much of it you had, and then you could make an accurate and complete grocery list and go shopping in a systematic, organized, grounded way.

Realizing this, change your mindset now!

Stop buying more.

Use what you have.

Set aside time *now* to go through your stuff and your spaces, one by one.

Vow that you will save yourself millions of dollars in stress, and give yourself millions of dollars in peace of mind, by knowing what you have and having clear access to what you have.

Vow that you will empower yourself to start making conscious choices that are in alignment with leading a stress-free, happier life—being happy with stuff you have, being happy with the space you have, being happy with the stuff living in your space.

If you are not using what you have, you will save "money" in stress by giving it away.

Don't lament how much "physical money" you spent on it. Touch every single item until you are finished with that space!

And, if you think it's not important, keep in mind that your closets filled with lifeless stuff are contributing to the lack of energy in you, your family, your kids, and your space! Every single time you walk into your space, you will subconsciously feel that dead and negative energy, because the stuff's energy is wafting in the air, permeating it, and touching you and your environment!

You don't even know that it's bringing you down because it has become a way of life for you. This crammed, cluttered stuff jammed into all the spaces of your home has become your way of life. You are accustomed to having to tackle the stuff you have to get to what you really want to use. You have numbed yourself to the pain you feel every time you encounter this battlefield. Do you get it? You and your family may not even know to want anything different yet, because it has become the landscape of your life and home!

One of my clients said to me recently, "What you just saw was our normal, so we were stunned when you helped us to make those transformative shifts. It was such a radical difference from what we were used to seeing and living with!"

Can you relate? Is this the truth of your life, and do you want it to change now?

You have a choice. Do you want to feel like a million bucks? Or do you want to be weighed down by million dollars' worth of stress? Do you want to feel peace, serenity, and joy? Do you want to be happy with your stuff? Or, do you want to battle your stuff and your space?

Choose now. See your spaces differently. Confront the truth of your stuff—all your stuff. And see what your stuff reveals to you.

I guarantee you that this new way of living—a simplified life, where you buy and have stuff that you truly need, where you honor each and every space in your house by leaving breathing space around what fits there, rather than leaving it crammed and jammed—will make you feel differently and will liberate you, and you will begin to see that it isn't about the stuff.

But guess what? By dealing with the physical stuff, and taking action, you will start uncovering the underlying layers of emotions, mindsets, and belief systems that accompany that physical stuff! That extra stuff you overbought in bulk was derived from a scarcity mindset.

While you're touching that stuff, ask yourself: *What mindset contributed to the accumulation of this stuff?* And then let go of it. Rather than looking at the physical savings on the fiscal level, start looking at the mental/emotional/spiritual bank account you are growing each and every day, as you start making conscious choices that make you feel happy, healthy, and empowered!

.

exercise. *true intentions behind buying habits.*

This exercise is about shifting your perspective regarding your time, money, and stuff. Write down your answers to the following questions:

Where do you accumulate stuff in your life?

Where do you hoard?

Where do you overbuy?

Where do you overstock?

Is the overbuying due to your belief system?

exercise. *change your habits with self-reflection and self-correction.*

If you tend to buy something just because it's on sale, ask yourself: *Do I truthfully have space for these extra items I got on sale?* If not, vow to stop buying more stuff just because it's on sale and you're "saving money." Remember your mental/emotional/spiritual bank account, in addition to your financial bank account.

raise your consciousness. *declare a moratorium.*

i just don't get it when people seem to have it all—the money, the lifestyle, the accoutrements of success—but their spaces don't reflect that success!

I mean, why not spend the time and money, if you have it, to make all of your spaces look like a work of art? For example, if you buy artwork, and you can't even see the artwork because it is buried amidst the stuff, it's time to shift your perspective. Raise your consciousness about *all* of your stuff in *all* of your spaces, and declare a new way of living.

Remember, our stuff carries the consciousness we assign to it, based on the meaning we give it and our opinions about it. The stuff's consciousness then affects your environment, especially when you have tons of stuff all thrown into one space.

Are you getting how powerful this is? When you keep throwing the stuff together, hoping it would organize itself magically, are you shocked and dismayed every time you open up your closet and find it exactly the same?

You—your heart, your mind, and your body—are affected by everything, whether or not you can see it or even believe it. The clutter in your spaces reflects the clutter in your consciousness. And the clutter of your spaces creates clutter in your bodies.

It always surprises me and excites me when people lose weight miraculously while they are decluttering. The internal stuff behind the physical stuff you're holding on to matches up with the stuff behind the extra weight you're carrying around in your body.

So, knowing how powerfully you are affected by what you have in your spaces, why not be conscious about the stuff you bring into your spaces and your life?

231

Why not raise your consciousness with the stuff of life you have chosen to live with and to purchase, and the stuff of life that has been given to you? Simply evaluate whether it aligns with the truth of who you are now.

Yes, often we are not aware of what choices we are making when we bring stuff into our lives. Our cluttered spaces have become the landscape of our lives, and we have become accustomed to having too much stuff in our spaces. So we don't think there's anything wrong with creating a pathway through our stuff from the doorway to our bathroom. We don't think there's anything wrong with sleeping on only one side of our bed because the other side is covered with books and paperwork. We don't think there's anything wrong when there are boxes and boxes of stuff to be returned. We don't think there's anything wrong when we have shelves of spices, but we don't cook anymore. It's because the stuff in the space has become the landscape of our life. It's become a way of life we are now accustomed to.

We continue to go shopping and buy more stuff, even when there is stuff still at home.

Clutter in our heart leads to clutter in our spaces. We want to pretend that it doesn't hurt— or that we aren't hurt—and bury the pain in our hearts in more and more stuff.

What is the truth behind my clutter?
That I really don't have it together.
That I really don't know what makes me happy.
That I really am confused.
That I am moving things around to keep myself busy so I don't feel my feelings.
That I am really sad and don't want to feel my sadness, so I will keep buying things to make me happy—or at least I think it will make me happy.
Yes, new things make me happy.
I keep buying new, fresh things so I can think that my life is fresh and new.
Is that an illusion?

Why keep buying and buying and buying, when you already have so much at home?

Do you *know* how much stuff you have at home?

This powerful exercise might shift your consciousness about your stuff and about what you believe you truly need to survive—what you truly need to be happy.

Declare a moratorium on bringing anything new into your home. Just use the stuff you have already. This practice will help you confront the truth of what you are using, what you will never, ever use, and where you are not being truthful with yourself, on many levels.

See what stuff you can live with. Be resourceful, and see what you can do with the stuff you have already.

For one month, do not go into a bookstore. Browse through your own books, and read only those books you already have. If you do not want to read any of these books, donate them.

For one month, do not turn on the television. Don't bombard yourself with images. Turn off the radio and cut off auditory messages from outside. Entertain yourself with what you have inside your home, or go outside your home into nature, and see what happens. Record your favorite shows on DVD and watch them after the fast. What did you miss the most?

Even consider not reading any magazines or newspapers for one month. Did you miss them?

Are you addicted to the constant bombardment of new images, new information, new data, new stuff coming into your life?

Remember, there are only 365 days in a year. If you subscribe to 12 magazines, and each one puts out one issue a month, that means you are going to have to read at least one to two magazines per week to get to the 144 magazines per year. If you have 300 books in your house, that means you have to read nearly one book a day to get through all the books you have in one year! That's 300 days of reading every single year. That leaves 65 days to get through your articles on the Internet, your reading from work, or all the music downloaded on to your iPod. I hope you're getting this.

If you regularly go grocery shopping when you already have all different kinds of food in your house, when are you going to eat the food in your pantry? Are you one of those super-efficient people who lets the supplies get low before you go out and buy what you will truly consume that week? Or do you have so much stuff in your pantry that you don't even know what's in there, and you'd rather go to the farmers market and get new, fresh stuff every week? Then confront that truth, and let go of the old, processed stuff. But if you go shopping every week at the farmers market and you still find yourself throwing away some of those veggies and fruits, then be truthful with yourself and don't buy as much stuff the next time. What's the worst that can happen? You will learn next time to gauge your supply needs.

So, for this month, try declaring a moratorium on bringing anything new into your home, and live with the stuff you have. Make the stuff you have work, whether it's clothes, books, food, or entertainment.

Live with the truth of your shopping excursions and how they feed you.

Get in touch with the truth of your heart. Get in touch with the truth of your mind.

Be at one with the truth for today. And see where that truth leads you.

Don't be afraid of finding out the hard core truth of who you are. Trust that the discovery of the answers that lie within paves the journey to a life where you will be clutter free, once and for all.

.

exercise. *moratorium on new stuff.*

Declare a moratorium on buying new stuff for one month. See how long you can go with just using the stuff you have, as stated above.

Journal about how it feels not to go shopping or step foot into a store.

Is shopping a habit, or a need?

Is shopping a luxury, or a necessity?

See if you save money by "shopping at home." See how it makes you feel.

Getting in touch with your needs, versus your desires, versus your addictions and habits, will lead to more conscious choices on a day-to-day basis, which will cause you to shift your behavior. It will also affect what kind of new stuff you bring into your home, body, mind, and heart, as well as what you determine to be old stuff you choose to let go of.

Enjoy the journey, and have fun giving yourself a break from shopping and from new stuff. Have fun using the "old stuff," and appreciating it and/or letting it go!

exercise. *shop at home.*

If one month sounds like a long time, declare a moratorium for one week.

Instead of going out to shop for that week, shop at your "own store"—the store where you have accumulated an inventory of stuff. Do you enjoy shopping at your store? Or do you just see junk at your store? Do you enjoy eating at "your restaurant"? Or do you not see anything appetizing at this "restaurant" of yours? If so, start letting go of the junk and giving it away. Trust that giving it away or throwing it away is the healthiest step you can take today.

your relationship with money. *the currency of the universe.*

oney is the currency of the Universe, and a conduit for the energy poured forth in this world. Do you have a handle on this all-important currency? What is your belief system about money? What attitudes have you adopted about money? Do you have a prosperity consciousness or scarcity consciousness regarding money?

I have chosen to declutter any thoughts about my weakness dealing with and managing money, and instead I have replaced those thoughts with new ones that represent me: I am a sound steward of money. More money flows into my life every day for me to manage, and I am managing it beautifully.

I have taken back control and empowered myself. I now teach others to take their power back. Don't just pretend you know how to manage money, if you don't. Hire somebody to teach you. Hire somebody to organize your finances, such as a bookkeeper. Hire an assistant who loves numbers to tally up the numbers so you can sit down and review the numbers. Hire an organizer or coach to build a fantastic system for you, so you can control your money and change your belief systems with money. Or do it yourself.

Whichever you decide, I want you to know that this was a huge issue for me, and I finally tackled it head on, took control of this all-important currency, and allowed more currency to flow into my life with this newfound confidence and empowered energy.

I used to think that some people were just naturally gifted and lucky with money. Yes, some may understand numbers and money more readily than the rest of us. They see the world in a certain way. I used to think that my brothers and my parents were very good with money; they seemed to always win money, save money, get returns on their investments, and make sound decisions regarding money. I, on the other hand, never understood how it worked and, frankly, was never taught. I just remember spending money, and I somehow always had access to money, so I thought it always just flowed in of its own accord and didn't think twice about it.

It wasn't until I started working after college, making my own money and paying for purchases with my own money, that I realized the value of money. I took it for granted. I didn't realize that working for one week paid me only enough money to buy me those boots I had been eyeing. The money I earned in one day was enough to buy everybody a round of drinks at a bar. Wow! I didn't realize how much my parents had sacrificed to give me everything I wanted and needed. They never complained. They never really talked about it. It all seemed pretty seamless, easy, and effortless.

So, I got into debt many times before I learned that I was ridiculously racking up interest charges on my credit cards, and I could have used that interest money I was paying to the credit card companies to buy a new purse or even a new car.

As I mentioned earlier, I got audited during my first year of acting, and I saw this as a wake-up call to get my finances in order. I sought assistance from my brother, a CPA, and my mother, a bookkeeper. They taught me the importance of keeping every single receipt to back up tax reports, helped me to organize my finances in a streamlined fashion, put everything into a notebook for the audit, and helped me set everything up on Quicken.

That is when I started learning that the "money" is just the currency of the Universe, energy generated and exchanged for services provided, and that if I wanted to acquire more, I better learn to be a better steward of my finances. *Yes,* I thought, *if you cannot handle this, why would God give you even more to handle?* I wanted to master the money arena of acquiring, managing, keeping track of my "currency/energy," and increasing its value in my life.

Finance is such a heavy topic, loaded with people's preconceived notions. People still often ask me if having an organized system really matters, and so what if they continue putting stuff into shoeboxes? I say, "You're right. Who cares?" The most important question to ask yourself is, *Do I care?* If you are fine with putting stuff into shoeboxes and scrambling at the end of the year to get your tax information to your accountant, continue doing what you're doing. I teach that the only stuff that should matter to you is your peace of mind and heart. I also teach that even your financial files can be a work of art behind closed doors, symbolizing clear pathways and homes for monies to flow in and out. Therefore, decide what your intention is for organizing your finances. If your intention is to know where every penny, dime, and dollar is being spent, managed, and invested, then you may want to think about a system where you can easily and effortlessly store, research, and evaluate this data.

My intention for organizing my finances and setting up all my systems is for empowerment, legal purposes, and for my own peace of mind and heart. I know on any given day what is flowing in or flowing out, and this empowers me to set up a new spending plan or set new goals based on the truth of my "money currency/energy." Legally, I can easily retrieve all the data I need for my accountants, and I can easily pass along tax information to them so they can do my taxes. When I have stockpiled receipts to be entered into Quicken, which I have many times, this still constitutes unfinished business for me, and I stress out and do not feel good about having this incompletion in my life. This year, I finished putting all pertinent information into Quicken before the April 15 deadline, so I was easily able to pass along the information to my accountants. I felt like a million bucks. I felt complete. Did this matter to anyone else, or did anyone else care? No. I cared, and it mattered to me—and that is all that mattered.

I continue to work diligently to declutter any thoughts that disempower me regarding my power with money. I confess daily that I love money, and money loves me! I confess daily that I am managing my money beautifully, and that money flows into my life easily and effortlessly, instead of thinking I'm a loser at handling my money and that it has to be a struggle.

I now think I am a winner with my money, that money is just a tool to serve me in the Universe, and that it is a very powerful tool. I do not discount the importance of money.

But I also realize that my thoughts and feelings about money determine what I create in my life. The healthier my feelings about money have become, the more money has flowed in for me to manage, organize, and be responsible for. The more I realize that money is in my possession to do something meaningful and powerful with—to bless others—the more money has flowed in. The more I think about what I can give rather than what I can get, the more money has flowed in.

Regarding the prices of your products and services, I always recommend you set the price you feel you deserve. If you charge more money than you think you are worth just because somebody else told you to, you are not being truthful with yourself, and your consciousness will cause you to lose that extra money anyway, because you feel you do not deserve it. If you lower the cost of your products or services just because somebody told you to, energetically you will be radiating an energy that says you do not feel great about offering your services or products.

Energetically, you want to be in a space where you are feeling clean and clear about your money, the currency of the Universe. This way, more money can flow into your life. More money can flow out of your life. And more money can flow back in.

When you leave this earth, you cannot take your money or your stuff with you.

So what is your relationship with money today? Can you change your relationship with it? Not just by getting rid of the credit cards or trying to pay off the credit cards, but getting to the root cause of the issue that caused the credit card debt in the first place.

Did I buy needless stuff I thought that I needed to make myself feel better about myself when I was feeling depressed? Did I feel like I needed new clothes while I was dating, because I felt I wasn't enough with my old clothes? Did I feel the new designer clothes made me feel like a million bucks, because without them I feel like a regular Joe Schmo?

Why do I need to buy new pillows and reinvigorate my space with new decorating stuff? Isn't the old stuff enough for me? Does this stuff really, truly, bring me joy?

Do I really need to spend so much money on gifts for my friends, or can I be honest with them and tell them the truth: "I would love to buy you a gift to thank you for our friendship, but the part that I treasure the most are the good times we share together. Can we instead spend time together?"

Do I need another pair of designer sunglasses? Why do I need to buy the latest and greatest seasonal item? To up my fashion quotient? Will this really add value to my life? Do I need the latest headset that has better sound quality, or can I live without the new one and live with my old one? Do I really need a new computer when I just purchased one last year, and there is nothing wrong with that last one I purchased? Why do I feel like I need the latest gadgets? Because my colleague purchased one. Because it makes me feel like I'm with it.

Money. Currency. Value. What do you value?

Understanding your TruthLoveMeaningPurpose regarding money and honoring it will save you years of grief. Understanding the *truth* of what drives your spending habits will help you make better choices with your money. Understanding why you spend money on items you don't truly *love* will help you get to the root cause of your spending mistakes, so you don't make those mistakes again. Understanding the *meaning* that money has played in your life will help you get to the root cause of what may be subconsciously driving you, so you can finally take your life back and empower yourself, and take charge of your money choices. Understanding the *purpose* of your money and what purposes best serve you will help you make sound judgments with your money.

Let go of all that is no longer serving you. Care about your journey. It's not about what everybody else wants. It's not about competing with everybody else, or comparing yourself with everybody else.

This journey you take with your money can be the most empowering, liberating, and uplifting trip you will ever take.

Honor your TruthLoveMeaningPurpose with your money, and see how powerful you feel. Your entire being will light up because you are consciously honoring that truth and living that truth. You will suddenly start making different choices that are more in alignment with your truth, and you will be happier living that truth every single day.

Love your money. Love your life!

•

exercise. *your relationship with money.*

How would you describe your relationship to money? Start journaling about your feelings about money.

What are some of your belief systems regarding money?

Do you feel out of control with money?

Without trying to solve every issue here and now, I want you to start focusing on how you feel whenever you spend money. Notice the exchange of money for the service or product you are purchasing. Become conscious of how great you feel when you pay money for something you loved. If you didn't, write down why you did not feel good.

Are your finances in order? If not, see if there is a correlation between how organized your finances are and the energy flow in your bank account.

Start getting your finances in order today. Get a software program that tracks your spending, such as Quicken, or sign up for mint.com. Or do it the old fashioned way and keep a written journal of what goes in and what comes out of your wallet.

If you are unhappy with your relationship with money, vow that you will change your views about money and start thinking differently about it, beginning today. Money means freedom, and it can be your best friend. Treat it with respect, and it will respect you as well.

exercise. *your new metric for money: TruthLoveMeaningPurpose.*

Apply the TruthLoveMeaningPurpose metric to your money, and see what choices you begin to make that are different from what you've done in the past. Only by checking into your unique TruthLoveMeaningPurpose will you begin to be a sound steward of the money you have been blessed with in this lifetime, and make choices that are in alignment with the truth of who you are.

How you choose to spend money, save money, use money, and treat money is entirely up to you. Just make sure you are following your TruthLoveMeaningPurpose.

You can confront your real stuff behind your relationship with money by asking some of these questions and writing down your answers:

Truth: What is the truth behind my money issues? How do I truthfully feel about money? Do I feel money is flowing to me, or flowing out of my life? Do I worry about money? Do I think about money all the time? Do I talk about money all the time? Even though I have lots of money in the bank, do I worry about money still? Truthfully, do I need help with my money? Do I spend money I don't have? Do I hold on to money I have, and am I worried about spending it?

Love: Do I love money? Does money love me? Do I love managing my money? Do I love spending money? What do I love spending money on?

Meaning: What does money mean to me? Freedom? Experiences? Stuff? What do you consider meaningful to spend money on?

Purpose: Is money serving the purpose I intend it for? Or do I stray from my purpose when spending money?

exercise. *underlying beliefs behind money choices.*

Now that you've more deeply considered your TruthLoveMeaningPurpose behind your relationship with money, I want you to think back to some of our earlier topics and think anew about why you buy what you buy. Explore the truth behind your money stuff, and write the answers to the following questions in your journal:

Do any of your beliefs represent a scarcity consciousness not just with money, but with stuff?

Do you ever think to yourself, "I don't want to run out of . . . ." What do you never want to run out of? Start a list.

Do you have a mindset that values buying in bulk to save a few dollars? If you do, are you truthfully organizing your stuff, and do you truthfully use it up? Or do you keep accumulating more and losing track of it?

exercise. *feeling prosperous with your stuff.*

Look at your collections of stuff. Is there any area of your life where you have accumulated stuff equivalent to thousands or even millions of dollars? Do these collections make you feel like a millionaire, or prosperous? If not, let them go. If so, take proper care of them. Journal about this as well so you will always remember this powerful lesson.

vigilance. *do you really need the latest and greatest stuff?*

a re you a "latest and greatest" junkie?

I admit that I am the first to go out and try something new. I tried the Surface when Microsoft came out with its version of the iPad. I tried various lightweight laptops after I was ready to let go of my Macbook Air, because the productivity tools I relied upon were incompatible with my Mac. I even had both for a while. I also tried some new time management tools, because I thought the latest iPhone apps looked super cool design-wise, and perhaps these other, more sophisticated systems would work better, but I kept coming back to my "tried-and-true" Microsoft Outlook, which I know works for me and for others. The bottom line is that I investigate other options because I'm in the time management/productivity business. But the truth is that I often find that many people who try the latest and greatest are not even fully utilizing an older system they have learned. What's the use of going to the next latest and greatest if you haven't even fully tested out a model that came before that? Sometimes the latest and greatest is not always the best.

Yet, in this day and age, we always want the better, faster, newer model. Why? Because our neighbor next door got one, or because our best friend has it. Because the ads are bombarding us with the message that life with the new model is better, greater, and sexier than life with your old model, and that you will achieve greater success if you buy the latest and greatest. Explore your reasons behind wanting the latest and greatest stuff.

We want the coolest cell phone with all the latest bells and whistles, or highest-tech television with the highest resolution and the flattest and most lightweight screen. New fashions come out every season that help us to express our creativity with clothes and make us feel we are with the times. New car models go faster and look better. New computers promise faster Internet speed and access so we can do more business in one day. New exercise equipment promises faster and quicker results with our bodies. New apps come out every day, promising to make us even more productive than the week before.

What about our old stuff? Does it still serve us? Yes, if you are still using it and it works, great. Keep it! Just like I have kept the same system for calendaring, contact management, and task management for twenty years. Of course, they keep updating the system, and I now use OneNote for all my notes instead of Outlook's notes program. But it's still fundamentally the same system.

However, that's not to say I won't take the plunge and make a big change if it truly improves my productivity. Even after years of being in this business, I myself have become virtually paperless. I used to keep paper files, but once I found out that I could send stuff into the cloud, I hired a scanning service to scan all my files and sent everything to the cloud. When I first did this, of course, I was afraid to take the plunge and to let go of the physical paperwork. But since then I've saved thousands of dollars on I would have spent paying my assistant to file the physical paperwork. I can now find anything I need within seconds, with the sophisticated search capability of the computer program. I now send everything off to be scanned, including receipts. The only paperwork I now have is whatever is in my Action Drawer, which houses only the stuff that is truly moving forward.

So I will be the first to encourage you to try a new system if the one system you have is slow, because you are losing your greatest commodity, which is time. Then, let go of the old, and replace it with a faster, better model!

I'm a huge fan of technology and love, love, love technology, when it is used for the most divine purposes of making our lives more efficient.

However, when we are bombarded with all the latest and greatest, we are often still holding on to our old computers, cell phones, and keyboards. There's a backlog of stuff accumulating in our homes, offices, garages, and storage units. C'mon, be truthful. When is the last time you really needed a spare keyboard? A spare mouse? A spare phone? With every new item you acquire, you must evaluate whether you want to keep the stuff you are replacing.

Why not give it away to a school or charity, where someone in need could really use this technology that is old to you, but would be new to them?

You must become vigilant as technology shifts.

It also means letting go of apps on your phone you are no longer using, or have never used.

It means letting go of the cyber clutter.

Stop accumulating stuff, right here and now, until you have fully touched everything you currently have, evaluated it, let go of the stuff you are not using, and organized the stuff you are using.

And with physical electronic stuff, don't use the excuse, "If it breaks down, I'll have it around!"

When that happens, something faster, better, and prettier will also be around, and you'll go out and get that! If you are a "latest and greatest" junkie, give away your "slower and not as good" stuff to someone who will think it's the latest and greatest! Recycle your stuff, and you'll feel lighter, not clutter up your space, and make the world a better place!

■

exercise. *purge electronic clutter.*

Go around the house and start gathering all your electronics, cords, and adaptors that are strewn all over the place, not being used. Put them into one area and look at everything you have.

Confront the truth of that stuff. When was the last time you used it? When was the last time you needed it? Do you know what it is?

If you don't know what it is, and you haven't used it for years, let go of it.

For the remaining items, label each item with a labeler on both sides of the cords, so there is no question what the item is, and put all the remaining items into a box labeled Electronics and Cords.

exercise. *let go of just-in-case fears.*

Do you have extra phones, cell phones, laptops, typewriters, computers, and printers laying around? Are you holding on to them just in case? When was the last time you needed these items?

Why not donate them to a school or a shelter? There are many places that would love to repair these older items and put them to use.

Also, while you are letting go of some of those items, start a new page in your journal and title it "Just in Case," and start writing about all the stuff you have kept or have done just in case. By doing this, you will become acutely aware of when this fear triggers you to keep or do stuff, and perhaps soon, you will consciously let go when you are immediately aware of when this happens.

exercise. *question new purchases.*

The next time something new comes out, stop and ask yourself, *Is the item that I am using right now functioning perfectly? Will this new item truly make my life more productive?* Be truthful with yourself, and if you realize you are addicted to buying the latest and greatest, dig deeper to find out the reasons why. And stop this vicious cycle by just saying *no* this time. Instead, continue using your tried-and-true item, and see if you can be just as happy with an older model that works perfectly fine.

EVERYDAY RITUALS. TOOLS & STRATEGIES.

mentally dump every day. *create space for action and ideas.*

i just got finished reading *The Power of Now* by Eckhart Tolle. What a powerful book! It helped me realize just how much I am living in the past or the future. When I'm in the shower, I'm reviewing the day ahead, instead of feeling the water cleansing away last night's nightmares . . . which I can't remember, but I'm sure I dreamed some frightful dreams. How come I can't remember them? I'm not supposed to. Oh.

Anyway, then I start thinking of which yoga class I should attend this morning, and if I'll have enough driving time to make it there . . . .

Finally, I remember to think of *now*: of the lavender shower gel refreshing my body, the smell awakening my senses—and then I feel the abrasiveness of my body not yet shaved, the prickly sensation of the half-grown stubble—oh, don't want to have hairy arms in yoga class . . . .

Boy, oh boy—I've gotta turn off this incessant noise, this chatter inside, about things that must be done today. I'm hungry—well, that's because I haven't eaten. Did I tell you that I forget to eat sometimes, because I'm so caught up in whatever I'm doing? I can't work until everything in my home and office are in their place. Only then can I write, do my marketing, do my client work, do my administrative work—in fact, just now I had to sort through some magazines that had piled up, and on a whim I decided to throw out most of them, only keeping the current issues of certain magazines for a treasure mapping project I had been planning to do for some time (gotta treasure map my life!). My stomach growls, reminding me to eat my breakfast—at 1:43 p.m. This isn't working.

Oh, right—I forgot my first rule of the day. Mentally dump!

As you can see from the example above, I am a huge fan of the morning mental dump, because if I don't do it, my thoughts lead me astray, bouncing me to and fro from place to place, all while I'm sitting at my desk. Before I know it, my thoughts have taken me far away to beautiful Bali, and the house where Julia Roberts's character was staying in the movie *Eat Pray Love*—oh, wouldn't that be a nice place to visit and spend a few months writing there? I'm doing it again.

My first rule for the day is to mentally dump. What does mental dumping look like?

It's just writing down everything you must do, need to do, and want to do! It's rambling on and on about the big stuff and the small stuff, your goals, dreams, hopes, and fears! At first, it may be difficult to write down everything, but once you do, you'll find that you cannot leave home without doing your mental dump. You will find that it is the perfect Rx for the wandering, confused, and lost mind. You will find that it is the perfect Rx for the broken heart.

Dump it into the dumpster.
Dump it on to your task list.
Dump it on to the page.

Write a letter to that ex-girlfriend, saying thanks for the memories and experiences, thanks for what you taught me, thanks for teaching me there is another way to live life and be in love and honor myself. Thanks for not getting me. Now I get that there may be other people out there who *will* get me, and love me exactly as I am.

Write down the one hundred things you want to do while you're alive. Climb Mount Kilimanjaro. Bike through the Italian countryside, staying at different villas, visiting spas, and sipping wine into the wee morning hours. Stop dieting for one year, and eat whatever I want, inspired by *Eat Pray Love*. Go on a whitewater river rafting trip with my partner, and use it as a mini-retreat, seeing it as a metaphor for the journey of life.

Thoughts can infiltrate our brain. Thoughts can run amok in our heads, polluting our minds, keeping us from thinking pure, clean thoughts—new thoughts that lead to new behaviors, which lead to a new reality.

Feelings can permeate our hearts. Feelings if left brewing inside us can lead to resentment, anger, and disease, clogging up the arteries that long to be free and clear for pure love to rush in—fresh, new love.

When left bouncing around inside our head, tasks can be a mundane, never-ending list of stuff that can deaden our senses. Once each task is on the page and out of your consciousness, you can organize it, wash it, calendar it, and take care of it, once and for all.

Projects can overwhelm us in our head, creating an ongoing list of to do's—where to begin, where to end, when to schedule. If left unsettled in the head, it becomes a maze where you hit a roadblock, just wanting to hide under the covers, go back to bed!

So, the goal is to mentally dump every time you start thinking about anything. Carry a notebook with you. Put it into your phone on the task list. Jot it down on a post-it.

I'm a fan of just putting it down. At least you can do something with it, written down.

However, what I most advocate is a system where you can organize the to-dos into categories, with like-items together. Just the other day, I was asked to think of another creative way to organize to-dos, since the idea of categorizing like-items is apparently worn out, old, used, used up.

But why do we need to come up with a fresh way to organize when the tried-and-true way is still the simplest way?

Why do we overcomplicate our lives?

Why not do something that has worked for years and has been tested by the productivity experts? Why try to come up with something inventive for entertainment's sake, for the sake of being new?

I get it. We've already talked about the numerous iPhone and computer applications that try to make this concept of "to do" as easy and accessible as possible to the layperson.

But could it be this simple:

1. Jot down your to-dos, thoughts, feelings, ideas, and dreams on one page or in a notebook
2. Organize them into categories, or like-items
3. Prioritize and pick three from each category
4. Schedule those priorities into your calendar
5. Show up and do that task

Yes, I'm saying it *can* be this simple. You don't need a sophisticated, creative, inventive new way to do this. Why not use what you already have first, and see how it works?

Let's use technology to help us automatically categorize our tasks, so we don't have to rewrite them. Then your system can act as your virtual personal assistant, reminding you when to take care of the task. I would highly recommend learning to use a program such as Outlook, which already has a built-in system for this exact purpose, so you don't have to reinvent the wheel.

Why carry your entire life around inside your head and heart? Why not live out your heart and your head in the present moment, open spaces for new experiences and adventures to come in and fill up your consciousness with new life, vigor, and miracles? Why not mentally dump all those new ideas that will soon become old, and allow them to manifest, to take shape and form, to become the dream actualized? Why not express your stuff today instead of waiting for tomorrow? Don't let another day go by with this stuff swarming around in your head like buzzing bees, annoying you. Each time you swat them away, they're going to keep coming back, creating a buzz, reminding you of the tasks you have left undone.

Lighten the load, and swear that today, once and for all, you will begin mentally dumping whatever comes into your head and heart. Smile as you think about how light you will feel. Smile as you think about your ideas finally becoming realized. Smile as you take that first step towards realizing your dreams, one to-do at a time. Smile as you become enthralled with the thought, *Can it be as simple as that? Can my life be that easy and effortless? A series of to-dos checked off my list, a series of dreams and projects and ideas on a page being carried out systematically? Can it truly be that simple?*

Yes! Yes! Yes!

Let go of the drama, struggle, strife, and suffering.

Embrace the ease and effortlessness of a simpler way to get things done, and make all your dreams come true. Yes, it can be that easy. Miracles abound!

■

exercise. *your master list.*

Get out a notebook or create a section in your journal, and start writing a list of every single to-do, goal, project, or whatever is on your mind. You can call this your Master List. If you are using Outlook or another computer program, the Task List or To-Do List will become your Master List. This was one of those wonderful lessons I learned from Jeffrey Mayer's book, *If You Haven't Got the Time to Do It Right, When Will You Find the Time to Do It Over?*

exercise. *three "next best" actions.*

Every day you will add to your Master List. Every day you will look at your Master List and decide what the three most important "next best" tasks, projects, or goals are. These are the tasks or to-dos you feel will "yield the most positive outcome in your life." I learned this wonderful lesson of how to gauge what is most important from Stephen Covey's *Seven Habits of Highly Effective People.*

Once any task is completed, you will put a line through the task in your journal, or check it off your task list on Outlook or whatever computer application you use to track your tasks.

Do not rewrite the task list or create a new list every single day.

The point is to get into the habit of putting all your thoughts on the page, preferably in the same place, every single day.

Get into the habit of dumping every single day.

Get into the habit of looking at this list every single day.

Get into the habit of deciding what the three most important "next best" tasks are for the day.

Get into the habit of only focusing on getting those three tasks done for the day.

Once you complete those three, then pick three other tasks to work on.

The point of this exercise is to get you to laser focus on only the three most important tasks, so you do not get overwhelmed with the multitude of tasks on your list. You can only take care of one at a time anyway, so why worry about the hundred other items on the list until you have the time to deal with them?

Congratulate yourself when you take care of one task. Jump up and down when you complete two tasks. Clap your hands three times when you complete three tasks, and scream out loud, "Yeah!" or "Yippee!"

homes & paths. *pave the way for miracles.*

ithin your home, and within every space in your home, have you created a positive energy flow that honors you *and* your stuff? Have you created a world where you establish clear *homes* and *paths* for everything in your life—nothing homeless, and no orphans? Your stuff can better serve you if it is housed in wonderfully cozy homes designed just for you and your stuff.

Why not house your like-items (or love items!) together? You can create homes—permanent spaces you love with clear boundaries you choose—for all the "families" of stuff that share the same traits, purpose, and/or qualities! Why not make them happy by bringing them together so they can live in the same home? Ah, I can hear the cries of joy when these long-lost brothers and sisters find each other again! You'll be hosting a reunion for all the Blankets of your world that can provide warmth and comfort to your TV-watching marathons, or a party for all the Balls that bring bounce and play to your children's lives. You'll be allowing your Housekeeping Supplies to help you, serve you, and rally together for the singular mission of "no more dirt" in your sacred spaces!

Do you get how powerfully deep this all goes? If you have decided to keep all this stuff, why not reunite the orphans with their families, and find homes for the homeless, giving them the love and the place of belonging they deserve? Why not spend the time and energy to create beautiful homes and spaces for your peeps, family, and community?

And please keep the pathways free and clear so you can move forward and get to where you're going—no traffic jams! Paths mark the direction in which your stuff is moving; your stuff has a path just like you have a life path or purpose. All paths should either lead the stuff back to its true home that reflects its heart and soul, or lead the stuff out to another journey—to the trash or the Giveaway Box—where it can become redefined as a treasure in the eyes of another beholder who sees it as beautiful. For instance, the hamper is a home for dirty clothes, and it's on the path to getting clean and back to its true home—the dresser or closet, where it can serve you and be worn again.

Likewise, the heart is both a path and a home for love to flow in and out, and to be given freely away. It can be a *path* for love for those who come in and out of your life to love for a reason or a season, and a way for your love to be distributed in the world. Your heart can also be the *home* for those you are choosing to love for a lifetime, such as your husband, wife, children, family, or friends.

If your love is viewed by another as "trash" and not appreciated as you deserve, and/or if love is not flowing back to you, please let go and find another to love or give love to, so somebody else can enjoy the love in your heart as you rightfully deserve—as a "treasure to be cherished." But don't ever just abandon, neglect, or forget about the stuff or the people in your care, whom you have chosen to love and/or have brought into your life.

Homes and paths are powerful tools for all your stuff, internal and external. Understand the difference between them, and allow them to serve you and your TruthLoveMeaningPurpose, so you can lead a life you absolutely love!

If you don't organize your stuff into clear homes and paths with clearly labeled and defined boundaries, the stuff will get lost, and so will you. If your home didn't have a specific address, how would the mailman know where to deliver mail? If every home and path looked alike with no addresses or street names, how would you or your kids know how to get home? If the path to your home is cluttered with stuff, how do you or your kids get through the door to the safety and security of your home? Paths like your mailbox can get stuffed when not dealt with and prevent new mail from coming in—like good news! So I'm passionate about keeping clear those pathways to miracles!

Homes and paths is also a metaphor we can use to declutter and organize our internal stuff. If your home is cluttered with stuff, where do *you* really live? If your heart home is cluttered up, where does love live, and can you receive love? If your mind home is cluttered up, how can new ideas and thoughts enter? Where do your dreams live, and to whom do they belong? What path are you on? Is your path cluttered with past beliefs that don't fit your current journey?

But we can't create homes and paths for our stuff if we're not conscious of its importance in our world.

When you're conscious of the purpose of every object, you will spend the time to properly create a home for these family of items so they can be of service to you and fulfill their life's mission and life's purpose for you.

Enjoy creating homes and paths for your stuff!

·

exercise. *create cozy homes for homeless stuff.*

Tour your home and collect one kind of item, such as batteries. Now put all the batteries into a home and label it Batteries. Start separating the batteries by voltage and creating mini-homes such as AA Batteries. Keep doing this until you have no homeless batteries, and all batteries now have a cozy home properly labeled to charge up your life!

exercise. *create paths for stuff that needs to be dealt with.*

Find three boxes or bags, and label one Returns, another Alterations, and another Giveaways. Now, start walking through your home and gather all the items you immediately know are items you want to give away, alter, or return to a store, and put them into the properly labeled paths. You can reuse these boxes or bags after the returns, alterations, or giveaways are complete, and permanently house them as well in their own permanent home close to the door or in your garage, so they will be waiting for you on your way out to run errands.

exercise. *create a permanent home for dreams to come true.*

Designate a journal or a poster board as a treasure map for your dreams. Label it My Treasure Map. Then cut out photos and images from magazines or books that inspire you and symbolize the dreams you want to manifest. Paste these images and words on to the board or journal, and place it somewhere where you will see it every day. Visit this home you have designated for your dreams to come true and cozy up to it, looking at it and reviewing it periodically.

Pretty soon, these pictures will become engrained within the powerful "television screen" of your mind. If you truly believe, these powerful pictures played out in your imagination will eventually become a powerful magnet attracting to you the experiences attached to these images. Your subconscious mind does not know the difference between what is real and/or not, so the law of attraction will bring to you what you imagine, feel and think about frequently. In this way, the treasure map is a powerful tool to house your dreams to become a reality. I learned the power of visualization from Shakti Gawain's *Creative Visualization.*

Taking action in the physical world by creating a permanent home for your dreams signals to both your conscious and subconscious mind that you honor your dreams and truly believe they will come true.

lighten the load. *travel lightly.*

as I was recently cleaning out my purse, I realized what a powerful metaphor this task was for life!

How much stuff do I really need to carry with me all the time? Am I really using this item on a day-to-day basis? Why do I carry it around?

Just in case. I'm afraid I might need it.

I have my breath mints, in case I have bad breath. My gum, in case I get hungry and need a sugar rush. (I haven't chewed that gum in two weeks, since I started this new sugar-free diet.) My second lipstick, in case I get bored of the one I use every day. (Okay, I used it once this past month.) My toothpick/mini toothbrush, in case I get something inside my teeth. (I certainly don't want to walk around with black sesame seeds lodged between my teeth. I use this nearly every day.) My fun Hello Kitty pens. (I love using them to write a check or to take notes.) My hair clips, in case I get tired of my hair falling on to my face. (I haven't used them at all.) My almonds, in case I need a quick boost of energy.

I already cleaned out my wallet this way, and I love how streamlined it is. I only have two credit cards, my health insurance cards, and my driver's license. I have touched and used all of these items in the past two weeks. I always empty out my coins into my coin purse in the car, so I will always have change for the parking meters.

It's funny: ever since I was little, I would always empty out the contents of my bags, evaluate my stuff, and then put the stuff back in that I really felt I needed, each time hoping that the load would get lighter. The same is true today!

Some days it does get lighter, and those are the days I'm happy. If I can take out one thing that will lighten the load, then I'm moving forward.

As you evaluate the items in your life, be happy with that one item you are evaluating, dealing with, and truthfully letting go of in this moment. It is a huge step in the right direction. Here's how cleaning out my purse is a metaphor for life: when you take one simple step toward feeling lighter, letting go of even the most seemingly insignificant stuff will trigger a deeper letting go of even more stuff. And then you will realize that letting go of your stuff doesn't need to be this giant, monumental, life-altering burden that will take all your energy to endure.

I'm not asking you to dump out everything from your purse today. I'm only asking you to let go of just one thing that you have been hanging on to just in case you might need it, and that you've now determined you truly don't need. Confront the truth of that item: *I thought I was going to use it, but I never have. The truth is I was holding on to it "in case of an emergency."*

Today I dealt with my eye tools: my mascara and my fabulous Shu Uemura eyelash curler. As I was writing this, I got all fired up about my eyelash curler, because it is truly amazing—it gives me an eye lift that makes me feel uplifted, doe-eyed, and like a million bucks! That's a definite keeper. The mascara? Every mascara I have gives me raccoon eyes— it's not worth it.

Okay, let go of the mascara. Keep the eyelash curler. Maybe tomorrow I won't feel the need to hold on to that either. Yippee, I'm celebrating lightening my load! At least I let go of my mascara.

Everything that I need is within.

·

exercise. *lighten the load you carry every day.*

Take out your purse or briefcase.

Go through every item; be ruthless and ask yourself, *When was the last time I truly used it?*

If you haven't used it for months, let go of it for now and lighten your load.

See if you miss this item in the next week.

Continue going through every single item, being ruthlessly honest with yourself.

Do this once a week, and see what happens.

Do you keep putting stuff into your purse or briefcase, just in case? Then just be aware that you are living in fear mode or scarcity mode or just-in-case mode, and it may not be your true reality.

This exercise will always help you stay vigilant about the stuff you carry around with you. You can't expect to stay organized and on top of it if you keep on piling stuff in your bag and you don't go through it. Every week, go through your wallet, remove the receipts, and put them into your Receipts file for the year. Every week, go through your wallet and organize your money so it's going in the same direction. Every week, go through your wallet, remove the heavy coins, and put them into your coin purse or container in your car for parking meters.

Performing these seemingly menial yet important tasks will help you to stay on top of your stuff, and you will feel empowered, knowing you are taking care of the stuff you are carrying with you every single day.

touch everything. *move out and move back in with clarity.*

d on't fool yourself into thinking that when your life appears neat on the surface, everything is organized. Neat does not equate to being organized.

Yes, the fundamental concept of organizing is placing like-items in one space with clear boundaries, but this is only one level of organizing. To go deeper, you must question if all the like-items are still part of you, and still resonating with your TruthLoveMeaningPurpose.

Ideally, the purpose of your stuff determines where you keep it, or the "home" you create for it. For instance, computer paper is used for the computer, while you use handmade paper to write letters.

So you must first confront the truth of that item, and whether it belongs to the home you have assigned to it. Then you must ask yourself if you truthfully need this stuff, even if the like-items are in perfect condition.

If you have touched everything in your space and have made a conscious choice to keep everything for now, based on the TruthLoveMeaningPurpose of this particular moment, then it is time to confront another truth: you can only move forward insofar as you can let go.

Think about a glass that is empty.
You pour water into it.
The glass is finite.
The water you pour into it will overflow at some point.

Think about running. You place your foot on the ground, and then you leap forward, releasing that foot to put the other foot on the ground. You cannot move forward with both feet on the ground. There must be a release—a powerful release, if you are to sprint forward.

Think about playing the piano. You place your hands on the keyboard to strike a chord. You must release the positioning of your fingers to strike the next chord and create a new sound.

Think about an oak tree. In the fall, its leaves go from a vibrant green to a beautiful burnt orange. Once the leaves turn color, the branches shed its leaves. The branches become barren, only for a season, so fresh, new leaves can be born again.

Empty your glass.
Release your foot.
Change notes.
Shed your leaves.

That's why, yes, I encourage you to move out completely and move back in.

Dump every drawer.
Empty every closet.
Clear out every item in every single space.
Group the items together into like-items.

Then, when you see the "family of items" you have just brought together, you will know if they belong in your "family."

Touch every single item, and make a conscious choice to let go or keep it.

Even if you just kinda sorta run your fingers over a box, this act of touching it will trigger your subconscious, which will register, process, and evaluate the item.

Then, move back in with only the stuff you deem valuable, and the stuff that brings you joy!

Label each group of like-items, so everybody knows which family they belong to, and you or anybody residing in your space is no longer confused about the purpose it is serving in your life.

The act of touching everything, moving out completely and then moving back in, is powerful—physically, mentally, spiritually, and emotionally.

Once you get into the habit of always being hypervigilant about actually touching every single thing (and not just dumping), your stuff will instantly come to the surface and you can deal with it in the here and now. There will be no more surprises, and you will remain pure, free, and clear.

But if a surprise insight or message does appear for you, thank God for the miracle of this splendid revelation, which will lead you to your next step.

Trust that you are divinely led, and the stuff will let you know when to let go—and enough, already!

Remember, the Universe is always conspiring to get you where you wish to be. Trust that the stuff of your life and heart and mind are all there for a reason: to teach you, guide you, bring you supreme happiness, and make all your dreams come true!

.

exercise. *touch every item in one space. create homes for each family of items.*

Are there spaces in your life that appear neat on the surface, but the truth is that you've shoved it all into some drawer or closet and it's actually disorganized? Write a list of those areas.

Pick just one area that is both neat and disorganized, and decide to tackle the clutter beneath the neatness to make it truly clutter free and organized.

Dump the contents of one entire drawer. Group into like-items. Then, touch one item at a time and ascertain whether all the items belong, using the TruthLoveMeaningPurpose criteria.

After you have made the final decisions, create a home for the same family of items, or like-items, by labeling it and placing it on a shelf or in a drawer.

Write about how you felt going through the stuff and what you learned.

exercise. *tackle three spaces, one space at a time.*

Now list all the areas of your home that are overflowing with stuff. This list doesn't have to make sense to anybody else but you. You just know deep down that you have bombarded the space or shelf or container with too much stuff, and you must let go.

Pick three areas from the ones you named. Go to your calendar and schedule at least one to two hours to go through each space, one at a time, ruthlessly applying the TruthLove MeaningPurpose criteria.

Continue going through each area on your list, until you feel that you have "just enough stuff" in each space, so that you are no longer cramming and jamming everything in, your stuff has enough breathing space, and where you can clearly see each and every item you possess.

take out the trash every day. *start anew.*

i know most of you are very smart.
But why can't you organize your stuff?
Why do your systems collapse?
Why do you organize your stuff, and it gets disorganized again?
Because you fell asleep and were not vigilant.
You did not stay current with the *you* of today.
You allowed things into your homes and offices without a second thought.
You kept saying "yes" to stuff but were not really conscious.
You didn't stop to breathe and ask, *Is this still me? Is this still serving me? Is this still working?*
You didn't take that extra step to take out the "trash."

I say that because I see so many people who take the trash out—somewhat.
"Somewhat" doesn't cut it. You either take it out, or you don't.
You cannot leave the trash at the front doorstep, in the front hallway, or in the garage.
When you do, you are littering up paths where miracles could come tumbling in!
You are not completely letting go of the "trash" in your life if you do not dump the actual trash into the trash bin. And if the trash bin in your kitchen is overflowing with trash, take it out to the backyard where the giant trash bins are.

Yes, not taking out the trash completely is one of my pet peeves. But most importantly, it may be a sign that you don't take out the trash completely in other areas of your life.

I wonder, "If you decide something is trash but still don't take it all the way out, where else do you do that in life?"

Where else in your life have you decided that something on the inside is bringing you down and you need to throw it out—such as negative thoughts, self-doubt, fears, or unforgiveness—but you don't expend the energy to fully dump this "trash?" Whenever you have processed something internally and have decided it is trash, and do not fully take it out of your consciousness, mind, spirit, and soul, here too you are not completely taking out the trash. This goes deep.

Are you leaving some of the stuff in the recesses of your consciousness, hoping it will just disappear on its own—that the trash man will come to the deepest, darkest place of your heart, knock on the door, and ask, "Do you really want me to take this trash? Is this really trash?"

Take out the trash this time. All the way. Internally and externally. Do whatever it takes to suck the life lesson out of the stuff and dump it where it belongs. You have determined it is no longer a treasure; it truly is trash. Take out the trash once and for all.

·

exercise. *create a new habit. dump your trash every day.*

For one week, at the end of every single day, empty out every single trash can in your house, putting the trash into the trash can outside or throwing it down your trash chute. Check in with how you feel as you are taking care of this all-important task. And check in with how you feel *after* you have dumped the trash.

Then try something different. For one week, at the *beginning* of every day (not at the end), empty out the trash cans completely, as described above.

Which one feels better to you?

Do you sleep better at night, knowing you have completely let go of the trash for the day?

Do you feel lighter as you leave the house in the morning, knowing you have completely let go of the trash for the day?

When you arrive home, can you feel a small yet perceptible shift in your space, knowing all the trash cans are empty?

exercise. *hone your clutter radar.*

Journal regarding your journey thus far of taking out the trash, and how you feel when you do and when you don't. Tune into the subtle nuances of not only your environment, but the powerful receptors in your brain and mind.

I want you to become the expert of your own space, instantly noticing when there is a shift in the space, or when something is amiss. I want you to sniff out the "clutter" or "trash"—internal or external—and habitually tune in to and exercise this "clutter radar."

Eventually you will know when the space is clear, and eventually you will expect your space to be free and clear without any provoking from me or anybody else. You will begin taking out the trash and the clutter in all areas of your life, and you will take care of this all-important activity because you will know it is for your highest good. You will do it automatically, and it will become a way of life for you. You will never, ever return to the way you lived before.

This new way of life, where you take your trash out completely every single day, will shift your perspective in all areas of your life. You will start thinking differently about your internal trash in the same way, even perhaps expecting miracles to come in as you dump your trash, inside and out!

travel every day. *happy homes for your daily adventures.*

i'm the official bag lady. I have bags for everything. I used to try to get everything into one bag, but all my stuff got confused and didn't know how to best serve me. It reprimanded me and asked to be separated so that each item could best serve me whenever it was utilized.

Once when I was renting a car while my own car was being repaired, the people at the rental shop (as well as the maintenance shop) asked me if I was traveling out of town, after seeing the number of bags I was housing in my car.

I laughed! Yes, I'm traveling every day.

I'm traveling to and from my activities, wearing different hats, juggling my roles, and balancing my schedule with organizing, writing, practicing yoga, working out, and spending time with family and friends.

So I have bags within bags, and I'm always in search of the perfect stylish bag to house whatever stuff I have in my life related to a particular task or role.

And why can't the bags we use to house the stuff we use every single day be stylish as well as functional? Picking a special bag that you love, love, love will bring a smile to your face every time you use it—every day! Can you also think outside the box, and repurpose that "oh-so luxurious" clutch you bought for your friend's wedding to go with that special outfit, to use it now to house your pens or phone or computer cords? Does the thought of using all the "wonderful stuff" of your life every day, even if it was purchased for special occasions, get you excited? After all—if I haven't shared this dictum with you before— "Every single day is a holiday and a special occasion to celebrate your amazing life!"

265

Now organizing my bags is a ritual that takes place every morning and night. There's my Client Files Tote, which holds all my client files for each day's sessions. Today the client files are housed in a bronze Treesje satchel. Sometimes I may visit three clients a day, so rather than confusing myself, I also have my Current Briefcase to house only the client I'm seeing that moment. Currently I'm into a sleek tan Prada briefcase given to me by a very special client. On days when I'm not seeing clients, my Current Briefcase houses the other files on which I'm currently working. Today it houses my Next Speaking Engagement Files.

I also carry a Computer Bag, which houses my laptop computer and all the stuff I need at my business meetings and/or for writing. I alternate between a Melissa Beth pink-tweed and white-leather tote, and a vintage Neiman Marcus black-and-white cowhide tote that I've had for ages. The laptop computer is housed within its own Laptop Computer Case. The extension cords and chargers are all contained in my Chargers Bag. I like to match the Charger Bag to the Computer Bag, so I alternate between my current faves—a red suede Gucci handbag, hot pink suede Fred Segal bag, or hot pink Juicy toiletry bag.

I have a Gym Bag to house my workout clothes I use at the gym: my tennis shoes, socks, boy shorts, gym top, my gym membership and picture ID, and my protein shakes and almonds I consume prior to a workout. Today I've put that into a fun rainbow polka-dotted giant LeSportsac duffle bag.

Then I have a Yoga Bag to house my yoga clothes, a towel, and hair clips and ties. I currently am using a funky white Betsey Johnson tote with floral interior for this purpose. I have a Yoga Mat Bag to house just my giant Manduka yoga mat. I've gone through so many yoga bags, but I love my orange Barefoot Yoga bag, which matches my boyfriend's brown one. Once I saw a woman carrying a furry pink bag, and I had to know where she bought it! When she said she couldn't remember, I became obsessed with having my mom make one for me!

This "search for the perfect bag for a particular purpose" is strangely addictive yet fun, and I hope you get turned on to my trick— haha—to keep you organized with TruthLoveMeaningPurpose!

Moving on to a very important bag that every man, woman, boy, girl, and baby should put together—I have a Self-Care Bag that houses those items that take care of me throughout the day. Here I keep snacks to take on the road with me and the toiletries I may need throughout the day, like my toothbrush and mouthwash. I don't want to have bad breath working with clients, and I don't want to show up to client sessions with a growling stomach! It also houses my Tide stain remover, as well as my Neosporin, in case I spill something on my clothes, fall down somewhere, or get a cut. Currently I'm using my Louis Vuitton clutch to take care of me throughout the day!

Then, of course, there's my purse that I carry day to day. I used to switch out purses a lot when I was younger to match my outfits. Nowadays I try to find purses that match any outfit. Right now, for my Everyday Purse, I alternate between the white and black Ferragamo purses my mom gave me. But even within my Everyday Purse, I have a colorful Toki Doki purse that I have turned into my Makeup Bag. It houses my at-my-fingertips makeup—blush, face powder, eyeliner, Quench moisturizer, dental floss, mouth fresheners—with sugarless gum in one section, and in another section, my keys. For this purpose, I'm always in search of bags that are lightweight, that are not too big or small, and that have compartments to house each family of stuff I need. I also love my two-zipper Kipling cosmetic bag, which is super lightweight and expands! I have an adorable hot pink suede Coach purse that I got from my sister-in-law, which I use as my Phone Bag just for my iPhone. And there's the orange Prada business card holder I received as a gift from my best friend that I actually use for my iPhone earpods. My handful of business cards are housed currently in a compartment within my Louis Vuitton amber wallet! And, for Speaking Engagements, I use an adorable sparkly grey mini-purse from Target, which houses a bunch of business cards. Believe it or not, all these mini-bags fit comfortably within my Everyday Purse!

I have to mention my "latest" bag—my pen-and-pencil case—which is now an essential for me. This purchase was triggered the day I almost lost my brand new, "high-end" stylus, which my boyfriend had purchased for me to take meeting notes with on my iPad. Mind you, this was probably the tenth stylus that had been in my possession, because I kept forgetting them and leaving them everywhere—such as at clients' homes. But I've discovered that when I spend the money to get something I love, love, love, and I treat it with the respect it deserves as the "special one," then I never lose it again. (I used to go through so many sunglasses and umbrellas, but once I got my "love, love, love" sunglasses and umbrellas, I somehow never lost them again!)

In addition to the stylus, I somehow always seemed to be misplacing my special silver Waterman pen I purchased at Flax, where I spent hours testing out at least a few dozen pens to find that one pen that wrote smoothly, flowed, and felt luxurious in my hands. (Truth: I went shopping for this pen during a time when I was having major doubts about having my book published and being picked up by a publisher. I bought this pen as a leap of faith to symbolize the most positive intended outcome I visualized—seeing myself signing my published book at a book signing!)

When I was growing up, one of my favorite things to purchase before starting school every fall was a pen-and-pencil case (oftentimes, a Hello Kitty one)! I realized that this was exactly what I needed—the perfect pen-and-pencil case for those special Writing and Office Tools! I went to one of my favorite Japanese bookstores/stationery stores in Little Tokyo and spent hours searching for the perfect case. Score! The perfect bag was awaiting me: a super cool, purple patent-leather pen-and-pencil case with—get this—inserts (or happy homes!) for the pen, stylus, and another pen!

A final note: Your purse and wallet should reflect your TruthLoveMeaningPurpose as well, and not be bulging with receipts. (On the other hand, let your wallet be overflowing with those green dollar bills and checks to be deposited! Cram and jam them in there!) I've gone "wallet shopping" with male clients to find the perfect wallet or briefcase to house their stuff, and shopping with female clients to find the perfect handbag or tote to house all the important stuff of life. Everybody is different, and one must check into their TruthLoveMeaningPurpose to discern when something is truly a "must-have," or when it's best to simplify and become a minimalist in this area. I could wax poetic and ad nauseum about this topic, as I'm so passionate about finding the best systems for every area of life—those that are the most time-saving, productive, and efficient, as well as stylish and beautiful.

For me, giving a home to the stuff that serves me and travels with me every day is paying respect to it in the best way possible! If these items were homeless and scattered all over the place, I would fight with the stuff, curse at the stuff, and waste many hours, because using the stuff would not be easy and effortless.

Travel every day with happy homes that house your stuff. Don't underestimate the importance of having your stuff in order. Love the homes. Love the stuff. And love the trips, the mini-adventures, you take on a daily basis! This is the beautiful stuff life is made of: loving all the stuff of your own beautiful life!

·

exercise. *organize your everyday travel purse, briefcase, or tote.*

Grab your purse, tote, or briefcase.

Dump all the contents.

Now group all the contents by either the type of item, or where you use it. For example, you could group all your makeup together, or group together everything you use at the gym.

Now find a beautiful, cool bag for each item or use. Put your pencils and pens into a Writing Tools Bag, or determine what part of your purse or briefcase you will always use to house your keys. The key is making a distinct choice and sticking to it. If you keep switching homes, you will get confused. Can you imagine if you moved to a different home literally every week? Would you know where you lived? You may end up with several bags within your purse or briefcase, and it may seem like a lot of different compartments.

Keep refining until it feels "just right." Only you will know if your purse or briefcase systems are working for you.

See if this way of organizing the stuff that serves you every day makes your life flow more easily and effortlessly.

And then continue to do the same with everything in your life, to make every facet of your life simple and seamless.

Have fun organizing the stuff that you use every day!

every day is a holiday. *celebrate you!*

W hat are you saving that for?
A special day?
A special occasion?
A holiday?

How many times have you stopped yourself from using something you just got, because you want to save it for something special?

Why not wear your brand-new sandals to the market to pick up the tomatoes you forgot to buy?

Why not wear your favorite new dress to the pharmacy to pick up your prescriptions?

Use your special linens for tonight's dinner.

Use your special pillowcases when you change your sheets.

Use your favorite handbag for your gym bag.

Wear your favorite suit today, which you have been saving for that special presentation you will be making in the future.

Wear that dress you wore to your New Year's Eve party, and reinvent it by wearing it with flip flops.

Why not start using your special stuff every day?

Then perhaps you will start to view your "everyday" as a special occasion to celebrate you, to celebrate the miracle of life.

Which came first—the chicken or the egg?

Did wearing that special outfit to the market elicit a special response from your being—that today is special—and created a chance special meeting with a long lost love? Did using the special bed linens make you feel like a million bucks when you went to sleep, knowing you were using your finest linens, and elicit the feeling that things are great and will only get better, and that you are special?

Why not treat every day as a special treat by using your finest linens and wearing your favorite clothes? Why not eat the Godiva chocolates now, treating yourself like the special person you are romancing and dating, rather than saving them for that special guest that might come over one day? Use your special china for dinner tonight, and when your husband asks why, say, "Today is special because of you. Every day with you is special."

When your friend sees you at the market all dressed up in your party dress, and asks, "Where are you are going—anywhere special?" why not say, "I'm celebrating today. Every day is a holiday and special day to celebrate life."

Don't wait for tomorrow! Party today as if it's your special day. Don't wait for a holiday or birthday to celebrate yourself and the gift of life.

Celebrate today.
Use your special stuff today because every day is special.
It's special because life is precious, and the fact that you are in this life is special.
Choosing life is special.
Being able to read is special.
Being able to breathe is special.
Your unique way of seeing life is special.
Find one thing that is special about today, and celebrate that.

When you do, don't be surprised if your perspective about your stuff shifts, and you start seeing everything as special. And if you find that you don't want to use your stuff even for special days, then why do you have it? Are you using the "old stuff" until it wears out? I challenge you to go deeper, asking yourself how you truly feel about your life, your stuff, and your self-worth, and search deeply for the answers.

When you think every day is special, suddenly your life and your time will be filled with everything you deem special—people, stuff, and events. Then, if you notice anything that does not seem special in your life, you'll know that it's time to let it go.

When you honor what is special to you, you are honoring how special you are on this earth.

"Special" is your TruthLoveMeaningPurpose.

Live today as special. *You* are special.

.

exercise. *celebrate! use your best stuff every day.*

For one week, use your special holiday plates for breakfast, lunch, dinner, and snacks. Think to yourself, and tell yourself and your family, "Today is a special day. We are celebrating our special lives!"

Journal every day about how you feel when you use your best table linens and plates. Notice what feelings arise when you do. Do you think, "I should save this for . . . " or "This is wasteful . . . "?

Do you feel differently eating your meals on these special plates? Do you feel good when you treat yourself like royalty?

What else has changed for you this week, since you started acting as if every day is special and treating yourself as special? Has your mindset shifted, even slightly? If so, great!

deal with it now. *not later—now, now, now!*

hello! I'm back again.

You may not have noticed, but I had run away from you. I've been avoiding writing, afraid to tell you what I go through with my stuff. Yes, I'm talking about the physical stuff, but mostly I'm talking about the heart and mental stuff that comes up as I'm dealing with my physical stuff.

I couldn't decide what to do with my leather jacket, so I just threw it in the closet, pretending that it didn't matter, not wanting to take it all the way through with the questioning. Yup, I do this as well. When the going gets tough, I do what I've seen some of my clients do when they think I'm not looking. They try to hide something from me, shoving a piece of paper or something else into their pockets, so that they don't have to answer my questions. They are tired, and they don't feel like going deep with this stuff right now. Later.

Later, later, later.

I'll think about it later. I'll probably give it away, so I'll throw it in there for now, hoping it will go away on its own.

I'll deal with it later.

Okay, June, deal with it now. As you teach others, question now and go deep now, and see where it will take you. Do it with this one thing, and you will be set free in other areas. It will permeate the other areas of your life, affecting you deeply. You will learn from questioning this one item, rather than shoving it aside, pretending this precious item doesn't deserve it, pretending it doesn't matter. It does matter. Your stuff matters. This leather jacket matters.

I give in. Okay, do I want to give it away? My beloved first leather jacket that looks kinda worn out and beaten up like it's been through a lot—like me. I think I've had it for more than ten years. And, hey, doesn't leather last forever?

I try to go deeper. I pretend I'm talking to a client: Does it look tired? Does it look beat? Does it look like it needs to be retired? Do I need to give it a rest, forever? Forever let it rest in peace. Perhaps I will give it away, because someone else will look at it with a fresh pair of eyes and see its value and beauty, and love its flaws and its beaten-up quality. Perhaps they'll enjoy the fact that the leather jacket has had the lining ripped and redone a number of times. Perhaps they'll see the beauty in the creases, wrinkles, and faded blackness. They'll see its glory.

Let me look at the jacket again. Do I see what they see? Or do I see what I still see?

Okay, I'm trying it on again. I'm taking it out of the closet, and it doesn't look bad.

It does still look pretty good. But is this still who I am today? It's not the me who would wear this out on a date night, but it's the me who would wear it after a workout or yoga session. Okay, I'll keep it.

OMG, this is not what I want to be doing. I'm trying to sort, declutter, let go. This is what I'm talking about.

But now I have to tell myself what I also have to tell my clients: Don't let go just because you want to let go and I told you to. Let go because it feels good to you, and only you. Let go because you have gone through conscious questioning within, you have gotten to the truth of the answers that run deeply within, and you have made amends with your past and this item, have paid them proper homage, and are ready to let go. Don't just let go because you think it's the right answer and pretend that "letting go is great!" Don't let someone else make the decisions for you—because someone else said you need to let go, or because someone else told you that it doesn't feel like you. Only you know what feels right, and what still feels like you. And certainly don't keep it just because someone said, "That's pretty expensive, and you could get a lot for it on eBay." Who cares what anyone else thinks? It's your life, so make decisions about your stuff based on what you think, since you're the one who's living it (and wearing it).

So . . . am I keeping the worn-out leather jacket? I'm giving it a new life by classifying it as a leather jacket to be worn only after workouts and yoga sessions. Cool. I'm shifting my perspective about my stuff and seeing it in a new light.

I love how this life asks me what I think about myself and my precious stuff. Sometimes it's so much easier to ask someone else, but ultimately, we're the ones we see each day in the mirror. You can't get mad at anyone but yourself, and you need to take responsibility for your decisions. Each and every one, even if you've made some wrong turns.

So today, why not get in touch again with your TruthLoveMeaningPurpose with just one item. Just one item, every day. Soon you will just know if you are avoiding or denying the truth of something in your space. Soon you will be forced to take action, because you will know when you're avoiding it by throwing it into some dark closet. Even when you leave your house, you will know it's there. This knowingness will seep into your consciousness and you won't be able to turn off the light anymore. The light will always be on. Great!

Deal with it. Now. Not later. Now. Now. Now.

.

exercise. *no more avoidance. deal with it now!*

Is there something you keep avoiding, not wanting to deal with it? Is there something you keep shoving under a rug to deal with later? What is it? Let's look at it in the light. Why are you avoiding it? Why are you kicking and screaming while dealing with this item? Write down all your feelings regarding this item and why you keep running away from it or think it's difficult.

Now, go through the TruthLoveMeaningPurpose criteria and write about the truth of this item. Write about how much you used to love this item and what has shifted. Write about how much this item means to you. Write about the purpose it served when you first received it or bought it. Now, write about the purpose it serves *not* being used. Thank this item for all the purposes it served. Thank the item for loving you. Thank this item for teaching you about the meaning of avoidance and running away, and lastly, for allowing you to face the truth of what's really going.

What's really going on with this item? What's the real story behind your wanting to deal with it later?

take it all the way through. *complete what you started.*

Unfinished business is clutter.

Don't leave unfinished business around. This unfinished business, especially if there is lots of it, is saying loudly to you, over and over, that you cannot complete something. It's an important concept to grasp. So take it all the way through. If you are working on a project or a space, take that space or project all the way through to its completion.

If you have lots of unfinished business lying around, in essence you are telling your subconscious mind that you are a loser, because you cannot complete this one thing. Even though you don't feel the impact of the physical stuff when you leave the stuff behind at your house, you are still carrying it around with you in the back of your mind.

The broken glass chandelier in your dining room is something you see every single day when you walk to the kitchen. The squeaky door is something you hear every single morning when you leave the house. The broken knob on your door annoys you every time you close the door and it doesn't shut properly. By the time you leave the house, you have accumulated this giant laundry list of stuff that needs to be done, stuff you haven't done, and sure, when you're in traffic, your mind focuses on what's in front of you and you temporarily forget about it. But day in and day out, seeing this unfinished business creates this massive traffic jam in your mind, leaving no room for anything else except the thoughts nagging you to take care of it.

That's right! Even when you're not consciously thinking about it, your unfinished business is still taking up space in your mind. It's preventing you from taking on new projects or welcoming new ideas, because your brain is screaming, "There's no more space in here for new stuff!" When you take care of this stuff in a timely manner, you are freeing up valuable brain space that could be used for other more important stuff.

Indecision leads to clutter. You can't decide what color to paint the dining room, so you wait for weeks, hoping divine inspiration will strike you, now with twenty swatches of paint on the walls. But since you can't decide, you decide not to paint. Weeks go by, and suddenly you lose the inspiration to paint the room. Now this indecision becomes unfinished business. How about deciding on one color and letting that decision inform your next step? Are you afraid of making the wrong decision and hating the color? So what? Paint it another color. Your fear of making a wrong decision prevents you from moving forward. After all, how will you know that you made a wrong decision or the right decision unless you make *some* decision?

Oftentimes, people move into their new homes and leave unpacked boxes lying around. Whether their excuse is "my house is so big and I don't know where to put things," or "I'm not sure I really want to keep this stuff anymore," this inability to decide leads to unfinished business. Unpack the stuff, don't be afraid of making a mistake, and take it all the way through. Even if it is not perfect, it is okay. It's better to have made a mistake than to have taken no action at all. What do you have to lose? You have everything to gain by being out of the boxes and feeling moved into your beautiful new home.

Leaving unfinished business around your space is like putting speakers around your house that are broadcasting to you: *I don't believe you. You said you were going to take care of me. You said you were going to decide. You were going to put the final touches on me. Can't you just finish this?*

Believe me, I get it! I totally get it!

I have been working on this book for years, and thought I was done five years ago! Life happened, and then, because I really thought it was done and I was going to self-publish, I told people about it—which was a mistake. Then people kept asking me, "Is your book out? When is it going to be done?" I felt like a failure at not publishing this book, but at the same time, I couldn't just put out a book that was still evolving with the truth of what I was learning. Still, this unfinished business clogged me up and made me feel guilty when I tried to tackle another goal.

So I really do understand how terrible it feels having stuff that is incomplete. Even though you're not carrying the physical stuff around with you, you are carrying around the guilt about not having taken care of your to-dos with you.

Finally, this year, I vowed once and for all to create the time and space to get my book done. I set the intention to do it. I set it as a goal. I then took my schedule and put it into my calendar. Then I showed up to write.

So the success of completion begins with one small step. One step at a time. One task at a time. Your goal is a series of action steps. When you think about all the steps it will take to accomplish your goal, you have already failed, because you have set up mental roadblocks for yourself, thinking about how difficult it will be to do all that.

Rather than thinking about how many steps still lie ahead, and how hard those steps might be, why not just start with the "next best divine step" that is calling for your attention? After completing this task, I guarantee you that your consciousness will signal to you the next step, and that next step will inform the step after that.

At the bottom of the hill of Temescal Canyon, sitting on my bicycle, I remember looking up and feeling intimidated, thinking to myself, *How I am going to get up this mountain?* Rather than succumb to my fears and doubts, and focusing on how difficult it would be, instead I focused on what was right in front of me. And I just started pedaling. I tried not to look all the way up to the top of the hill, because I was not there. I just focused on the piece of ground right in front of me, and I kept confessing to myself that the journey would be easy, effortless, fun, and enjoyable—and guess what? That's exactly what happened. I tackled every inch of that hill, one pedal at a time. Suddenly, I was at the top of the mountain. The rush for me was pedaling one "cycle" at a time, enjoying the journey, and all of a sudden, I was at my destination.

With this book, it seemed daunting to think about all the steps to getting it published. But the one step that I kept coming back to was—just write! Just keep writing chapter after chapter after chapter! After you are done writing, then organize it, but you cannot do both at the same time. The creative process of writing was getting jumbled with the mental process of organizing, and the two processes were colliding into each other, creating this traffic jam in my consciousness.

Finish one thing. Take it all the way through to completion, and see how you feel.

That one drawer. That one room. That one phone call. That one letter. It doesn't matter how small the project is. Don't overanalyze. Make a decision to finish it, and see what happens. See how you feel. You will feel better, because at least you finished.

And after you have finished that task or project, then ask yourself, *What is my next best action step?*

Keep doing this with every to-do that constitutes unfinished business in your life, and you will soon clear away the clutter of unfinished business. Then you will develop supreme confidence in being able to take something all the way through to its completion, which will set yourself up for success in other areas of your life.

Next time, your mind will say, "Okay, I believe you, and I know you are capable of taking this new task all the way through to completion as well. So I will start it, believe I can complete it successfully, and set more goals!"

Keep the faith. Believe you can take it all the way through.

No matter what, you are a winner for today, because you decided to take one definitive action step, and you took it all the way through!

.

exercise. *take one action today on your unfinished business.*

Start a list of unfinished projects in your life.

Now, just pick one that really bothers you.

Write about it. Write about how good it would feel to get this project done. Write down what the next best step is to complete this project. What is one step you can take today? Go and do it.

Then, after you have done it, ask yourself the same question about what the next best step is that you can take, and do it.

Eventually, you will get into the habit of just taking that next best step, rather than thinking about the gazillion steps it might take to complete the task, which would immobilize you.

Today, just take one action step all the way through, and let that step inform your next step.

And celebrate, giving yourself a pat on the back for taking this one action step. Now you are one step further along in your project! You are one step closer to completion!

Continue to celebrate every step you are taking all the way through! Congratulations!

wear your feelings every day. *inside-out expressions!*

i love, love, love fashion and clothes! Clothes have memories and thus trigger emotions for me, so I am constantly reevaluating the stuff in my closet to stay clutter free, ensuring that my clothes' energy and style reflect the energy of who I am inside and who I am today!

I fondly remember and associate certain moments of my childhood to the clothes I wore: my low-waisted corduroy red bell-bottom cords that I wore to the Grand Canyon, my super low-waisted light blue Ditto pants in sixth grade when we moved to Monterey Park, the super-fitted white jumpsuit with beautiful red flowers that my mom made for me, all the fun triangle halter tops I wore in the summer of seventh grade, the yellow dress I asked my mom to make from *Teen* magazine for my piano recital, my eighth-grade white flowing graduation dress that I had my mom make right out of *Vogue*, the short midriff cutoff shorts and tie-up shirts that showed off my flat belly that my grandparents bought for me while visiting from Japan, the black-and-gold-trimmed top and matching capri pants with gold shoes, along with the rabbit fur coat my mom bought for me when I was going to an Earth Wind and Fire concert in college; the red peacoat and red skirt my dad bought me in Japan . . .

No matter how much I declutter, I find it hard to get rid of that miniature pink furry coat Mom made my Barbie when I was seven. It reminds me of the exact replica mom made for me, and how to this day I still love things that are furry. They make me feel like a girly girl. Anything with fur on it, faux or not, makes me feel luxurious. I know it's not politically correct to say I have real fur stuff, especially when I am so into animals and am rooting for the goats when they're being chased down by wolves on *Planet Earth*! But I'm sorry, rabbits—I still have my rabbit furs! Do I need fur collars and fur stoles to make me feel special, or do I just love them because they're luxurious and make me feel glamorous?

I love my J red leather jacket that my dear friend custom-made especially for me. When I first wore it, Dad asked what the J stood for. Joy! I'm wearing it now, and it always makes me feel special. Do I need a jacket with my first initial to remind me I am special? Is there anything wrong with wanting to feel special?

I love my black Ferragamo leather purse Mom bought for me. It's the perfect bag that matches everything and is the perfect size, depth, and width. It always looks chic no matter what, and it makes me feel special.

I love my most recent purchase of cute furry white legwarmers that I bought from this store on Abbot Kinney in Venice called Waraku. I love that store, which carries everything from Japan and the latest hottest styles from Tokyo. The faux fur was sitting in a basket with other socks, all alone, screaming at me, "Buy me! You would know what to do with me!" At home, I put them on over my white Juicy sweats and my white tennis shoes, and they amp up my style quotient, immediately making them special. It actually looks like I'm wearing furry white boots! I also put them on with white boy short undies and a cute white thermal top, and I think it looks sexy. It's an entirely new look, all for the price of $12.99.

What else stands out in my closet as something that is special and I don't want to let go of, and that has survived and made it through several passes of decluttering in the past two years?

My chunky necklaces with real stones. I've worn them periodically over the past years, but I love the way they decorate my closet shelf. They add pizazz to my closet and make me think that one of these days, I will go back to just wearing a plain white tank top and jeans with these necklaces. The agate, turquoise, and coral necklaces are just what that simple getup would need to make it special. So here are the questions I ask myself to get to the truth and the heart of the matter, so I can decide whether to keep them, or let them go: Are these tried-and-true favorites? Or am I holding on to the past with these items—a past way of dressing and my past style? If so, can these pieces be "reborn" with a new item in my closet? For now, I decide that I love, love, love these necklaces, and I am holding on to them. Sometimes there doesn't need to be a logical explanation or defense for why you are holding on to something. It can just be that you feel it from your heart.

Okay, let me go over and look at the bag of clothes I wasn't sure whether I would let go of or not. I was going to give it to one of my friends who hasn't gone shopping for a while, and who needs some clothes. Some of the clothes I'm letting go of aren't trendy anymore, but they might be trendy for her. Let me see what happens if I look at them today—two months later.

(Cardinal sin: Don't let anything you have decided to give away sit in your closet or in your home for more than a day. Otherwise, you will have to go through everything again, as I'm doing today, wasting valuable time. Once you make the decision, take that decision all the way through—as one seemingly wise person, me, once said! Ha!)

Why did I want to let go of these clothes? Had I changed? Had I shifted? Had I grown? Had I evolved?

Okay, it's not as deep as that. I had gained weight! Two months ago, when I was going through my closet, I was getting frustrated that everything I tried on didn't fit in the morning, and I would have to try on several pairs of pants to find that one that fit comfortably. There's nothing like going through your day feeling uncomfortable and wanting to come home and change. It reminded me that I used to not even have to worry about my weight, but now that I'm no longer a chronic cardio queen, I have to think about these things.

I'm hungry.

Getting back to the stuff—when we have stuff that doesn't fit and that doesn't belong anymore, we're also carrying around the thoughts attached to the stuff, so that we feel bogged down and heavy, rather than light.

So, to give it a rest for a while, I took the clothes out that no longer fit my new body, put them in a box labeled CLOTHES SIZE 2—TRY AGAIN, and retired it for a few months to see if this new body is going to be my body forever.

Now let's see how I feel a few months later. Will I keep the clothes because I love them on this body? Or will I let go with love, trusting that the body I have now is just fine, that these clothes are just a representation of the body and of the me I was in the past, and that it's perfectly fine to let go of them for now? I may someday fit into them, but am I going to wait until that someday comes along, carrying that box with me from size to size? Will those clothes ever be in style again? Perhaps, but perhaps in a slightly different form.

So, for now, I re-evaluate the clothes and try them on again. Do I love them? Yes, I still love the red silver grommet tank top that shows off my belly. When my belly is flat, it is passable. But if my belly looks fat, I will surely need to pass it on to someone who will enjoy showing off their belly, big or not.

I decide to keep the black polo top that I just got last season. I didn't wash it in a delicate cycle, so it looks kinda worn, but I'll see if my wonderful dry cleaner can repair it. If not, I'll let it go, as I don't like to wear things that are showing signs of wear and snags.

So, with every piece, I evaluate it with a fine-tooth comb, and it makes the job of getting ready in the morning easier when I know that everything that is sitting in my closet is good to go and good to wear at a moment's notice. No more searching around for something that fits, because everything that's sitting in there does fit. No more trying on a few pairs of pants to see which one fits.

When I'm staying current with my stuff and being truthful with my stuff in every moment, it saves me heartache, headache, and time when it comes to getting dressed in the morning. Putting on my clothes becomes a joyful way of expression for me, from the inside out. I know I took the time to put on what I love, something I care about, and I know it represents me and how I feel today.

So, the clothes are not just stuff. Going through clothes is not a waste of time, nor is it a frivolous or luxurious thing.

It is important because the clothes I wear on the outside and into the world reflects my inner stuff and true being. It matters, because I understand how powerful the stuff makes me feel.

Today, just to go to the coffee shop, I put on a party dress with cowboy boots to feel dressed up for this special occasion: writing for you! This act of getting dressed and picking out the perfect outfit just for today is important, because it serves as a metaphor for me and my life.

Pick an outfit for this one day, because every day is precious. I'm not "throwing on anything" just to cover up my body. I'm honoring my body in this moment, honoring my current feelings and how I want to feel wearing a certain outfit. I'm allowing my clothes to represent how I feel today!

It doesn't matter that I'm wearing my party dress outside, and it doesn't matter what anybody else thinks. "Where am I going all dressed up? I'm dressed up for life. My life!"

I love my clothes and my life! They are all me, it's about how I feel, and that's what counts.

.

exercise. *dare to wear what you are vibing today.*

Check in with how you feel today. Don't go into "automatic mode" and just put on something you'd typically wear to work, to work out, or on date night. What is your attention drawn to in your closet? Are you vibing that bright orange scarf? Are you feeling blue today? Were you inspired by *The Great Gatsby* movie and want to don a hat? Or are you feeling like sporting khaki cargo pants, pretending you're on a safari in the African savanna? Build an outfit around that one article of clothing you are vibing today. Use this exercise to get in touch with your feelings, and allow yourself to express how you are feeling today with that certain accessory or piece of clothing. I dare you! And if somebody asks you what you're all dressed up for, just say, "I felt like it!"

exercise. *dare to wear your party outfit to the best party of your life. today!*

Today pick an outfit that you would normally wear to a party, and wear it out and about. Set the intention that you are celebrating you, your amazing life, and the miracles of life! See what happens as you go about your day, and see if this outfit evokes certain feelings of well-being and happiness for you. See if the outfit makes you feel embarrassed or self-conscious.

The party you are going to is your party—every single day.

What if you lived your life like this, pretending every single day is a party celebrating you? What if you lived your life every single day as if it's a special day? How would this "living" shift your perspective about you and your life?

Would you start acting differently because of the outfit? Would you start being a different person because of the outfit?

This exercise may give you hope and strengthen your faith that every single outfit or item you possess does affect you and your vibration deeply, whether or not you believe it. Which came first, the chicken or the egg? Did your outfit cause you to generate great experiences today and act more boldly, and therefore feel great, or did those wonderful, out-of-the ordinary experiences happen because your outfit made you feel wonderful? It doesn't matter.

I would love for you to begin to realize how powerful the stuff in your life is, whether you're wearing it or carrying it physically, mentally, or emotionally. That's what matters. It's all connected.

delegate. *let go of being and doing all things.*

When is it time to let go and hire the experts? Only you know inside. But in making this decision, you must remember to put a price on your time, your relationships, and harmony in your home, in addition to the expense of hiring an expert.

I used to have paints, paintbrushes, hammers, nails, and screws in all different shapes and sizes, but the truth was that although I kept accumulating them, I never got around to using them myself.

Once I painted my bedroom walls white, to freshen up the room. It seemed like an easy enough task—I mean, how hard could it be? Well, I soon learned that there is a proper technique to painting even white walls, and if you don't know the proper technique, and/or have the patience to learn it, even streaked and swirly layers of white can start looking drab, which was the opposite of my intended outcome. And once I put up a closet organizer in my closet, where the shelf was just a few inches off. When I hammered it in, it looked even and straight—I mean, who would really notice? Well, my clothes certainly noticed, as they slid over to one side!

The truth was that I knew prepping was the most important part of painting, but I didn't have the patience to prep. There is a method and art to painting that I could learn, but is that truly my passion? Similarly, putting up closet organizers requires measuring precisely—and is measuring my true passion?

My passion is designing, decorating, and styling a space to honor each person's TruthLoveMeaningPurpose.

My passion is finding and hiring the artisans—rather than mere technicians—who can not only bring passion and art into my space with their craft, but inject the power of their own passion and love into my space.

I don't have the patience to precisely measure everything, so I rely on professional closet organizers to install systems. I even used to joke that I can't even screw a light bulb—which is actually kinda sorta true, because when there are so many different light bulbs for every space, the truth is I would much rather prefer to hire the handyman expert to find the light bulbs that exactly fit each space and lighting fixture, and who loves shopping at Home Depot, rather than going there myself in a state of frustration and overwhelm. I have realized that whatever "time" I would spend perusing the aisles is costly in two ways: (1) it would take me twice as long as someone familiar with the products, and (2) it costs me peace of mind, as my frustration would cause a downward spiral of energy.

But let's say you *are* a handyman extraordinaire—and you are also a successful investment banker who doesn't have time to do the little things around the house your wife has been nagging you to do. Do you think insisting on doing it yourself is fair to your wife, whose "office" is the home and kitchen?

Let go of the belief system that you must be everything to everyone. Yes, you are good at it—but does that mean you are the only one who can do it?

Let go of your ego. Let go of thinking you have to do it because you're the man of the house. Let go of thinking you can do it better than somebody else. The truth is that when you hire a handyman to take care of all the little stuff that would take you all weekend to do, you are saving the cost of stress and making a deposit into the relationship bank with your wife.

When you take this action, you are still the man, delegating what is no longer your passion to somebody else whose passion and business it is. Most importantly, your priority will shift to valuing your weekends, spending precious time with your kids and your wife, and/or spending precious time by yourself decompressing from your busy work week. Also, when you pay somebody else to do something you would moan and groan about doing, you are letting go of your resentment at having to take care of those important matters on your precious weekends, and your wife can let go of her anger at you for putting off those tasks that are important to her. You are also building a new belief system that says doing what brings you joy and bliss will bring an influx of infinite riches into your household.

By employing somebody whose passion it is to be a handyman or handywoman, I also believe that you will be contributing to the beautiful intended flow of the Universe, where everybody working out of their passions will be compensated handsomely and richly rewarded—just by their desire to be of service using their God-given gifts.

However, what if dilly-dallying and tinkering around the house is a stress reliever for you? What if it is a meditative exercise that helps you forget about the office? Then, the truth is that you should schedule the time to take care of this stuff that your wife and family need completed to keep the household running smoothly. Or, better yet, use the handyman for this important stuff, and find a project to work on that is not going to affect your family and your household, such as building something from scratch.

So confronting the truth of what stuff you are capable of doing, as well as the time and energy involved, is paramount to your peace of mind and harmony in your household. Weigh out each scenario, and think about the time, stuff, and people in your life from a different perspective. Examine your intentions behind your actions, and make sure that your actions are in alignment with your priorities, loves, and passions, and honor of your loved ones as well.

Enjoy the journey of letting go and delegating stuff to those who are passionate about the tasks and activities you can't find the time to do or have the patience to do. Infusing your life with the passion of these amazing team members will amp your own passion in the areas of your life where you are focusing your attention, such as your job and relationships. Soon you'll see that it will elevate the energy of your entire environment and being, and will bring miracles into your life!

.

exercise. *delegate one task.*

Name one activity you do not enjoy doing. Can you delegate this task to somebody else? Can you think of somebody else who absolutely loves performing this task?

Can you hire them? Can you barter this activity with this person?

Get creative! Think of solutions that will help you to let go of this "passionless" task, so that more of your days can be filled with things you love and enjoy doing.

exercise. *be grateful for the blessing behind this task.*

If you choose to continue doing this task you do not particularly enjoy doing, take charge now. Stop complaining. Get creative about how you can make that job or task more fun.

Feel the gratitude in your heart for your life, for being alive and healthy enough to notice what you want more of in your life. See the greater lessons you are learning from performing the task or job. Journal regarding the gratitude you have in your heart for being healthy enough to do this task and discover the blessings behind the task.

The more love and passion you infuse into your everyday life, even with the seemingly trivial tasks, the more love and passion you will continue to attract into your life!

everyday vacation. *your home as your favorite retreat.*

Y our house is a world in and of itself you can learn from!
Why do you need to travel to distant, faraway, exotic places?
Are you craving excitement, adventure, and a sense of spiritual renewal?

Guess what?

It's right here.
In front of you.
In your home.
In your office.

Bring order to the stuff in your life in your own home, in the way you desire, and you will create a flow of energy that will yield far greater benefits, satisfaction, and fulfillment than any one-week trip you could go on.

You go on vacation halfway across the world. You get excited about packing your bags. You plan the trip far in advance. You plot out the sights you want to visit, that are "must-sees." You decide which of the best restaurants you don't want to miss out on. You schedule a tour that will take you efficiently and expediently to the hot spots of that region. You don't want to miss a thing! You take photos, journal, and blog about your adventures, so you can share them with your friends, colleagues, and family! You send postcards from these locations: "Miss you . . . wish you were here!"

You return home. You might not unpack your luggage for a few days, a week, or perhaps until the next trip. You leave the bags at the door, too tired and exhausted to unpack. You may even need a break to recover from your "vacation," to get yourself grounded again.

Why are you sabotaging your space and the greatest adventure of your life—your everyday life?

Why not go on a different trip this time?

Remove your bags from the foyer, where they are constantly reminding you of how much fun the trip was—and now you're back home, dealing with your "oh-so-mundane" life. Unpack immediately to take this past trip all the way through to completion, and fully receive the gifts and enjoy the treasures from this last trip. Unpack immediately to be ready for your next great adventure. Unpack immediately so you don't "trip" on the baggage that you are still carrying around from this last trip!

Now, why not go on another trip "around the world" in your home, your office, and your life?

Why not pretend that the home you live in is your favorite resort and vacation spot?

C'mon—would you dump stuff in your foyer, where it would greet you every day with a frown? Would you let the leaves on your indoor plants brown? Would you let the flowers you received last week sit in the stinky container? Clean out the container, and get ready for more flowers to arrive on your doorstep. Get ready for new leaves to sprout in your life! Do you see how deep this goes?

Why not treat yourself and your home or home office with the respect it deserves?

I once created this "everyday vacation" with a client who loved staying in hotel rooms. She loved the crispness of fresh hotel linens, and the fresh scent of the fluffy white towels folded neatly on the silver rack in the luxurious bathroom. So I called her favorite hotel, purchased all of it, and we recreated the "hotel spa-like feeling" in her own home, even down to the beautiful floral arrangements. After that, she no longer felt compelled to go out of town to get rejuvenated. She was so inspired at home that she ended up cancelling her future trips for the year.

When I go traveling, I spend the first hour or two getting my hotel room "clutter free and organized" to energetically match the beautiful feeling of my clutter-free home. I will put away the hotel signs and rearrange the hotel furniture so it feels peaceful to me. I will unpack my suitcase of its contents right away so I am ready for my vacation adventures—even if I am there for one night. I am notorious for leaving a hotel if I don't feel it matches the vibration of where I live every day.

So why not get excited about your life's travels every single day within your own life and home? Why not create a home you love, where every item is a treasure and something you relish and love, where every single day in your home feels like you're on vacation?

Every day would feel like an adventure, because every space you'd enter would be fresh, new, and filled with positive energy! Every day would be magical, because all the stuff in your space would be oozing with so much life force that you could feel the energetic pull of love infusing the space.

Why not create an office that you get excited to work in, that inspires you to create, analyze, dissect, communicate, build? How exciting would that be?! You spend forty hours a week at your office. Why not make this space as amazing as the hotel you carefully researched in Dubai? Why not make your home as beautiful as the restaurants you hung out in on the French Riviera?

Once and for all, create a life you love in the space you live in every single day of your life. Spend the energy and time to travel through your home, your office, and your stuff, and create a life you love in each and every space. Spend the energy and time to travel through your closet, rather than going shopping (again). Spend the energy and time to travel through your foods, your fridge, and your pantry, and cook up something exciting rather than ordering out (again). Pretend you are at a marketplace in France, searching for treasures. What would you buy? What would you pass up?

Look at your life and where you are here and now from this radically different perspective, and see what souvenirs you have brought into your life from this life trip you are on. Notice the stuff that seems unimportant now. Notice the stuff that seems out of date, or old. Notice the stuff that no longer seems exciting to you. Let go of the stuff that feels old, worn-out, and boring.

Keep only the stuff that feels exciting, new, and positive.

Now, walk through every space, and see if you get that same exciting feeling you get when you go to a foreign country or exotic place, or while checking into a fresh, brand-new hotel room. See if you get that same feeling, where you love coming back to your room, knowing you are on vacation.

Why not take a vacation in your own home?

Why not live life as an exciting adventure in the space you live in every single day of your life, where your spaces are filled only with stuff you love?

.

exercise. *create your favorite vacation spot at home.*

Write about your favorite or dream vacation spot. What do you love about this spot? What feelings arise when you think about this spot?

Would you like your home or a part of your home to be like this vacation spot?

Write about how coming home to this "vacation spot" every single day would make you feel.

What are three action steps you could take right now that would take you closer to this goal? Do them now.

Continue taking action until your space feels more and more like your "favorite vacation spot."

life force spaces. *let it take your breath away.*

every space has an energy, vibration, and life force you can feel when you enter it! Evaluate the spaces you reside in or work in.

Even if a space is familiar to you, if there is a current of positive electromagnetic energy flowing through it, it is unmistakable and undeniable. The best way to describe it is that the space will literally take your breath away.

One time, when my significant other and I were looking at new places to live, we felt this kind of shift every single time we returned to our space. It only confirmed that the space we were already living in was "so us," and filled with so much positive energy, that we couldn't deny it.

I'm not just talking about aesthetics or beautifully decorated pieces, either.

I'm talking about the energy of the stuff, the energy of the space, and the placement of stuff within the space, all merged with your own energy and/or the energy of you as a couple or a family, which will literally sweep you up into its powerful life force and draw you in every single time you step foot into that space. For example, even though I grew up in my mother's house, where she still lives, I still get that "ooh and aah," wonderful feeling when I visit her newly remodeled home. I asked my mother if she feels the same way, especially when she has been away for a few months, and she said, "Yes, most definitely!"

I am a big believer in feng shui. When I first move into a new space, I will call in my feng shui practitioner to assess the space. Even if the space has nothing in it, it still has an energy, or "chi." And when you place stuff in that space, it must be in alignment with the space and with you; otherwise, you are creating negative energy, which impedes the flow of positive energy. I am not an expert in feng shui, so I call in the expert to evaluate the space and inform me about the cures we can put into place to maximize the space's potential, so it can serve me, my life, my prosperity, my career, my health, and my relationships.

I would love, love, love for you to be in love with your space, for your space to be in love with you, and for you to love feeling that *love* with all your spaces. Can you imagine, a love fest in your living space?

Yes, it is possible!

Recently I recommended a few changes to a client's home: simply letting go of the stale, dusty pine cones in the dish on the dining room table, and buying a fresh, live plant. The other day, I received a photo of the newly recreated dining space, with softly lit candles on the table and a vibrant green plant in the corner of the room, and just looking at the photo took my breath away!

I have made these subtle changes to my space myself, over and over, and sometimes just the slightest repositioning of stuff and/or editing of the space can bring that feeling I am seeking. When the changes are in alignment with the truth of the space, no matter how small, the space will feel like it's singing to you, it's so happy with the changes!

It is always striking to me how much even small creatures, like cats and small children, can feel the difference. Once the space is resonating with that much positive life force, it is a like a giant magnet, attracting everyone to this space, which is radiating sheer love and positive energy!

Once I organized, simplified, and redecorated a garage for a client, whose only goal was, "We want to be able to eat off the floor of the garage!" Twelve hours later, the garage was spotless, impeccably organized, and decluttered of past energies—and lo and behold, the family was picnicking on the garage floor when I left them. And as soon as we started clearing the space in the garage, all the kids and their friends wanted to play in that clear, living space, rather than inside their 3500 square foot home!

Imagine. Dream. Believe. Create. Yes, yes, yes! Begin with allowing this magical energy to infuse the smallest of your spaces, and then expand your vision to encompass the bigger spaces, and your entire life!

.

exercise. *elevate one space.*

Right now, where you are, think about a space you want to evaluate. See what space your energy is drawn to.

Now walk to that space, and close your eyes. Feel its energy. Don't think about it too much. What's the first thing that pops up in your mind?

Now touch each item in that space, feeling its energy as well.

What is the space, and the stuff within the space, saying to you? Is it authentically and truthfully still you, now? Do you still love it? Does it still have meaning? Does it still serve a purpose? If the answer doesn't come, that means *no*.

If you have to work to come up with a reason you love it, even though it serves a purpose, let it go.

Continue going through the space and touching everything using this methodology.

Put all the items that are not of your TruthLoveMeaningPurpose right outside the door outside of the space.

After you have completely gone through everything, walk out the door.

Wait for one minute.

Imagine what you want the space to feel like and look like when you walk in.

Now, walk through the door with a new perspective. Does it feel like and match what you visualized? If not, close your eyes and ask, "What else needs to go? What else needs to be moved?" Then open your eyes and see what strikes you.

Oftentimes you will be surprised at what the stuff says to you, but if you allow the process to unfold naturally without controlling it, you will love the feeling you get with the stuff gone.

Keep moving more stuff around and out of the space, and continue walking out and walking back in, until you feel a perceptible shift in your environment. Keep moving stuff around and out until the space is so beautiful that it takes your breath away!

exercise. *feel the energy of just one item.*

After you have done the exercise above, find one piece you absolutely love and place it in the "new energy" space to see if this piece belongs in this particular space.

Now pick another piece that you don't really love, and place it in this "new energy" space.

Notice how the two pieces make you feel. Only you can tell the difference between something that makes you feel great and something that makes you feel de-energized.

If you are sharing the space with somebody else, everybody should have a say about the stuff in the space and the energy in the space itself. Doing so honors all the inhabitants of the space, so the space becomes uniquely tailored to the energy field and loves of all the inhabitants.

honoring boundaries. *love boundaries, so you can be boundless.*

i used to get lots of parking tickets—and get very upset about it—until I shifted my perspective.

In college, I would recklessly park my car somewhere to get to class on time, and then rack up hundreds of dollars in parking tickets. Then I would show up in court to cut the parking tickets in half. I was extremely irresponsible (sorry, Mom and Dad), and I wasn't thinking about the cost of my time or my parents' money for this stupid mistake.

Later, after I learned to carefully read signs and thought that I had learned my lesson, I would still get parking tickets, because I was thinking about something else rather than staying in the moment of parking the car. I would drive around, trying to find a parking spot, visualizing the perfect spot, and get rock star parking! Oftentimes, I would see my girlfriend after I parked, in the middle of putting coins into the meter, but in all the excitement of seeing my girlfriend, I wouldn't really be paying attention to what I was doing. So I would often not put enough money in the meter, or put money into somebody else's meter.

Sometimes I didn't fully read the signs on the streets and parked in spaces where there was clearly a two-hour parking limit. I would return to the car to put in more money for two more hours, but because I didn't read the sign all the way through, I would still get ticketed because they had marked the tires.

So, all my life, when parking my car, the lesson for me has been to stay in the moment of what I'm doing now, pay attention to all the signs, don't let myself get sidetracked or distracted by even a phone call or another person, and take care of the task at hand!

How many times had I also walked up to my car when the meter maid would be writing up the ticket, and it was only one minute past the expiration, and was frustrated: "C'mon, it was only one minute"?

However, whether it's one second, one minute or five minutes, it still means, "Time's up!"

I get it now.
Take responsibility.
The parking meter had expired.
The signs clearly read 60 minutes only.
I exceeded the limit by only one minute, but nevertheless, I still exceeded it.

All these messages made me think about "parking" and "expiration dates" from a different perspective.

We are borrowing someone's space for the interim. In this case, the city where we reside owns the parking space, and there are rules we must abide by. Parking in somebody else's space is a privilege. The city owns the street, and it has graciously created temporary parking homes for my car that I need to honor. If I dishonor that rule and don't park within the boundaries or don't honor their time limits, well, then it is clearly my right to get a ticket and pay the fines for the infractions.

This makes me think about the home and community space that everyone in a partnership or family enjoys. If there were rules set up in the home that everyone created together, would there be more peace in the household and less clutter if there were clear consequences and infractions given to the people who broke the rules of the household?

Also, what if every item in our household had expiration dates on it? And what if we held on to them past their expiration dates? What would be the consequences? Would the item disappear into the ether? Would we act differently if we got fined one dollar for every minute we kept an item past its expiration date?

I just noticed the orchid arrangement we have on our coffee table. The flower just dropped and the leaves are wilted. It's time to let go. There is no tag that says "expires in 90 days from purchase" on that plant. But I held on to it, because I was hoping that another flower would blossom. I immediately went over and dismantled the arrangement. Eating food in the fridge that might be spoiled would yield terrible consequences, and that's one area I don't play games with. Even enduring one day with a stomachache or food poisoning would cost me days of perfect health.

This goes deeper. What if Planet Earth had rules we had to abide by, like recycle your plastic and paper containers? What if Planet Earth had rules that clearly stated the waters will get polluted if each household dumps more than 100 gallons of trash out every week?

In Japan, they have strict rules about trash and recycling. Everyone has a certain allotment of how much trash they can throw out at once. What would we do in the United States if there was such a rule? When I first separated trash from recycling, I was stunned! Nearly 90 percent of my "trash" is recyclable. I create so much trash—recyclable or not—with only two people in my household!

Just talking about parking triggers a whole slew of issues related to citations. Although I'm the first to say "f*** the rules!" when it comes to acting a certain way, I am also the first to admit that without the rules, there would be anarchy. And, in a country or city or household, without clear boundaries for stuff, everybody would be running amok.

What is the difference between freedom with no rules and freedom with rules?

At least when it comes to parking, it has taught me that when you own something, you have every right to enforce a rule for stuff you own that you are sharing with the world. In this case, the city shares their space with the public, and therefore we the public should respectfully abide by the rules, or park elsewhere.

I choose to follow the rules of the parking space, remembering I am a guest in the parking space, and will now gladly pay two dollars, or whatever the cost is, to "borrow" or "reside in" the space for a while.

So for me, honoring the boundaries created by others and creating clear boundaries for my own stuff gives me freedom to be boundless with the other most important stuff in my life, such as my imagination, creativity, health, relationships, heart, mind—almost everything else.

Boy, have I changed and shifted my perspective from long ago—it must mean that I'm growing up! Taking ownership of myself, my stuff, and my life—and it feels so good!

.

exercise. *three expired items.*

Write about three items in your home, office, or closet that you feel have expired, and yet you've been holding on to them past their "expiration date." Why did you hold on? Were you were aware of it? Why didn't you let them go? Can you let them go now with this awareness?

exercise. *pay for the lesson gladly to learn the lesson completely.*

Next time you get a parking ticket, laugh out loud and say, "I deserve it!" And, then, go home and gladly pay the ticket immediately, without holding on to your mistake. By doing this, your soul immediately gets the lesson and takes it in stride, but it will also remind you next time you're parking, "Did you check all the signs properly?"

exercise. *let go of every expired item.*

Go to your medicine cabinet or refrigerator and throw out everything that has expired. Just doing this will free up dead energy. Why have you held on to these items? Were you defying the rules and boundaries created by others? Or do you not believe the boundaries and rules created by others? Just food for thought, but an interesting way to shift your perspective.

veer from routine. *stir change.*

Sometimes in order to stir change inside of you, you must go down another path. Do something differently every day. Take a different road to work. Eat something new on the menu. Eat at a different restaurant. Start your day fifteen minutes later. Stay at work thirty minutes later.

Pray that you want to stir change today in yourself for the highest good, in order to move forward. Pray that you want to stir change in others to help them. And see what comes up for you to take action upon that may be different from what you do every single day. The Universe may bring up something to take action upon that is quite different from anything you've ever done before.

My prayer before I go in to teach class or lecture is to simply be a blessing to at least one person in class: to inspire them to feel and live deeply, to create space in their consciousness and minds for miracles to flow in, to transform and improve the quality of their lives. This prayer to be a blessing to at least one person gives me the permission and the courage to be bold enough to maybe even get "kicked out of the room," (as one of my acting coaches would say). Setting an intention to be of service, to freely "go on the ride" with the students without any preconceived idea about how I should be or do or act, gives me the courage to truly tune in to what the audience may be needing at that particular time.

In one class I taught, I "veered" from my workbook, and I kept talking about being "conscious" and "making conscious choices, making conscious decisions, having conscious awareness," in response to questions from the students. Later during the day, I berated myself, just for a minute—okay, all evening on Saturday—thinking, *How could I have*

301

forgotten to mention that important part of the workbook? But I know there must be a message . . . what is it?

Finally, it came. When I did yoga on Sunday, the instructor skipped our usual shoulder-stand pose, and during corpse pose, she said, "How many of you are thinking we didn't do shoulder-stand? You should welcome the change of routine. Go with the flow. It's all perfect."

This message reminded me that it's good to veer from our routines once in a while, to stir things up, so that we can make a change. *Hello, June! In order to make a radical change, you gotta do something radically different, or at least do "something" different! Isn't this what you teach?* Ha! Cosmic joke is on me!

During my private one-on-one sessions with clients, I always pray before the sessions to be a blessing and to get my ego out of the way, so we can work on whatever is for the highest good for the client. I think about what might be best, knowing what we worked on from the past, and I could have an agenda planned out, but I have found that my best work comes when I trust Infinite Intelligence or God to walk through the room and listen to my intuition about the next best divine steps. So I veer from what I think is best and allow the veering to be guided by some other power beyond my mind, which is only an extension of the past and things known. I allow the unknown to factor into the equation of what is for the highest good, and access the superconscious mind connected to the Universe, which is all knowing of all things past, present, and future.

I have felt that the success of my business has been built upon my ability to go on the ride, trust the ride, and take action on whatever is coming through at that moment. Well, even with this book and my teachings, I'm learning to go on the ride so that my teachings will be fresh. I have to honor the fact that they're constantly evolving along with me, and it's okay to veer away from "the book" and what I thought it was going to be about in exchange for what is coming through right now for the highest good of those who are reading this book.

Change is the only constant in life.

Veer from your usual routine when you are called to, and do not be afraid. This is where the miracles occur.

.

exercise. *do one thing differently today to activate change.*

Today, change something in your routine. Order a new food for lunch. Stay at work fifteen minutes later to clear your desk. Write an e-mail to an old friend. Call your child or significant other just because—to say, "I love you." Don't exercise today if you exercise every day. Go to sleep early. Don't eat dinner if you don't feel like it.

Write about this the following day and see how you felt doing something differently from what you normally do. Did you feel a pep in your step or excitement at the prospect of veering from your usual routine? If you didn't, keep on stirring yourself up and activating change by doing three different things today. If you did, vow to stir it up and do something differently every single day.

You want a radical change? You want to change? You've got to do something differently. Just one small thing can make all the difference in the world.

do it today. *or let it go.*

1 ife is too short to be doing things we don't want to be doing. Let go of those to-dos on your To-Do List today. Get rid of them.

If a to-do (or task) has remained on your To-Do List (or Task List or Master List) for a year, and you have not made the time to take care of it, then delete it now. Why keep looking at it on your To-Do List, making yourself feel like a loser because you have not taken care of it?

If you truly believe in your heart that this to-do is important, and you must take care of it or else you will feel like a loser, then put it into your calendar this week and do it.

If you still keep on dismissing the to-do and/or your reminders to do the task, and/or you conveniently find other things to do in the time slot you have designated to take care of this "all-important task," then it must not be that important, or else you would have taken care of it.

What is the worst thing that would happen if you do not do this task? What is the best thing that would happen if you do this task?

Confront your truth, and decide, once and for all, if you are still going to hold on to the guilt of not doing this task, and/or let it go. But don't just let it go on the To-Do List so you do not see it anymore.

If you think that erasing the task from your To-Do List where you see it every day, and erasing the reminders that pop up on your computer to take care of it will erase it from your consciousness, your mind, or your heart, you are fooling yourself. You will be carrying it around with you, even though you cannot physically see it. You will know it's there in the back of your mind, and you will be reminded of it every time something triggers you into remembering it.

Letting go completely of a to-do means being at one with the truth. You will finally let go of it and delete it from your To-Do List, because you know the truth is that you do not want to create the time to take care of the task, so it must not be that important. Being at one with the truth means being truthful with yourself, admitting that it is actually a lie on your To-Do List, that not handling that task is not that big of a deal, and that it won't make or break your life. Let go of the importance of that to-do, and make amends with yourself, admitting that it is not a priority in the big scheme of your life.

While writing this, I was reminded to buy a gift for the body shop where I took my mother's car, and they fixed a minor scratch for free without charging me. I immediately added it to my Task List when it happened and when I was so grateful, but over the past few weeks, I had kept putting it off, thinking, *Should I buy flowers, cookies, or a cake? Should I go by in person?* My indecision was cluttering my mind. But just now, I reminded myself to take care of this task now, because it is important for me to express my gratitude for the gift I received from them. Not being charged was a gift from the Universe into my bank account, and in my consciousness I am truly grateful for any gift that somebody gives to me. By acknowledging the gift, I am acknowledging my gratitude for these kinds of gifts from people and asking for more, telling the Universe that I believe in miracles of this sort, which can occur daily.

Okay, I just completed the task. I asked my gut what the best gift was, and I decided a box of cookies that could be shared by the staff who helped me was best. I just spent thirty dollars which will come out of my bank account in physical dollars, but today I feel like a million bucks, because I have deposited millions of dollars in peace of mind and heart getting this to-do off my list, and allowing the energy of gratitude flow from my heart into the hearts of those special people who performed a deed of kindness for me.

Speaking of unfinished business and tasks on my Task List that keep popping up and reminders I've snoozed through oh-so-many times: I just got up in the middle of writing and decided that those new jeans with annoying white creases down the side are not worth repairing and dyeing, as I would rather get a fresh pair of jeans for going out. However, I still love them and have only wore them a few times. So I just took them out of the Repairs Box, letting go of that to-do and item in the Repairs Box, and I put them into their new home alongside my sweatpants that I wear for my evening walks. Who knows how I will feel about wearing the pants with creases for a walk, but for now, I feel awesome letting go of something that was unfinished business.

What can you do today to give you peace of mind and heart, which will make you feel like a million bucks? What can you do today that will set you free?

.

exercise. *confront the truth of one to-do you have been avoiding.*

Is there one task on your mind or To-Do List that you have been avoiding? What is it?

Journal about it.

Is it that important to you? If you haven't taken care of it, why not?

If it was that important to you, wouldn't you have taken care of it a long time ago?

Can you let it go?

Can you scratch it from your To-Do List or mental mind chatter?

Continue doing this until you come across a to-do or bit of mental chatter you can let go of.

exercise. *let go of a seemingly important task from the past that really is not a priority now.*

Today, let go of one to-do that seemed to be important in the past, but now that you have confronted the truth of that seemingly important task, the truth is that it is not as important as you thought it was, and it is time to let go.

imperfect doing is perfect. *do it now, and it's perfect!*

I love Jeffrey Mayer's book, *If You Haven't Got the Time to Do It Right, When Will You Find the Time to Do It Over?* This book appealed to me and my inclination to want to be perfect, yet it also made me face the truth about whether I would honestly do something over.

Since I was little, my mom and dad taught me to be grateful and to express my gratitude by writing thank-you letters promptly: when visiting someone's home, when being treated to dinner by somebody, or after having received a gift.

However, when receiving gifts from Japan, I would delay writing thank-you cards to my relatives, because I had to write the letter in Japanese (which is not my first language, and I'm not fluent). When I was young, my mom would make grammatical changes to my letters and change my elementary "babyish" language to more sophisticated Japanese, and then I would have to rewrite the letter. I felt like the entire process took forever and was unenjoyable for me.

After visiting Japan after college graduation, my relatives found out that I cannot speak fluent Japanese, and that my Japanese is more "'childlike" and not perfect, so I decided not to play this "polite, perfect game." Why write sophisticated letters when they were not really coming from my true self? I decided to just write my letters with simple Japanese characters, hiragana (phonetics) rather than kanji (complex characters).

Luckily, too, now there is Google Translate, so I used that last time, writing the letter in English from my heart and letting the words be translated by the computer. Everybody commented on how "funny and imperfect" the translation was, but guess what?

I didn't care, because at least I wrote the thank-you letter that expressed the truth of my heart. I released my desire for perfectionism, and I also released my fear about what they would think if it was imperfect.

I laughed and said, "Oh, well," when my mother told me that they thought it was funny and cute.

I'll take funny and cute and imperfect over not doing something because it needs to be perfect. I would rather finish something now completely than have that "unfinished business" sitting in my consciousness for a long time, making me feel like a loser with an ungrateful heart because I didn't write the thank-you card expressing the truth of my heart, which is that I *am* truly grateful. (And, by the way, thank you, Google Translate! Love, love, love you and appreciate you so much for helping me to get it done!)

Now I tell my clients to write thank-you letters or other letters to people they are thinking about—today, not tomorrow—and it is not important to have the perfect stationery and/ or find the perfect words, but the act of doing it now imperfectly is more important. So, oftentimes, they will jot a note on a post-it and send it off—imperfectly.

Write from your heart today. Write a letter on a shopping bag. Write an e-mail. Text someone. Write on scratch paper. Whatever you decide to express today in whatever way you choose to communicate it is perfect. Your heart is the perfect expression of how you feel here and now. Do not fret about leaving something out. You can always write another letter. But for today, you followed your heart and expressed your heart, and your heart is freer and lighter because of it. You have taken action on something that was in the back of your consciousness, something you had put off for fear of not being perfect. Whenever you do so, you will be released from your perfectionistic fear, the fear of not getting it right.

Just now, I thought of my friend Pam's mother and father. Pam was one of my best friends who passed away nearly five years ago of a brain aneurysm at age forty-five, and I had always wanted to write a letter to her parents to thank them for the wonderful daughter they had brought into this world who had made a difference in my life.

In fact, I first thought of them when I was rereading the chapter in this book about "doing it now." I thought, *Write that letter you've been meaning to write to them.* But I thought to myself, *What am I going to say?* So I shoved that thought to the side until now. I decided to just start writing, and the words flowed. Still, however, doubt and fears crept up: *I haven't talked to them in five years. I've never had a deep relationship with them. What are they going to think? Do I want to remind them about their daughter who passed away five years ago?* Despite the fears, I pushed the send button on my e-mail, also copied to her husband, son, and brother—as I wanted them all to know what a difference their loved one had made in my life.

Taking care of unfinished business in your heart will free up space for miracles to come along. Miracles in relationships. Miracles in business. Saying "thank you for this gift" will free up space for more gifts to come into your life today.

Let go of trying to be perfect.

Just doing it today is perfect.

■

exercise. *one perfect "imperfect" thank you.*

Think of somebody you have meaning to write a letter to. Grab a piece of paper, post-it note, or even scratch paper. Start writing the letter with whatever words come out in this moment, and just finish it. Date it, sign it, and put it into an envelope. Express your heart and tell the truth: say that you have been meaning to write, and you are sorry it has taken so long. Even share that you are reading a book that dared you to write this letter today, imperfectly, and that although your words may not be perfect, you just wanted them to know you had been thinking of them.

Get into your car, drive to the post office, and drop this letter into the mailbox now! Or, write the letter in an e-mail and push the "Send" button now!

Now start a list of other letters you have been wanting to write, or people you have been wanting to call. Schedule them into your calendar. Perhaps do one a week. By taking care of this unfinished business, I guarantee you will start feeling lighter. You may even lose weight.

You may even start taking care of other unfinished business because the "dam of resistance" and "dam of inertia" has broken. You have unleashed amazing energy and creative power by telling yourself that it is more important to take care of the business today rather than waiting until tomorrow. And you are telling yourself that imperfect doing is better than not doing something at all!

Rejoice, celebrate, and pat yourself on the back!

stay current. *embrace the gifts of now.*

The phone keeps ringing. Why not let it just ring and ring and ring? Why the compulsion to pick it up? Who's trying to get our attention?

Just like the ringing phone that always feels like it's right in your face, the stuff lying around your environment is calling out for your attention.

Just this morning, I saw a stack of magazines sitting in front of me that I had been meaning to go through. The stack was screaming, "Deal with me!"

So I did.

I tore out the articles I wanted to read, and I tore out the images I wanted to put into my fashion treasure map. What, might you ask, is a fashion treasure map?

A fashion treasure map is just a map of fashion pieces and outfits that I like this season, and that I want to create and wear in my own life. They can either be pieces I need to buy and add to my wardrobe, or just ways to wear my clothes this season. It's my way of having fun with new styles, ways of being, and ways of expressing myself in the world.

So, I went through the magazine stack, I threw out three magazines, and I ended up with just a few cutouts that I added to my treasure map.

I feel current.

I've always had this issue with magazines and wanting to stay current, but when they pile up past three months, I feel they aren't current anymore—so why read them?

Do I read them to know what I missed? Do I read them to make myself feel better, so I'm not wasting the money I spent subscribing to the magazine?

Magazines are my eye candy, bombarding myself with images at home so I don't have to go shopping at the mall. It's my idea of window shopping at home, and I get my shopping fix. The most important part, though, is going through the magazine, cutting out the images I want, and then throwing the magazine out.

If I don't throw it out, then I feel incomplete. I feel like I didn't really go shopping at all, that I just stayed at home and didn't get through anything. There's no sense of accomplishment.

It's wild that I feel this way with magazines, but I do, and I always have.

There was a time when I would collect issues of magazines for one year, neatly organize them by month in chronological order, and even label the shelves *Real Simple, InStyle, O, Architectural Digest,* and *Vanity Fair.* But why? I never looked at those magazines once I read them. They were fun to read for that moment, and blast myself with those images of that moment, but months later, I never touched them, because there would be newer issues out that I wanted to go through.

So magazines are for me an act of staying with the current—and staying current.

If I don't go through them *now*, then they lose their appeal and edge, they're no longer current, and so I need to recycle or toss them.

I feel guilty about tossing them without reading them, but the magazines are probably talking to me saying, *Hey, you haven't read me—but there's more current stuff coming up in the next issue. Don't worry. You haven't missed anything. Let go.*

Stay current.

·

exercise. *use magazines to get in touch with your current truth.*

Gather all the magazines from your house.

Ask yourself, *When was the last time I looked through these and touched them? Am I truthfully going to read them in the next month?* Be ruthlessly truthful with yourself. If the answer is that you don't know, recycle them or donate them to a local library or school.

Trust that by letting go of these magazines, you are not letting go of important knowledge. Instead, focus on the fact that you are creating space for new, current knowledge and information to come to your attention for you to focus upon. Focus on the fact that you are letting go of having to know all things, and trust that whatever you need to know will come into your periphery.

exercise. *stop magazine subscriptions for*
one year to discover what you truly read.

If you subscribe to many magazines, feel overwhelmed with the number of magazines you are receiving, and feel guilty about not reading them all, try this:

Stop all subscriptions to all magazines for one year.

Take yourself off of all subscription lists on e-mails as well.

When you think of a magazine, go and buy it when you have the time to read it.

Stopping all subscriptions will get you in touch with what you truly desire or miss.

When the one-year self-imposed exile from subscriptions has ended, be hypervigilant and super-conscious about what kind of magazines you want to subscribe to, and what kind of energies you want yourself exposed to. Why not start with just one subscription and see if you are truly reading that magazine every single month before subscribing to another magazine?

live your life as a work of art.
you and your life are a masterpiece.

if I opened up my heart to every single item in my house, I would be a basket case.

Just this morning, I revamped my client files for my business and decided to use fun purple files to house the paperwork for my clients. And, I decided, I'll make them special by using black and gold tape. My clients are special. They deserve black and gold expensive tape. They have spent money to be organized, have allowed me into their homes and lives, and have given me these beautiful opportunities to serve them. Their paperwork deserves the best. Purple folders with black and gold labels.

So I began switching out the plain, first-position manila folders with these purple ones, and the drawer actually started feeling better. I mean, I felt better, and I could tell that the files were so much happier in these purple files. I was excited to use these purple files this week and I was excited to see what other ways I can be of service to my clients—all because of the switching to these purple folders. It's as if the purple color enlivened, re-energized, and brought a new life back to the paperwork inside of them. It's as if the purple folder enriched and empowered the paperwork inside. Wow, that's deep.

Okay, what about this? I took out my past client files, those I hadn't seen or visited in more than one year, and I thought, *Do I really need to do these, too?* I rationally thought, *No, you're no longer seeing them, and some of them are very old clients from years ago. You don't need to spend the money to put them into purple folders with black-and-gold label tape.*

But these folders were calling out for my attention. I began going through each folder, switching the paperwork out, and the names of those clients started taking on a life of its

313

own. Perhaps they will never call again, but I know that I'm ready for them if they do. *I'm here to be of service, and I'm grateful for the past times we spent together. I'm grateful for that past opportunity to serve you. I still care about you. I still think about you.* Switching out these folders was my way of paying homage to my past clients who helped me to build my business and helped me to get to where I am today. It's my way of being grateful.

Where else in your life do you settle and compromise—or not go over and beyond—because no one will ever know but you? Do you talk yourself out of taking certain actions because no one can see them?

What would happen if you lived your life as a work of art? What if you pretended your life was put on to a projector in a museum, and everyone—the people who knew you and the people who didn't—saw how you lived your life on a giant screen? Would you live your life differently—being different and acting different—if you knew an audience was watching?

Here's one way to tell. Do you shove stuff into a drawer or room when company is coming over? After all, no one will know except you, because you'll have that drawer shut or that room door shut.

Do you only organize and keep clear and clean the spaces that are on display and for show, rather than the spaces behind closed doors that no one will ever see?

I am a strong advocate for organizing behind closed doors, even though you and your family may be the only ones to see that space. You will know the difference. When you walk out the door, you will feel great! Why? You will feel great because you will know that no matter where you go in your life, whether it's your garage or your closet, you will not feel ashamed of that space.

When your stuff and spaces are in alignment with your TruthLoveMeaningPurpose, and you are feeling great about your life, you will carry that awesome feeling of integrity and authenticity within TruthLoveMeaningPurpose wherever you go! You may not look different, but trust me, people can feel that difference.

Do you get how deep this goes?

Why not live your life as a work of art behind closed doors? For nobody but you.

You will then know whether the full range of your public *and* private thoughts, spaces, and being are in alignment with your TruthLoveMeaningPurpose.

What do you see when you look outside yourself, and inside yourself?

Do you love what you see? Is the stuff you see on the outside truthfully you? Is it meaningful to you and not just to somebody else? Is the stuff you see truly serving a purpose for you? Does this outside view match up with the true you and what you believe to be truly you?

For instance, I once had a client who loved modern and minimalist style—at least, on the inside. But when he looked out into his office or home spaces, he saw the direct opposite. The spaces looked like an antique store, cluttered up with small, big, and old stuff. There's nothing wrong with that design preference, if that is what you truly visualize as your ideal self, ideal life, and ideal space. But if the inner you *and* outer you do not align with your TruthLoveMeaningPurpose every time you look out into your spaces, this lack of alignment creates chaos, confusion, disorder, and more clutter within and without.

Do you get how powerfully deep this goes? It is all connected. Now that you are aware of this information, and understand that the key to leading a clutter-free life is to honor your TruthLoveMeaningPurpose and live your life as a work of art, you can no longer close your eyes and pretend.

Honor the stuff within you and without you that represents the true you, and honor this amazing life you have created. And, if you don't like what you see, let go now.

See the spaces and stuff of your life as an extension of you.

And see that you can make the spaces you inhabit into a beautiful work of art.

Then, as the inner stuff of your soul flows seamlessly into your outer stuff and outer spaces, and there is no separation between your inner world and your outer world, the landscape of your entire life will become a work of art.

You are a masterpiece. Your life is a work of art. The artfulness of you and your life should inspire you. There will never, ever be another person like you, with your unique preferences, likes, dislikes, and passions, so why not breathe life into every stroke and subtle nuance of your stuff? Make your masterpiece life authentic, and not something that can be easily replicated, duplicated, fake, or phony. All the stuff you possess inside and outside makes you who you are. So why not see that you are creating anew on the blank canvas you were given when you were born? Recreate and redefine, or start all over, if that's what you feel like.

You will no longer pretend it doesn't matter. Because it does matter, if you dig deep and question it.

So I know it may seem silly to spend hours switching out my manila folders with purple folders. No one will ever see the folders that return to the Clients Archive Box, but I'll know.

I'll know that the purple, black, and gold folders elevate my business, my clients, and—most importantly—myself, my life, and my perspective.

And that's all that matters. *I* know.

∙

exercise. *one space you are ashamed of.*

Write about one area or space of your life that no one else sees but you, and that you are ashamed of, or at least not proud of. It could be your junk drawer, your garage, or even your paperwork files.

Write about how you would feel if you cleared the space. Write about how long it has been that way, and how you are now committed to clearing the space for you and you only. And write about why it matters now to you.

exercise. *turn shame into pride, even if you are the only one who knows.*

If it's a drawer, set aside one to two hours to clear out the space and get it organized.

If it's a garage, set aside twelve hours on a weekend, and set yourself up for success by hiring helpers, enlisting family and friends, and ordering trash bins and trucks to haul away the giveaways and trash.

Write about how you feel after you have achieved success with the space—particularly about how much better and lighter you feel!

LET GO.
CREATE SPACE.

pain perspective. *create a new story.*

i once was taught that pain and suffering are optional.
But how do you get out of the pain?
How do you release the pain?
If everyone could choose to release their pain, wouldn't suffering no longer exist?
Is it really true that suffering is optional?

Yes, suffering *is* optional, because whether or not we suffer depends on our viewpoint of a certain event or experience.

When we decide an experience caused us great pain, and we choose to continue to carry that perspective with us, we suffer.

What if we chose to shift our perspective? Would that help us release the pain?

Yes. Because the pain lives in our perspective, not the event itself, it is our perspective that needs to be released.

In order to liberate yourself from that pain, reframe what happened to you in a different light.

Okay, let me be vulnerable and share my own stuff, so you can understand how to take this "system" for "letting go of pain" all the way through!

Think of something that happened to you, and tell the story as if you were a victim.

Poor me! Those experts convinced me to go into debt to buy stuff for my space that they thought would elevate me and my life, and I believed them!

Now tell the story as if you were a hero.

Now that I have once again listened to others who professed to be experts and gone into debt to do what they told me they thought was best for me, I now know better. Superwoman that I am, I can share my deeply learned message with the world. Don't let somebody else tell you where you are, and remember to examine the messenger. Do they have their stuff in order and deserve to be an expert in your life? Do they truly have what you desire, or are they just preaching to you without embodying what they teach?

Now tell the story as if God/Universe gave you this experience to learn a powerful lesson that would lead you to become who you are today.

Powerful lessons learned this time around! I had to go through this again and again and again to finally learn that I am the expert in my own life. Yes, I will hire experts when needed, but I must run everything by my intuition first and foremost. And if somebody is rushing me to make a decision, that's a red flag for me to stop, pause, reflect, and go within for the answer. I do not have to allow somebody else's timing to stress me out or pressure me to make a bad decision.

The stuff we tell ourselves causes our pain, suffering, joy, bliss, and power.

Do I deserve to be in pain and suffering rather than bliss and joy because I created this scenario—gave my power away—again?

What stuff are you stuffing down that you don't want to see or feel?

I am stuffing down anger and frustration at myself. How could I make the same mistake again? I thought I had learned this lesson. I don't want to feel like a loser again. I am so ashamed at having caused this scenario again. I am also stuffing down anger at the other person.

What stuff from your past are you burying, so you don't have to feel the pain?

I don't want to feel the pain of making the same mistake again. I don't want to believe that I am at fault, rather than the other person. Ha! I don't want to feel the pain that I am causing my own pain! Deep stuff. I am burying the fact that I am a powerful being.

Whether or not you consciously know it, your inner being knows it, and is holding on to this stuff.

I am holding on to anger, blame, and frustration at myself.

What system can you use to let go of the stuff that is holding you back from fulfilling your greatest potential?

(Ha ha, this is the system I am sharing with you now!) Yes, that's the reason I had to go through all of this again—so all of you can understand how our perspective causes us to suffer, how you can let go of the perspective that's causing you pain, and hopefully you won't have to go through what I've gone through so many times.

This stuff is telling you that you are undeserving and unworthy, and is preventing you from being a powerful magnet.

Financial issues and debt trigger big-time feelings of unworthiness, because I feel like it's something I was never able to master as easily as others in my family. How many times do I have to go through this to learn this lesson?

The stuff you are stuffing is clogging up your pathway to miracles.

I get it. I no longer look at this scenario as a pothole or rabbit hole I cannot get out of, but as a minor hiccup in my life I can overcome! The most important lesson to take away is to recognize that I have been giving my power away to so-called experts because I didn't want to take responsibility for being my own expert in my own life. It was easier to pretend that I didn't know what I was doing. I must declutter my self-worth and belief that I deserve to be a master of monies from all feelings and beliefs to the contrary.

Once and for all, take a look at *all* your stuff.

I just did, with all of you as witnesses!

Be at one with your stuff.

I am. Thank you, God, for my stuff. Thank you, God, for bringing these issues to the forefront of my consciousness so I could finally deal with them, examine them with a fine-tooth comb, forgive myself for my shortcomings, forgive others, and love my life with all its ups and downs. I would not trade anything in for the world. (See how I'm turning a seemingly negative experience into a positive, uplifting experience?)

Did you wrong someone?
Did you feel betrayed?
Were you hurt by someone?
Did you hurt someone?
Did you lie?
Did you cheat?
Did you do something you felt was wrong?

It truly doesn't matter what the world thinks.

What matters is what you—your true self inside—thinks, believes, and feels about what you did and what happened.

No one can persuade you differently.

You can go through years of therapy, trying to come to terms with what happened, but if you do not believe you have been redeemed, vindicated, restored, and forgiven on the inside, nothing will shift in your life to create a radical change.

The radical shift comes from within you.

As I shared with you above, sometimes the first step that is needed is being vulnerable enough to admit that you were wrong, or that you made a mistake, and sharing it with just one other person (or the world, as I did!) so it is no longer a secret. Sometimes that is enough to activate that radical change you desire.

Your unique perspective on your life experiences and your stuff will make all the difference you need to move forward.

Release the pain, suffering, and attachments to the stories you tell.

Let go of your stories.
Let go of your attachment to the pain.
Let go of playing victim.

Shift your perspective with your stuff.
Take ownership of your unique experiences.
Take your ownership all the way through and suck the life lesson out of the experience.

Step into your power.

Act as if you knew the answers to the questions you have about how to move forward that you are aching to hear.

Sometimes just the asking will unleash the answers we already carry within our hearts and souls.

This is exactly what I did as I spoke my words aloud to you, and trust me, it brought up a lot of stuff that I didn't know was still buried inside of me. Trust me when I say this stuff works, if you allow the answers to be revealed to you.

Ask, and the truth will be revealed to you.

Move forward now.

·

exercise. *cut the attachment to the old story and create a new story.*

Write about an incident that you feel badly about. You could be the victim or the perpetrator. It doesn't matter. If you think about this incident, and it stirs you up inside, you are carrying it with you and still holding on to it, no matter how many years have passed. You have not forgotten it, released it, and come to peace with it. Now is your opportunity to release it, and to learn how to release anything else you may be carrying with you.

Write about the incident and experience it in full detail. Describe how it made you feel. Describe what you could have or should have done instead. Write everything you can remember. Write down your feelings about it, as I did above.

Now write, "I forgive [yourself/someone else]." Write why your soul may have created this experience by writing "I learned . . ." and write everything you learned from it. Write why you are a different person today because of it.

Write over and over:

> *I forgive [yourself/someone else], and I promise from this point forward not to harbor any negative feelings towards myself or others, because it is only hurting me and preventing me from moving forward.*

Every single time you think of this person and/or this experience, imagine cutting a string of attachment with scissors, and keep saying,

> *I am letting go now and releasing it to the Universe.*
> *I forgive [yourself/someone else], and I have learned this important lesson that I am carrying with me.*
> *I am getting lighter and lighter every day, releasing everything that I am harboring in my heart.*

You may have to reread what you wrote and cut the strings numerous times to truly release the pain, suffering, or anger, but it's worth it. Just remember that you are retraining yourself to see this experience or person from a different perspective. You are learning a new way of being, living with what happened but not letting it define you. You are redefining who you are and the way you see yourself. You will start looking and acting differently once the release happens, because there will no longer be any negative energy around it, and it will just be a part of your amazing life, part of your past to honor, and will no longer impede you from moving forward to embrace the miracles of this present moment and your glorious future.

moment-to-moment clutter. *let go.*

i 'm kind of ashamed to admit this, but you know those little pet peeves or grievances that seem so petty but can nag at you like pesky mosquitoes? I'm embarrassed to even share my latest grievance with you.

Silly me—why am I now ashamed, after I've shared all that other stuff with you? Here's another example that will show you how deep this seemingly "unimportant" stuff goes, and how easily we can let go of this internal clutter.

Last night, I was in a great mood, having completed much paperwork in my office.

Suddenly the doorbell rings. We are startled because we live in a security building, and they usually ring us if someone wants to come upstairs to visit. We chose the building precisely because of this "security factor," where everybody has to check in; no one could just come up and ring our doorbell.

When my boyfriend answers the door, there is an Asian woman at the door asking for me by name. She pronounces my name perfectly.

I wasn't expecting anyone, and I was planning to meditate at this hour. I looked at it as an intrusion into my life and privacy.

Yet as I motion to my boyfriend to make her go away, he signals to the door, motioning for me to go to the door—so I reluctantly go to the door.

This woman asks me if I have voted, and tries to convince me to vote for some measure that will improve the schools as she hands me a flyer. Annoyed at the time and intrusion, I

324

asked her if she was "allowed into the building," and she dismissively says, "Yes." I quickly tell her that I'm voting, and yes, I would vote YES on that measure.

After she leaves, I air my grievance to my boyfriend, telling him that it bothered me that she could just come up at this late hour, campaigning at 8:45 p.m., and that perhaps I should tell management because this has happened before.

"Oh, well," he shrugs. "If you only get disturbed one or two times a year, that's not bad."

We meditated for twenty minutes.

And guess what kept coming up during that meditation?

I have to call downstairs and let them know. Security has gotten lax.

Others have gotten upstairs to leave business cards on my door.

Others have just come up with no warning from downstairs.

Why do I pay to live in this building?

I have told them before, but for some reason, they are not getting it.

I have been stalked before, so I have this issue about people just showing up on my doorstep with no advance warning.

I don't care if it was one time in one year. It still disturbed my peace.

I choose to live in a building like this, so I should be protected from these invasions of my privacy.

At first, I rationalized it out. I have worked on campaigns and know it's hard work. I admired her perseverance to get the word out to support the schools. She probably has kids at home that will be affected. She is Asian, I am Asian, and I have empathy for her just because we are both Asian. I know: *truth* was coming out. I had compassion for her. What is my boyfriend going to think? I already felt stupid for reacting in such an annoyed manner when he was being so matter-of-fact about the situation.

Nevertheless, I could not shake it.

I felt it was an intrusion into my privacy at such a late hour.

I'm sure the security guards wouldn't have approved unless she said she was my sister, aunt, or cousin.

Yes, all this was coming up during my twenty-minute meditation, while my mind kept going to back my mantra.

Let go, June.

Let go of this.

This is silly, I tried to convince myself.

But after meditation, I called downstairs to report what had happened. The guard listened with an open mind and assured me that he would pass the word along and that this would never happen again.

I'm so happy I did, because I would have been holding on to it during my sleep—during my important sleep travels where things brew even more and whatever I am thinking about gets increased.

Yes, some would argue—"Who cares?"

It was just one time. But this one time will sit in my consciousness for who knows how long until another grievance similar to this one arises, so I feel it is best to take action and deal with it here and now, express the truth of my heart and feelings, forgive whomever I need to forgive (the campaign lady, the guards), and let go.

And, I'm happy I took action, because this is the *truth* of my heart and the *truth* of who I am. My boyfriend has not lived my life and my experiences, and he would never know the fear of being stalked. Perhaps being disturbed does not matter to him as a man, because he can easily handle it. Or perhaps he is just more easygoing than I am. But it doesn't matter who he is.

What matters is who I am and honoring the truth of who I am. What matters is taking responsibility for my feelings, my life, and my stuff, and speaking my truth without fear of what he or anyone else thinks.

Why?

Because it is important to me. And that is what truly matters.

So many times, people have tried to convince me that "That issue is better left alone," or "Don't bring it up, as it will bring up other stuff," or "Don't rock the boat," or "Don't bother saying that, because it won't matter," or "You're just being too sensitive," or "Will it really make a difference?" or "That person won't ever get it."

But the truth is that only I know how much it matters to me in the long run. These seemingly insignificant issues can soon become a giant mountain of clutter in my heart and mind that will get in the way of my achieving my desires. I choose to believe in the bigger picture: every action I take, no matter how great or small, has consequences and impacts the world. Perhaps the vulnerable expression of my heart can make a difference in the lives of others, too. So I'm speaking the truth about my grievance because I don't want to carry it with me and allow it to pollute my mind and heart. I want to take the lesson away and leave the rest behind.

What stuff am I leaving behind? Annoyance with the lady. Frustration at the guard who messed up when he let her upstairs. Annoyance that perhaps she lied. Annoyance that this Asian woman looked trustworthy and could have looked like my cousin—and do the guards think we all look alike? Annoyance that my privacy was disturbed. Feeling badly about not feeling sorry for her. Feeling badly about not having more compassion for her as a mother. Feeling badly about not having compassion for the fact that she was campaigning. Feeling badly that I complained. Feeling stupid that it affected me so much.

What lesson/blessing/miracle am I taking forward?

I am proud of myself for taking responsibility for my feelings and taking action, instead of shoving the truth under to pretend it was not important. I am proud of myself that I respected myself enough to speak the truth to my boyfriend, the guard, and to her without fear of judgment. I honor the fact that I put a high price on my privacy and respect my privacy. I love our space, and the security and privacy it gives to us. The money we are paying for this place is totally worth it. I love our home! I love my life!

.

exercise. *let go of the grievance by expressing your heart and keeping only the lesson.*

Write about a grievance you have. It can be something that happened recently or something somebody said to you, or it can just be something you overheard or a pet peeve you have. It doesn't matter how big, small, significant, or petty it seems to be; it is important because you are carrying it around with you. Start writing about it, and continue writing about it until you get the entire story out on paper.

Now, decide what the lesson to be learned from this experience is. What is it teaching you about yourself, others, life?

Is there any action step you can take to "declutter" this experience? Can you express your feelings and thoughts to the person or people involved in a letter, e-mail, or phone call? The mere act of writing a letter you may never send off can be all it takes for you to declutter and get it off your chest. If, however, this issue/experience keeps coming up, and you can't stop thinking about it, you must take some kind of action. You may even imagine yourself using scissors to cut the strings of attachment to this incident and say out loud, "I am now releasing this to the Universe, forgiving myself and others, and holding on to the blessing behind it." Keep doing this until you feel a release, and keep doing this every single time you think about it, until it no longer comes up in your heart or mind.

Here are some powerful affirmations you may want to start saying, in addition to taking physical action:

I let go of past grievances! I forgive myself and others. I let go of my past.
I take away the insights and lessons learned. That is the true miracle!
I create space for miracles in my heart, mind, and consciousness.

crack your heart wide open. *there's no other way to live.*

C rack your heart wide open!

The heart that is shut down is dying day after day.

Clear your arteries today by dumping betrayal, resentment, anger, and unforgiveness into the trash.

How do you get in touch with your heart?

The heart knows all things and knows no boundaries.

The heart is boundless and infinite in its power to feel, express, and motivate one to action.

Day after day, year after year, the most compelling piece of unfinished business in everyone's lives involves the matters of the heart.

Unfinished business in the matters of the heart, left unresolved and unexpressed, keeps you from moving forward.

So, all you can do today is ask: *Is there something I've been holding on to that needs to be out there in the Universe? Is there something I've been wanting to say to another person that I haven't, for fear of rejection or what they might think of me? Is there somebody I need to call to express my gratitude for things they did that I am appreciative for, even the people I see every day?*

It's never too late to say "I love you," or "Thank you," or to even air grievances, because those feelings left unexpressed inside your heart are creating a thick armor that is preventing you from moving forward in other relationships.

It is all connected. The clutter in my heart is preventing me from having more good stuff coming into my heart, because the bad stuff is infecting the good stuff that is in there.

What's the price I'm paying for not giving my heart?
Risk loss.
Risk hurt.
Risk pain.

God help me in this relationship to manage my fears, to allay my fears, and to deal with them.
To move past my fears of loss and not being good enough.

I can say that I feel confident of who I am and my talents and gifts.
I can say that I am worth a million bucks to anyone, and that this man should see me this way.
But why don't I feel this way?
Yes, I do at times, but not always.

Focus on what your heart desires.
Focus on what is important to you.
Don't get attached to the form.

Focus on your visionary man—and yes, you want it desperately to be the man you are with right now, but for now, your heart is telling you to keep believing and trusting you will be with your visionary man, who will confess to you that he doesn't want to spend a moment without you, that you do it for him, that you take his breath away, that you capture his attention, and that when you are in the room, there is no one else.

That's what I crave, feel I deserve, and desire.
I will not settle.
So, God, tell me, how much longer do I continue giving?
I know the book is inside of me, dying to come out.
The book on organizing, simplifying, and decluttering.
And here I am decluttering my heart.

My heart is in a state of uncertainty.
Now I understand why people shut down their hearts.
Fear.
Fear of getting hurt.
Fear of putting out and not getting back.
Fear of getting rejected.
Fear that I am not good enough.
Fear of disappointment.
Fear of betrayal.
Fear of having these painful feelings of envy, jealousy, and unworthiness.

I want to release all my fears, and no longer live in this state of perpetual fear with him.

I don't want to think that he does not truly love me for the long run, that he is with me just for the interim, that he will leave me for someone younger, prettier, smarter.

I don't want to think that he will move on to grander adventures.

I am afraid I am not enough to hold his attention.

I guess the part I fear most is that if he is thinking these thoughts, he will hold them in and not share with me, and then, suddenly, one day he will be gone. And I will be in so much pain. Why didn't I see it coming?

This is the most challenging thing for me, then.
Let go of all my fears. And create space for what is possible.

To be in this relationship with this beautiful, gorgeous, stunning man—handsome, smart, spiritual, adventurous, cute, funny, charming, ambitious, passionate—and to know that I deserve him, and that I am good enough.

The truth is that I want so much in life.
The truth is that love is so important to me.
The truth is that I crave to be in love with someone who is in love with me.
The truth is that I want to be loved for who I truly am.
The truth is that I want to be desired by my visionary man, craved and lusted for.

What need am I trying to fill inside of me that isn't being met?

Truth?
I don't want to be alone.
I don't want to die alone.
I just want to believe that all my dreams can come true.

Expose your true stuff. Be vulnerable.

When I'm love coaching, clients are often shocked at my suggestions.

What shocking things do I say to them?

"Speak the truth of your heart."

"But, but, but, but . . ."

"But what? How hard is it?"

Yes, it's difficult for some, because oftentimes we are trained to be careful when it comes to matters of the heart. There are many books written on how to get married, how to be a bitch, or how to play games to get the man or woman of your dreams.

I never really got this. Here's my theory, and why I think this is total crazymaking.

You know how I feel already about just coming from your TruthLoveMeaningPurpose.

You know what that is if you do the work—what turns you on, and what doesn't. We all have different preferences, different likes and dislikes.

So why would you change who you are when you're looking for love, to get the man or woman of your dreams?

Is the person whom you consider the man or woman of your dreams truly that, if you have to change who you are to win their heart?

Let's say you change who you truly are to get this man or woman.

Then what happens when you get your dream love?

You have to keep being this changed person who's not really you, suppressing the true you, to continue engaging with and keeping this person interested in you.

What clutter!

Let go of the clutter and speak the truth of your heart to the love of your life from the very beginning. Always. Now. Feel the liberation that comes with just being you. Keep it simple. Don't overcomplicate, or sabotage yourself regarding what is possible.

And please—stop asking people for advice who aren't "experts" in their own lives with their own relationships. Are they in a fulfilling relationship that is out of this world? Perhaps if they are, they might know a little something about how to get the kind of relationship you are seeking. But it always surprises me when people ask their close friends for relationship advice, and these friends are always armed and ready with lots of advice on what to do and what not to do. Before following their advice, ask yourself, are your friends practicing the advice they are dispensing to you, and is it working in their own lives? Are they themselves in successful relationships? Remember to look at the source of the advice, and remember that you are a unique being with a unique relationship. Honestly, I don't think you can buy a manual on how to be "successful" with the person you are in a relationship with. The only manual you need is written in your heart, and comes from your TruthLoveMeaningPurpose. So listen to your heart, and speak the truth of your heart always.

Can it that be simple? Yes!

Allow somebody to fall in love with the true you, the real you!

I've done this so many times, and I can tell you without a sliver of doubt that it works. When I say it works, I mean that I myself have many times revealed the truth of who I was vulnerably—insecurities, arrogances, and all—and found those who loved me for exactly who I was. And, of course, there were many who did not get me or who thought I was weird, and did not "like" me. Yet I look at each of one of those seeming "rejections" of me as blessings. Thank you, God, that they didn't like me or love me back if they didn't get me, and/or expected me to be somebody I am not, and have to deal with all my neuroses. Those who have loved me and gotten me fully are those who have allowed me to be all of me, accepted all of me and my idiosyncrasies, loved every nook and cranny, and seen it all as a beautiful part of my authentic spirit/soul/heart.

In fact, with my boyfriend, when I shared my heart the way I shared it with you, he confessed that he was inspired to share more of himself and reveal his true heart, and he said that there was just that much more of me to love and fall in love with.

I love the movie *Hitch,* and in another life, I would be that matchmaker, as I love, love, love encouraging others to fully be themselves, snots and all, and see what happens, especially in a new relationship. This is the fastest way to declutter what you don't want—somebody who will not fully love you for who you are.

So the journey continues, and I'm so passionate about all of you just being who you are with your unique TruthLoveMeaningPurpose and creating a world you love, love, love filled with "love magic" and "love synergy" just by cracking your heart wide open, even wider than you could ever imagine.

Experience the miracles of love when you speak the truth of your heart and expose your true self.

.

exercise. *three lessons learned from a past or current love relationship.*

Where is your heart shut down?

Think about a lost love—a love from the past, or even the love you are in now.

Write about the relationship. What happened?

What were the three most powerful lessons you learned?

How did you grow as a being in this relationship that made you stronger, better, more evolved?

How did you contribute to this relationship? Is there anything you would do now, knowing what you know now?

Is there anything you need to resolve?

Is there anything you wish you could have told this person?

Write it down now. And don't stop until you have completely decluttered your heart of its burden of unexpressed feelings. Express everything, no holds barred, trusting that no one has to read this letter but yourself.

Get angry at yourself. Scream, yell, cry!

Allow yourself to get emotional. Allow yourself to confront your truth of fears and doubts.

exercise. *forgiveness paves way for true love.*

Now, forgive the other person. They were doing the best they can. He/she/it was a messenger in your journey—an "xyz" factor that you must believe was created in your life to learn something powerful. Let go of the attachment to the form, and don't be upset at the form. Instead, channel this energy, and be grateful for the lesson learned.

Forgive yourself. You were doing the best you can.

Let go of regrets. Let go of the past.

Trust that you are where you are today because of your past.

Embrace the present being of who you are and your past experiences, which make up the core of who you are.

Keep on coming back to this exercise with every single relationship in your life that you are still holding inside your heart.

Everything you are holding on to in your heart in a negative sense is taking up valuable space and keeping the doors to the heart shut down. Instead, reconcile all the negative memories and feelings, and release them into the Universe, trusting that the only way to have pure love and deep relationships in this lifetime is by continuing to keep your heart cracked wide open. The only way to do this is to realize that no matter what happens, you will be okay. No matter what happens, your heart is resilient. Keeping it open, free to love and be loved, and exposed to the light, is the only way to live life.

love mirror. *unconditional love.*

What's behind my heart clutter?

I'm sorry that I left you, Jerry.

I'm sorry that I was too selfish and too self-absorbed in my own drama to fully explain to you everything that I was going through.

I now think back, and yes, I was too selfish to think about you.

I'm sorry if I neglected you.

I'm sorry if I just left you there.

I hope that I didn't make you feel unloved.

I loved you so much.

Thank you so much for coming into my life to open up my heart.

When asked if we could adopt you or else you would be euthanized in fifteen minutes, I said *Yes*, although I was stressed about being responsible for another being and wondered how was I going to manage and handle you. I felt so out of control.

Little did I know that the *Yes* I said was a *Yes* I desperately needed.

You came into my life as a breath of fresh air.

You immediately ripped open my heart.

Your life force was so apparent.

I was shocked that you understood me.

I was shocked that you looked directly into my eyes and gave me love.

I was stunned when I looked back into your eyes to give you love and saw that your heart melted, and you shyly closed your eyes.

You were acknowledging me: "Aw geez—shucks, June—love you, too."

When we watched television, you watched the screen along with us. When there were commercials, and we started talking, you turned away from the screen and looked at us, to converse with us.

I was so upset to leave you all by yourself for the first time, when I had to leave for work. I didn't want you to feel alone. You cried when I left. You cried when I came home.

You were loyal, faithful, and unconditionally loving. You greeted me at the door every single day. I was always surprised that you would know when we were coming home by the sound of our car two stories below. You would get all excited and run to the door to greet us. How did you know we were coming when I, the human, couldn't even distinguish our car or hear anything downstairs? Did you feel by psychic vibration? I know, I know—you just sensed and felt me.

When Pam came to visit, and we were watching her favorite show, *Entertainment Tonight*, you kept crying to get our attention. You climbed up to the top ledge so that we could "rescue" you and give you our full, undivided attention—you did it at the beginning of the show and at the end, while the music was playing.

When Pam slept in her room with the door closed, she noticed your cute, furry paw making its way under the crack in the door, and laughed. You had fallen in love with her and her energy, and you wanted her to open the door so you could sleep with her.

Pam fell in love with you, not knowing a thing about cats. She asked me if all cats were like you. Yes, I told her, when they are safe and feel loved, they show us their hearts and act from them.

When her parents came by, she wanted to show them how wonderfully loving and personable you were, but instead, full of fear, you retreated underneath the bed. Just like me, when I'm nervous or scared, you hid your true self beneath a mask of fear, which doesn't give anyone an opportunity to get to know the true you. I told Pam, "Jerry didn't feel as comfortable and safe with your parents, so that's why he was scared to show up as himself, vulnerable and exposed. You understood him, and saw his true heart and his true colors, so that's why he shared all of his heart with you."

When we went out of town and left you with Dino every other day, you were so angry at us that you turned your back to us when we came home, instead of being happy to see us. I know your feelings were hurt. So we hired Alicia, a pet nanny who came twice a day to brush you and play with you, and you seemed happier. I know you were telling me that you needed attention and love every day—just like I do.

I loved when you would snuggle next to me and put your paw on me, needing to touch me at all times. You didn't like it if I moved so that we weren't touching anymore. I know you liked to stay connected at all times.

The more I think about you, the more I think you mirrored back to me who I was.

I, too, am somebody who always craves love and intimacy, and wants to be touched every single moment and every single day.

I love you, Jerry.

You left an indelible impression on my mind and heart.

I think about you often and cry every time I think about you.

I am not proud of how I left you during the divorce.

I left you in somebody else's custody, whom I know loved you as much as I did, but I also knew we had a very special connection.

You gave me your unconditional love every single day. And I'm sorry I took you and your love for granted. I hope you can forgive me and know now from heaven that I am truly sorry from the bottom of my heart.

I am so grateful for all the gifts you gave to me.

Before you came along, I was not open to loving an animal so much. You taught me that animals are beings with authentic feelings and emotions, and desire love just as much as human beings.

Thank you for loving me unconditionally, for teaching me to go deeper with my capacity for love, and for opening up my heart!

.

exercise. *express gratitude for one "being" who made a difference.*

Think of one person or being in your life that has made a difference in your life.

Write a letter of thanks to them.

Tell them three qualities that you appreciate about them.

Tell them three experiences you remember.

Now think about how these qualities are a reflection of you.

Think about what those experiences taught you.

The point is to exercise your gratitude muscles and realize that every person and being can be a powerful messenger for your journey, and every experience can be a tremendous gift, if you choose to see them as delivering messages meant to propel your life forward. After all, you are here to complete a particular life purpose and mission. Doesn't it make sense that you would be led to particular experiences, encounters, and beings who would activate that life purpose and/or bring messages to you that would allow you to live that life purpose more authentically? The love of somebody or something is a reflection of the love and the beauty—and a particular truth and meaning—inside of you.

keep loving. *clear the clutter of your heart.*

decluttering the stuff of relationships, and getting to the truth of why a relationship existed and how it served you, is powerful—especially when a relationship is over.

In order to move forward with self-awareness and stay clutter free in your heart, I believe you must examine the intentions behind each and every relationship, and why things came to an end, to grow from the experience. Suck out the life lessons from the relationship, be supremely grateful for the lessons learned, and walk away with the love, memories, good times, and lessons. Leave the rest behind. Let go of the clutter in your heart.

In every relationship I have experienced, when either it was ending or we were in tumultuous times, I always felt as if a part of me was dying. I feel everything so deeply, so it makes sense that I would feel every single stab as it pierced my heart. Yet time and time again, no matter how painful it was, if I consciously return to the lessons behind the experiences, I always find a deeper understanding of why my soul "chose" these relationships. Every relationship helped me to grow in a different way. Sometimes I learned how to love others more unconditionally. Sometimes I learned how to love myself more.

When one boyfriend broke up with me, I couldn't believe it. How could somebody break up with me? What did I do wrong? And then suddenly I wanted him more than ever. Was that my ego? Why did he break up with me? Ha, I thought I was perfect and a great girlfriend! Apparently not. Falling asleep on him when he was visiting was not a very attractive trait and did not made him feel special. So I had to examine my own behavior and decide what I could do to be the best girlfriend I could be to somebody.

One man couldn't handle my having so many friends. After that relationship ended, I vowed that I would be with somebody who didn't feel threatened by the way I wanted to live my life, whether I had one hundred friends or two friends.

In another relationship, my boyfriend thought I was weird. He kept saying, "You're so weird!" but not in a loving way. This man didn't appreciate the quirky stuff about me. And I learned to not suppress my "weirdness" and to be more "weird," so that I could fully embrace all the wonderful stuff about me, weird or not!

Another man didn't appreciate it when I was vulnerable and said, "I miss you." I felt he was rejecting an authentic part of me, so I vowed never to let somebody tell me to be less "emotional," "vulnerable," or "loving," but to be even more vulnerable! My mantra became, "I am now attracting somebody who loves not only my head, but my heart, too."

Then, in my next relationship, I attracted a man who said he had to "cheat" to appreciate me. I wanted to be with a man who did not have to cheat to appreciate all the wonderful qualities in me. Why didn't I listen to my intuition when I knew he was lying?

Did I learn more about what I wanted in my next and ideal relationships by going through these relationships? Perhaps.

I then attracted a man who accepted all my quirks and eccentricities and loved everything about me—because that is what I had asked for. And I received the gift of being loved for being vulnerable in this next man. He was totally into me in all ways.

So every relationship has included more and more of what I desire. And with every relationship, I have walked away with so much love for these other people whom I viewed as tremendous gifts. Had I not experienced some of this stuff, I would not have known what to ask for in my Universe. How could God give me what I truly desired if I didn't know what it was I truly wanted?

Yes, rejections and betrayal can pierce the heart and leave a scar for a long time, sometimes forever.

But I'm asking you not to let it leave a permanent stain.

I'm not asking you to erase the painful memory from your heart, but can you release the pain?

Can you release the anger, resentment, and hurt?

Yes, you can—but only by forgiving the other person who betrayed you and angered you.

And only by forgiving *yourself*, for being stupid enough to believe in this person, or believe this person was good, or believe this person was good for you, or believe that this person would never, ever do that to you. Forgive yourself for going on that ride with this person.

You had to go through this experience to finally realize something about yourself.

This person held up a mirror to you, so you could question who you truthfully were and what you were about. This person triggered you big time, and without this person, you would not be the person you are today.

This person and this relationship actually defined the person you wanted to be and the relationship you wanted to be in.

Once again, you cannot learn these lessons in a vacuum. You cannot just read books about how to be in love and be the best lover and partner without going through the range of emotions and the depth of stuff you experience in a relationship. There are so many variables in a relationship that books cannot address, because you are so unique, and what you have experienced is unique. And when you're in a relationship with someone who also has their own stories, stuff, and essence, this union is in and of itself unique. Nobody could ever predict how you should be or what you should do, because no one has ever experienced this union before.

Get it?

So it is in the loving that we discover who we are. It is in being all we can be in this moment that we become more of who were born to be. It is in gratitude that we attract more of what we desire into our experience. And isn't this what love and life are about—feeling love in every corner of our spirits, and gratitude for our unique hearts?

So today, let go of the clutter in your heart, and create space for the miracles of a new and renewed love.

.

exercise. *your best self.*

Write your ideal vision of you. Your best self. Who are you? What qualities do you possess?

exercise. *yourself, mirrored in your relationships.*

Now write about every single relationship you have been in and how each relationship brought you closer to your ideal vision of yourself. If a relationship didn't bring you closer to your ideal self, write about how that relationship took you away from your ideal vision of yourself. Keep on writing, and you should see a pattern emerging: are you getting closer to your ideal vision, or farther away?

exercise. *your vision of ideal relationships.*

Now, from where you are today, write down your ideal vision of your future relationships. Write down exactly what you envision will happen, in the best possible sense, to propel you forward into your new life where every vision and dream is coming true.

Write down what will be required of you for this to happen. Courage. Trust. Belief. Faith.

exercise. *a letter from your old self to new self.*

Write a letter from your old self to this new future self. Give your new self advice from your old self. This should give you a different perspective on the ways you are constantly changing, whether or not you want to believe it. Changes *will* happen, and your perspective will determine whether they are positive or negative. Why not believe you are positively progressing, and look at every single experience as a gift from the Universe to you? Why not believe that your new self is craving this knowledge from your old self? Why not trust and believe that every single one of your dreams can come true, with the proper mindset and faith?

MOVE FORWARD.
A NEW WAY.

just because . . . *you feel like it.*

W hy do I ask someone when I go to a restaurant, "What are you getting?"

Am I curious what the other person is ordering?

Am I not sure about my choice, and I want that other person's choice to inform my decision?

Am I comparing myself to the other person and my choice to their choice?

Is it more or less than what I am eating?

Is it healthier than what I am eating?

Is their choice better than my choice? Am I missing out on something?

When I was twelve, I would ask my best friend Karen, "What are you wearing to school tomorrow?" Why did I ask that? Because I wanted to wear the same thing as somebody in my tribe. Because I didn't want to stand out with my unique choice. And just because it was fun to dress up every day coordinated. Just because.

Finally I got to the point where I didn't have to ask anybody else what they were wearing, and I just wore what I felt like wearing! I felt great when I wore whatever I felt like—like I felt as a kid. I didn't care if it was a dressy event or a casual event, and I didn't care what the dress code was.

All I cared about was that I felt comfortable in my own skin, wearing the clothes that I wanted to wear on that day. If I felt like wearing a dress when everybody was wearing pants, why not? If I felt like wearing a tiara, why not wear a tiara?

What was I afraid of?

Being judged.

Standing out.

Being asked, "Why do you think you're so special? What gives you the right to dress like that?"

Or just being confronted with questions about why I'm wearing this, and why I like it.

Adults think it's cute when little girls wear their Cinderella costumes for the day. Or when little boys wear their cowboy outfits. Why can't we as adults be like little kids, and not care what others think? Why can't we just wear whatever we feel like wearing?

We can. Just today, I saw a girl in downtown Los Angeles wearing "heart ears" and thought, *Okay, she either forgot to take off her Halloween costume from last week, or she decided, "Why not? I just feel like it!"* I smiled, thinking of her boldness in wearing whatever she felt like wearing today.

Today I felt like wearing my cute pink, black, and gray argyle ski cap that I bought in Mammoth to go with my all-pink ski outfit and that I used to have in my Ski Wear container. I took some of the ski wear out of the container and decided to just wear it whenever I felt like it. I felt happy wearing it! Once a neighbor saw me dressed up and thought I was going skiing or to the mountains, and I just laughed without explaining anything.

Do we always need a reason to justify our choices? Can't we just feel it in our heart? Can't we feel it in our gut? Can't we just feel that happy feeling inside—do we need to come up with logical, physical, empirical evidence to back up that choice we made?

Aren't these reasons good enough?

Just because.

Just because I feel like it.

Just because it feels like me.

Just because I love it.

Just because it's fun.

Just because I'm vibing it.

Just because it's me!

Just because.

．

exercise. *wear something you have never worn before . . . just because.*

I dare you to wear something you would not typically wear every day. Today, I dare you to wear something you would wear to a special event or occasion. Wear it because your heart sings when you do. Wear it without having to make up an excuse if somebody asks. Say, "Just because . . ." and smile or laugh!

This exercise will cultivate your "think outside the box" and "feel your heart" muscles through your day-to-day choices. Exercising those muscles through your seemingly insignificant choices will affect how you make the seemingly significant choices, and will start a revolution within your body, mind, heart, and consciousness. You'll be living your life on purpose, following your bliss and your heart, rather than your mind's rationalizations or your shoulds.

exercise. *order what you want . . . just because.*

At a restaurant, if you are in the habit of asking what everybody else is ordering before you make your decision, don't check in with everybody else this time. Instead, check in with yourself. Feel your heart, and ask yourself, *What do I truly feel like eating? What sounds delicious?* Then stick to that, and see how that makes you feel.

This exercise will uncover the truth behind your asking everybody else what they are ordering. Is it curiosity? Comparison? It will help you cultivate choices that are independent of what others are doing or eating.

exercise. *do what brings you joy . . . just because.*

If you find yourself constantly comparing yourself to others and checking what others are doing, declare a media moratorium. Don't read the news. Don't go on the Internet. Stop reading Twitter messages. Don't go on Facebook for a while. Retreat into your cave and check in with yourself first and foremost, and do those things that bring you joy. Read those things that bring you joy. Eat those things that make you feel joy. Don't use others as a gauge or backdrop to your life. You are the star of your own life. Be the star, and wake up each morning making decisions that are in alignment with your TruthLoveMeaningPurpose first.

set intentions. *clear pathways of clutter.*

i 've discovered that the "letting go of stuff" process can be magical and mystical if you set a clear intention every time you work in your office, begin a project, start on a task, or even throw stuff away or give stuff away.

I'm compulsive now about getting rid of the stuff I have made a decision about. If I let the giveaways reside in my space for too long, they start to question me like a crying child: "Don't you want me still? Why are you letting me go?" Then I start to have doubts, and I have to spend the energy and time to revisit the stuff again and again and again, wasting valuable time, especially if I arrive at the same conclusion. Worse, if I decide to keep it, a little part of my surety of self starts to wither away.

I love working on a desk with clear surfaces, because then I can laser-like focus. In my clutter-free environment, I set the intention to easily and effortlessly get through my paperwork. If I have other stuff on my desk, it distracts me from what's in front of me. When I say "easy and effortless," that means the opposite of struggle, strife, and drama. I have a clear pathway set in my mind and am prepared for everything to flow.

I encourage my clients to do the same with any new project they are beginning. The thoughts flashing in your mind are just as powerful as the paperwork you are dealing with. If your boomeranging thoughts are colliding with each other, it creates a massive explosion of confusion and overwhelm, and your blood pressure will start rising. That, combined with the massive stack of paperwork in front of you . . . don't you just feel like screaming and running away?

But, wait—there is an easier way. Be at one with your decision that the task before you is an important task to tackle. Realize you will feel so much better and lighter when you accomplish this task you have been putting off.

Say out loud,

> *I am easily and effortlessly accomplishing this task, and feeling better and better in every moment.*

Then, only take out the paperwork and stuff related to that one task, and let's see what happens!

When you set your intention and you are clear about the purpose of your task, you are sending a signal into the Universe, marshaling all of its forces, heralding the angels and all their assistants to come to your divine assistance.

Combine setting your intention with setting a clear boundary for your time, and I've seen miracles happen. The task that might have seemed impossible, that you thought would take five hours, now only takes five minutes. It is as though the doorways are wide open and the pathways are clear for miracles to take place. There are no longer any cluttered intentions colliding with each other, asking each other which one wants to play first. The sole intention you have decided upon comes to the forefront of the task, space, and time, and together they synergize and conspire to assist you in getting it done now, easily and effortlessly!

When you combine a clear intention for your task with a clear time boundary, you are setting the Universe's wheels in motion to help you achieve your heart's desires. To help you get it all done now. To help you simplify your life. To help you appreciate who you are. To help you honor who you are. To help you align who you are truly with the stuff you have. To help you let go of false truths and embrace your authentic self. To help you get to a place where you can say, "I LOVE MY LIFE!"

Set your intentions every single time: When you're driving, to hit all green lights. When you're going to visit your mother, to make sure that by the time you leave, she will feel on top of the world. When you're going on a date, to have meaningful and fun conversations and interactions, where the truth about whether you want to spend more time with this person will come to the surface. When you're going on a job interview, to help the employer see and feel your best qualities, and know the truth of whether this job is for your highest good. When you're going to work, for your work environment, personal interactions, and projects to flow harmoniously, productively, and joyfully.

Do this every time, and see what happens in your life.

Declaring your intentions clears the clutter, paving the way for miracles to happen.

.

exercise. *one powerful intention for one task today.*

Just for today, set an intention before you set out to achieve any task, no matter how small or big. I want you to exercise your "intention muscle" and get into the habit of being supremely conscious of whatever activity you are engaged in and combining that with a heartfelt intention.

While you take out the trash, say out loud,

> *I am letting go of [this trash], and creating space in my life for [what your heart desires].*

When you practice this, you are telling yourself and the Universe that you know there is a connection between letting go of something and activating new space for creation.

exercise. *declare an intention and time limit for your task.*

Try declaring an intention and setting a target deadline or time frame before any task. Say out loud,

> *I am easily and effortlessly going through the kitchen and letting go of what is not healthy for me, and finishing this within one hour.*

Now set a timer, and go do the task.

Then journal about what happened.

Did the task seem easier?

easy and effortless. *don't make it so hard.*

did your task in the previous exercise go quickly, easily, and effortlessly for you? That must mean it was meant to be!

I'm so excited for you! Change is good! Be at one with your change! You must have needed it and wanted it, and it is for the highest good!

If you are feeling uneasy or uncomfortable, you're probably overthinking the change! Let go of your worries, fears, and doubts, which are based on your past!

Change your belief that you must work hard, that things have to be a struggle, that you must spend lots of time in order to change.

Why can't your life be easier and more effortless? Why can't your health improve miraculously? Why can't money flow in easily and effortlessly? Why can't you get your dream job with that magic number?

The only thing between you and your dreams is your mind: its worries, fears, and doubts.

Let go of your preconceived notions of time: how long something will take, and how it will happen.

Create space in your life and in your mind for change, and the infinite number of ways your change could come about.

Change your mind about what is possible and what can be. Shift your mindset about what good can come your way.

Commit to this decision you have made about your new vision for yourself. Be at one with it. You are always free to change your mind later.

Why not entertain the notion that all your dreams are coming true, rather than believing things will stay the same and be the way they've always been? Thinking that thought will make sure you receive the same results you have always been getting in your life.

Are you addicted to struggle? Are you addicted to everything being hard? Did you make a pact with yourself that in order to get your heart's desires, you must work hard for it?

In the past, I used to believe that things had to happen in a precise order: first, I was going to study with the best acting coach. Then I would land featured roles, then co-starring roles, and then starring roles. Why did it have to be that way? It didn't. But I ended up creating that exact sequence of events because I was so locked into that single reality where everything had to happen in order. There was no space for anything else to happen outside that 1-2-3, A-B-C-D reality, which I was envisioning and attached to day after day.

Where do you do that? In your relationships? With your job? With your career? With your kids?

Stop right now and think about a different way for things to turn out. Can you imagine an easier way? Get giddy and excited about everything flowing easily and effortlessly.

Do you think I was lucky because I was destined for luck? Or was it because I thought I was lucky and created that luck? Did I think it was going to be easy, and those thoughts created that reality?

Yes, yes, yes—get enthralled with this idea of you being lucky, where things flow easily and effortlessly. You are getting rock-star parking wherever you go. You are the first person in line at the store. When you start to see it happen with the little stuff of life, you will begin to believe it can happen with the bigger stuff!

Let go of struggle. Let go of strife. Let go of drama. Let go of things needing to be so hard.

Welcome, Easy and Effortless! Hello, Lucky You!

•

exercise. *let go of the struggle and drama.*

Write about where there is drama, struggle, strife, and suffering going on in your life.

Now, are you ready to change the drama, struggle, and strife to a life of ease and effortlessness?

Are you willing to at least shift your mindset? Are you willing to do whatever it takes to lead a life where you are fulfilled and happy?

Write about this idea, and how committed you are to it.

exercise. *identify unhealthy thoughts that must be purged.*

Start writing down the thoughts that constantly bombard your brain. Identify the unhealthy thoughts you have repeated to yourself over and over throughout your life.

Now, vow to let go of these old friends, these companions on your journey who have stood the test of time. Gently say to them,

> *I am now letting go of you, as I realize that it is unhealthy to keep repeating these thoughts.*
> *I am now replacing these thoughts with new thoughts that make me feel alive and make my life happier.*

Then, replace that old mantra with a positive mantra that makes you feel lighter, happier, better.

By doing this with every single thought and feeling that arises, you will realize that changing the thought/feeling is a choice, and hopefully you will feel empowered to change. Change your thoughts, and your feelings surrounding the thoughts, and change your reality.

exercise. *create a new life of ease and effortlessness.*

Imagine that you are a powerful creator, and that you created these struggles for a reason. Write about all the reasons why you created these struggles in your life.

The truth is that you *are* a powerful creator. All you have to do is start confessing today,

> *My life is flowing easily and effortlessly.*

Say it every single day. Catch yourself when you say, "Oh, this is taking too long. Oh, this is so hard. Oh, this is never going to happen. Oh, this is a struggle. Oh, what a drama!" Start reversing this mindset in the middle of that thought and start confessing over and over,

> *Easy and effortless.*
> *Everything is moving easily and effortlessly.*
> *Everything is happening easily and effortlessly.*

See what happens to your day as you start filling your mindset with this mantra. Notice whether your life starts flowing more and more. The difference may be subtle, but slowly, day by day, you may begin noticing you are letting go of the battle and surrendering to the flow of ease.

miracles in action. *believe and you will receive.*

i'm such a believer in miracles—that everything and anything can magically appear in your life—just based on the stuff that has happened to me and the stuff I witness in others' lives every single day! When I'm with others, and a miracle manifests in front of their very eyes, they are incredulous. Sometimes they attribute it to me, or they chalk it up to being a coincidence. They question whether life could be this easy, and then rationalize that what just happened was a fluke.

Manifest what you want by saying a thought out loud and setting a clear intention, and poof—the magic dragon, Tinkerbell, the fairy godmother, the miracle appears!

Money. When I first began acting, I created a file folder called Acting Income. The following week, I booked my first commercial, and I received my first check for acting income. Could it be that easy?

One of my clients was an actress, and I asked her if she had a home for the infinite riches she expected to pour in. She said no. I asked her if she truly expected money to flow in, and she hesitated. I taught her to practice her faith by taking a physical action in the Universe to demonstrate her faith and belief that money would pour into her life by creating a home for incoming checks. At first, she took out a small box, and I said, "Let's create a bigger box, acting with expectation that a *lot* of checks will come in." That week, she called excitedly to tell me that more checks than she had ever received before came into her life unexpectedly, and she was able to put them into that new home.

I asked another client what her dream job would be and what her magic number would be for her annual income. We jotted down the job with the magic number on her Goal List.

She named a number that was twice what she was making. I asked her if she really believed that she would receive this and felt she deserved this, and she said, "Yes." Then she came up with excuses about why this would never happen, and I admonished her and said, "Don't negate the miracle by talking yourself out of it. Your head doesn't know. Your heart knows and told me the magic number." Less than twenty hours later, she called me excitedly, and said, "You're never going to believe what happened. I was offered a position at my job with the magic number—do you think it is connected?"

Faith in action on the physical level.

Even without taking physical action in the universe, you can begin to practice your ability to manifest in small ways, such as saying a thought out loud, expressing that intention, and truly expecting it to happen on the physical level.

Parking spaces. I always manifest rock-star parking spaces because I think about what I want, I say it out loud, and voilà, at just the right time, a parking space will open up. I was taking my assistant out for her birthday and drove to a popular restaurant on busy Santa Monica Boulevard on a Friday evening. I said, "I'm going to manifest a rock-star parking space," and right after I turned the corner, a car pulled out of the parking space right in front of the restaurant—one of only two coveted parking spaces!

Finding a mailman or mailwoman. Just this weekend, I was reminded by my boyfriend how he had witnessed this particular miracle not just once, but three times with me. When I first learned about the power of creation and manifestation, and how you can use your words to stir up the Universe to deliver what you want to you, I took it literally and started practicing on the mail delivery system.

I had learned that I should start small, get success, and then move on to bigger things I wanted to manifest. So I would use the letters I wanted to mail out to manifest mailmen or mailwomen wherever I was. Traveling in between clients, I would say, "I want to see a mailman or a mailwoman," listen to my intuition as I was driving, turn down streets that I normally would not take, and voilà—a mailman or mailwoman would be coming out of an apartment complex at the exact time I had turned down a street. I would jump out of the car and say, "Thank you—what a miracle you are!" and they would smile and be pleasantly surprised at how surprised and excited I was to see them.

I did this numerous times, and with every manifestation of a mailman or mailwoman, the idea was cemented for me that the Universe is oh-so powerful, always delivering what I ask for. One time, I was driving from Westwood to Santa Monica for a client appointment, and I forgot I had a letter to mail out. With five minutes to spare, as I was driving down busy San Vicente Boulevard with cars racing by at 35 mph, I started praying for a mailman or mailwoman to appear. Suddenly, I saw a USPS car pulled off to the side of San Vicente under a shade tree, in between the gigantic houses. As I pulled up behind the truck, get this! I didn't even have to get out of the car! It was brilliant—like those drive-through restaurants, the mailman actually walked up to my car window, and I exclaimed, "OMG! You're a godsend! A miracle! Thank you sooooo much! Expect miracles in your life, too—I truly hope you get a miracle, too!" I always wish them miracles at the end—as they had just given one to me! But can you believe it?

Okay, I have to share with you two more amazing, miraculous stories!

My boyfriend and I were so excited about our brand new, beautiful his-and-her matching vintage-looking Gary Fisher cruiser bikes, so we made up a rule for that weekend that we had to take our bikes everywhere, and we could not use the cars at all— just for the weekend! Cutting our carbon footprint while getting exercise, we were proud! Of course, true to form, lots of errands came up unexpectedly, like "OMG, I have to deposit this check at the ATM—gotta take the bikes," to "We're out of stevia—gotta take the bikes to Whole Foods," and on and on.

On that same Saturday afternoon, after we had already taken the bikes to the bank and to the market and returned home, suddenly my boyfriend realized that he had to mail out a package by today. In true form, we started racing to the post office before they closed at 4 p.m. I said, "No worries—easy. We'll manifest a mailman or mailwoman!" He laughed as we continued biking on California Avenue to the post office. I looked down every street looking for the USPS truck, and suddenly I saw one.

This isn't as easy as it seems! Manifesting a USPS truck is easy, but manifesting a mailman or mailwoman in person requires amazing synchronicity. They are all over the city on any given day, so the mailman or mailwoman must be coming out of a building and walking on to the sidewalk to another complex, or you must catch them while they're at their truck grabbing their next batch of mail to be delivered, at just the right time! The Universe has to time this perfectly for the divine synchrodestiny meeting between you and the mailman or mailwoman to happen.

When we walked up to the USPS truck, there was no mailman or mailwoman to be seen. I said, "Wait, let's wait! I know someone will appear!" but my boyfriend was anxious to get to the post office to drop off his very important package before it closed, and insisted we continue biking to our destination. As soon as I started to pedal, she appeared! I loved it! It was the first time he saw the miracle of this "Universe delivery" in action!

Now, for the ultimate story. A few weeks ago, while biking to a café about two miles from our house, my boyfriend and I decided to take the beach route, which is a very steep road down to a short street with just a few houses before we hit the beach. I forgot to drop off my letter in the mailbox at our building, and I had it in my hand. My boyfriend said, "I'm sure we'll see a mailbox somewhere." But instead, I excitedly screamed, "Better yet, we'll manifest a mailman or mailwoman!" getting excited about the power of manifestation and welcoming the challenge!

So we got on our bikes and sped down Entrada, a very steep road, at about 25-30 mph! Check this out: at the bottom of Entrada, the light (usually red) was green, and we were turning left on to Channel Road, when suddenly a USPS truck came driving down another street from the opposite direction! I actually biked past her as she waited for me to cross. I made a quick sharp right and was beaming soooooo giddily as I biked up to the truck, and said, "OMG, you're an answer to prayer—you're a miracle! Thank you!" as I handed her my letter! She was surprised at how excited I was and said, "You're welcome!" As I pedaled off, I kept screaming to her, "Expect a miracle!" and she said, "I need one—it's my first day on the route!" And I said again, "Expect one; you'll get one. I did!" And she smiled and took off in her truck.

I was so giddy and incredulous. There were only a few more houses until the street ended and we would have been biking on the beach, with no more chances of encountering a post truck or mailman/mailwoman. We take this street all the time to the beach, and I have never, ever noticed a mail truck on this short route, let alone run into a mailman or mailwoman!

My boyfriend was beaming from ear to ear in disbelief, laughing, and we were suddenly filled with a miracle consciousness, knowing that God/Universe is always ready to deliver the miracles when we ask and truly expect that they will come along! Trust me, my boyfriend is now a believer, and he asks for miracles out loud like I do, and he has seen the amazing results that come with this method of manifesting!

But remember, the only way it works is if you truly believe. I once took a miracle workshop with a fantastic evangelist, Tim Storey, and he said that many people wish and pray for a miracle, but they don't really believe they will get one or truly expect it. If they've gotten only one, they somehow limit themselves to that one. He taught me that if I'm going to ask for a miracle, I better believe I will receive it and act as if I will receive it. I need to truly expect it and prepare for it!

Players. Okay, I have to share just one more story to demonstrate this point! Just this morning, we went for a walk in Palisades Park and down to the beach, as we always do. We brought a special Frisbee, the Flying Ring, so we could get more of a workout chasing after the Frisbee in the sand. There were hardly any people on the beach, so it was a perfect time to toss this Frisbee, which is the longest flying Frisbee ever, and sometimes uncontrollable.

We passed one group of volleyball players, as others were arriving to play their games. Suddenly my attention was directed towards two little boys, probably about seven years old, playing soccer between two goals, competing against each other and trying to get the ball into the goal. I have never played soccer, but I became a fan after watching my nieces' soccer games and watching the World Cup this year. I thought it might be a fun way to get some exercise, too! I had completely forgotten about it until I saw the little boys playing with each other, and thought to myself, *It would be fun to play soccer—I wonder if we could play with them just for a few minutes?* Then I immediately lost that thought when I saw the Flying Ring flying toward me and I had to race after it to catch it!

We were about fifty yards past them, when suddenly from a distance, I saw one of the little boys approach my boyfriend. He had walked all this way to ask him something. They talked briefly, and then my boyfriend resumed throwing the Flying Ring to me. I asked him, "What did the little boy say?" He said, "He asked us if we wanted to play soccer with them!"

I was incredulous! I screamed, "What did you say?"

"I said no, we're playing Frisbee. C'mon, let's play . . ."

I screamed again, "OMG! You don't know—I just asked for that! OMG, I can't believe they asked us to play! Do you know how many times we have walked on the sand? Has anyone ever approached us? Have I ever asked? This is the first time I ever thought that thought, *I want to play*—and OMG! The little boy asked us to play!"

We are always broadcasting signals to the Universe, because we are always vibrating at a certain speed, and projecting and attracting a particular life force, like a magnet. If we choose our thoughts carefully, and we are very, very clear, the signal will always register loud and clear. The call we make will be answered!

Only when our channels become cluttered up with other stuff in our minds and hearts do the requests come back tainted, tattered, and even infected with our own polluted thoughts. Does this make sense?

The cynics who believe "it will never happen" will continue not receiving, and things will continue not happening in their world to prove their point. The Universe loves proving your points, especially if you are attached to a particular reality. The disbelievers who say, "I don't believe it. It's too good to be true," may receive gifts, but then sudden misfortune strikes, and the gift is taken away—because hey, the Universe had to prove the point that "it was too good to be true."

I could go on and on about miracles, and the miracle ground you could be standing on every single day, with numerous stories to demonstrate my point. I witness it in the "small things" like finding a mailman, and in the big things, like seeing a friend defy the odds and recover from a terminal illness, or a seemingly infertile couple end up having not just one kid, but two kids, after they were told it was impossible. When I tell these stories, people are always incredulous that things like this happen in my world, but the truth is that I believe in miracles. I expect miracles to happen, I expect the extraordinary to happen in my life and others' lives, and that is why it happens.

I don't know which came first—my luck, or my mindset. I once took a workshop where they asked us what our belief systems were, and what was something we've always known about ourselves. When my first answer, without missing a beat, was, "I'm lucky—I've always been lucky!" the workshop leaders were surprised, since they had never heard that answer before. But it's true.

I believe it's true because I expect and believe in miracles. Because I do, they happen. I believe good things happen, and I believe in happy endings. I believe that fairy tales come true.

When I was little, people used to make fun of me and call me Pollyanna. Without even knowing who she was, I hated being called by that name. I finally watched the movie a few years ago, and I loved the tale of Pollyanna— how effervescent, optimistic, and full of faith and hope she was, how she always saw the glass as half full rather than half empty.

They're right. I am Pollyanna. But is it because I think I am, and therefore I create that corresponding reality? Or did that reality come first, and perpetuate my belief that I am lucky?

Whatever the reason, I don't question it anymore. I know that it works. I'm not saying that every single desire I have asked for manifests immediately like the illustrations above, but when it does, it is a sign for me to continue believing. To continue clearing the clutter in my own mind. To pull up the weeds of self-doubt and fears. To pull up the weeds of disbelief and believing something is impossible. To pull up the weeds of others' voices telling me I'm living in a fantasy world, and how can it be that easy? Who knows—maybe I sometimes create complications and difficulties and struggles so I don't have to feel guilty about how easy things can be for me. I am so aware of when I have caused "missteps" or "accidents" or sabotaged myself, because the easiest way would have been too easy, and I admit that sometimes I have wanted to say, "I worked hard to get here!"

But not anymore. Now, I'm over it. I want the best, and I want it easy, effortless, and fast—no holds barred.

Now I don't care what others think, and I will run away from anything that smells like negativity, cynicism, or sarcasm. Those ingredients are toxic to a ground that is breeding miracle consciousness.

There is only room for believing, expecting, preparing for, receiving, and manifesting on that miracle ground you are standing on!

And, finally, I have to add, I always scream, "Bring it on! Bring on the miracles, God!"

.

exercise. *develop a miracle mindset.*

Start exercising your miracle mindset muscles. Focus your intention on the belief that you are a powerful creator, and say out loud,

> *I am now manifesting [list desired miracles here].*

If you're mailing a letter, manifest a mailman or mailwoman. If you're driving, manifest a parking space. Try it with the little things and then, with confidence gained, move on to bigger manifestations.

Please write to me and let me know the miracles you manifest when you do this exercise, no matter how big or small! And let me know if it's okay to publish them! I believe that sharing miracles brings on even more miracles. Universe/God wants us to share our miracles, so that others can witness them, hear about them, and believe in them, to create a giant vortex of miracles flooding this earth!

words and thoughts are powerful creators.
what world are you creating?

in your world, what language do you speak? What words do you choose to use in your everyday language? What does your vocabulary consist of? What are your favorite words?

The words you choose send out a broadcast signal to the Universe, creating a vortex of energy that bounces right back to you in a physical form. The words you speak are powerful, because your words create a certain vibration. Therefore you create what you are speaking, and attract that creation to you.

When I realized this, I stopped saying "I can't." I started saying, "I can." I started focusing my words on what I wanted to create, rather than what I didn't want in my life. I started saying, "I am . . . " rather than "I desire . . . " knowing that loving who I am is the most powerful manifestation principle in the world. I started saying, "I expect miracles every day," and "My life is flowing easily and effortlessly," instead of thinking, saying, and believing, "Life is a struggle."

For one summer, I spent three entire months listening to affirmations from Louise Hay's *Love Yourself, Heal Your Life Workbook*. The only words I remember are "I love and accept myself exactly as I am," and they are etched forever in my subconscious and conscious mind.

This affirmation was huge for me, because in my eyes, I felt that I wasn't good enough as I was. I was always in a state of perpetual growth and forward movement, thinking I needed to acquire more knowledge, look better, and think different thoughts in order to be the person I thought I wanted to be.

Finally, I got it.

I got that my reaching, striving, and searching was putting me in a state of mind that said where I am is not where I want to be. I could never be satisfied with what I had and what I had achieved, because I thought that not moving forward was death. I thought that life was about change, and changing for the best. I thought life was about goals, and achieving goals.

That's why this quote by Arthur Ashe is still one of my favorites and reminds me of what's important:

"Success is a journey, not a destination."

Yes, I was so focused on the destination that I didn't even notice or enjoy the journey. I would race through my tasks and activities without truly being in the moment and enjoying and appreciating the sights, smells, and people along the way. I was so focused on getting to my destination, wherever that was. And the crazy thing is, because of my ambition, my destination kept on changing every day and every year. Every year, I would set new goals and destinations without focusing on the mountaintops that I had climbed and conquered. I never paused to acknowledge and reflect upon the many lessons learned, because I was too caught up in getting to the next destination. Even after a monumental significant accomplishment, I would say, "Next!"

For example, when I ran my very first LA Marathon, I felt disappointed at the end. It seemed anti-climactic. Now I know why. It's because I was so looking forward to achieving this goal, yet the goal itself turned out to be fairly easy since I had trained so diligently for six months.

What I didn't realize then, which I know now, is that the training for six months was the journey and the destination. All the lessons and insights I gained were the rewards. The race was actually the icing on the cake!

Now I realize that there is no "waiting," ever.

This is it.
All we have is today.
Today is the day to seize your dreams, and take one step towards them.
Enjoy the journey.
Live in the "I am" of where you are right now, and who you are today.

Now my language is filled with everything in my life that I am creating:

> *I expect miracles.*
> *I expect my good to come every single day.*
> *I love and accept myself exactly as I am.*
> *I am perfect.*
> *Everything is perfect and divine.*
> *I am always in the right place at the right time.*
> *Everything is happening in divine order and timing.*

Yes, I admit Pollyanna is a truthful depiction of me.

Throughout my life, I have been confronted with people who try to negate my reality, saying that I'm living in fantasy when I surround myself with happy people, and how unrealistic it is. Or they might say that things are handed to me on a silver platter. To those other people, the glass is half empty, not half full. They don't truly believe that life *can* be that easy, and sometimes the good things in life don't have to come about through blood, sweat and tears.

I have had to do much to reverse those naysayers' belief systems that were lodged in my consciousness, so I would no longer feel guilty when things were great, happy, and easy.

I now choose to believe that I can create whatever world, people, and experiences I desire—and that is my reality. I now choose to believe that life really is all about being happy, believing in miracles, having a positive outlook on everything, believing all things are possible, believing that all my dreams are possible, believing in Prince Charming, believing that I am Cinderella, the princess, *and* the queen . . .

I now believe that I am royalty in my world. I do believe that I am the star in my life and my world, and I can choose to create my world with the images that I hold in my mind, body, and spirit.

As I said before, I witness miracles every day. I've manifested a roommate on the last day of the month when my other roommate left one month earlier. I've manifested an amazingly loyal "rock-star" personal assistant who has been with me for nine years. I've manifested my ideal love relationship. I've manifested money into my bank account. I've manifested the people and resources I needed "out of the blue," at the exact time I needed them. Even at the eleventh hour, when most people would have given up, I have received miracles in the way of amazing opportunities and synchronistic encounters that have propelled my life forward.

And when people see this happen in my life, they are incredulous.

Truthfully, I wake up every morning, confessing that today is going to be a great day filled with miracles and amazing surprises. Most of the time, that is exactly what happens.

Truthfully, the world that I live in now has a lot to do with the unsexy work I do in my quiet times, in my times of solitude when no one else is watching, the conversations I have with myself in the car, in the shower, and in the moments I'm between stuff in my life.

This powerful inner work is the secret ingredient of how you, too, can create your own world of miracles! Actually, it's not a secret anymore, if you've watched or read *The Secret* by Rhonda Byrne—a wonderful film/book about manifestation, creation, and the real secret to getting anything your heart desires.

So, today, choose your words, and create your own language and your own world where anything and everything is possible. Where your fantasy becomes reality. Where miracles happen every day.

And if somebody chooses to call it fantasy, that's their trip and their perspective. Get off their train ride of cynicism, and live in eternal optimism.

I'll stay with my world of make-believe where there are happy endings! I love my castles, tiaras, and miracles!

.

exercise. *three favorite words.*

What are your three most favorite words? Why?

If they are words that powerfully reflect the reality you wish to create, use them every single day by speaking them out loud to yourself. Notice if your reality shifts to include experiences that contain these words.

Pick three more words that you would want to describe the new ideal life you are dreaming about. Start using these words in your everyday life. Notice what happens now to your reality. Does your reality shift to accommodate and include these words into your experience? Did these experiences occur now because you decided this was your new way of life? Or did you decide first, which caused those experiences to occur? (Which came first, the chicken or the egg?) It doesn't matter for now. Just know how powerful your words and language are, and how what you think and say automatically draw exactly that to you.

A friend recently gave me a metal keychain with the words "Magic, Miracles & Wonder" etched on to one side, and "Live Life Like A Fairytale" on the other. You can bet these words are at the forefront of my consciousness every single day and remind me what I truly believe in. Of course, this friend said he had to buy me the keychain, as it reminded him of me! Bring on the magic! Bring on the miracles! I am in awe and wonder every day at the magic and miracles of life!

exercise. *i choose to . . . i can!*

For one week, notice how many times you say "I should" and "I can't."

Replace these words with "I choose to" and "I can," and see what happens in your reality.

See how you feel as you are going about your day. Do you feel a pep in your step? Do you feel better using these words?

exercise. *create a new reality.*

For one week, instead of thinking that life is difficult and what a drag this or that is, stop complaining and lamenting. Do not speak negatively about yourself, anybody, or anything. Instead start saying,

> *Every day in every way, my life is getting better and better.*

follow your passion. *it's your gift to the world.*

i believe that following your passion and living in your passion equates to success in life, and that passion will always lead to happiness, joy, infinite riches, and money pouring in. If your heart is in the right place, and you desire to be of service to the world and/or God with the God-given gifts you have been blessed with, then there is no reason you will not be a success.

Everybody's passion is different and tied to their TruthLoveMeaningPurpose. Only you know what turns you on, and what makes you wake up in the morning with a pep in your step, excited to give yourself to the world. Only you know if you're excited about driving to work, being at work, and doing and being what you are doing. Only you know, if you truly go within for the true answer.

Are you following your passion? Are you following your heart? Are you living passionately?

Once again, it might look differently for different people. It might mean being the best parent you can be and raising children—as my parents did. It might be researching the cure for cancer in Germany. It might be healing people through Reiki or acupuncture. It might mean rescuing animals and volunteering at the local animal shelter. It might mean teaching special needs children and helping them to achieve the goal of writing their name. To me, passion and success are interlinked, and it is all about fulfilling your greatest potential and utilizing the gifts you have been given to use.

I have a girlfriend who knew that she wanted to be in public relations when she was in high school. Her college classes and her internships were all dictated by that choice, and she quickly leapt into her career as a public relations specialist and was a whiz kid in her early twenties, far surpassing her peers. Now she's a successful entrepreneur with her own PR firm.

It's so easy to look back and say, "I wish I coulda shoulda!" It's so easy to look back and say, "I wish I had studied harder in school and gotten straight A's . . ."

But the truth is: Your journey is perfect. You are perfect. Whatever encounters and experiences you have had until now are what got you exactly to where you are today. You would not be the person you are today without those experiences.

In my early years, my journey toward decluttering was evident even during my career choices. I tried on everything that I thought was me, like I was trying on different coats, and then I decluttered each choice after I had fully worn it for a season and decided it didn't quite fit me or resonate with me. I could only discern the right choice by fully immersing myself in each career, giving it my all, and doing whatever it took to figure it out and decide.

I tried publicity. I tried music. I tried producing. I tried television news. I tried real estate. I tried property management. I tried advertising.

After trying on several careers and figuring out which ones were not quite me, I kept asking for the truth to reveal itself. What was fun? Creating systems? Bringing order to an environment? Counseling?

I kept trying on other careers until one struck a chord in me—acting. Acting challenged me to go even deeper with my imagination and feelings. It gave me permission to go on the self-actualization journey and was like therapy for me! As I shared with you before, my journey with acting led to organizing, decluttering, and simplifying, which was also challenging for me.

Now I believe that I am still growing and evolving, and that the most divine "career" for me is still transforming before my very eyes. I still love feeling deeply, even crying, and expressing my feelings out loud. I love teaching, writing, speaking, and sharing my stories and experiences with others! I love connecting the dots and helping people to declutter on the deeper and inner planes, not just with the physical stuff. I love helping people have the relationships they desire and declutter what is holding them back from loving or receiving love. I love helping people set up systems for their businesses uniquely tailor-made for them. I love finding ways to save time and expand time, and be more productive. I still love fashion and interior design and making sure all of it is a truthful reflection of one's unique TruthLoveMeaningPurpose.

I have realized that there is an underlying theme: helping to curate somebody's life so they can live a life they absolutely love, love, love! This means helping people see that their lives are a work of art, and they are already a perfect masterpiece as they are. All they must do is let go of the clutter that prevents them from seeing this truth! I also realized that I get bored when I'm only staying on the surface, so my other passion—which I believe is my life purpose—is *going deep*. That life purpose infuses all that I do: inspiring and moving people deeply.

As I have said before, whatever is my passion in my career must also be fully played out in my life. So that's why I'm passionate about my own life, going deep within for the answers, living my TruthLoveMeaningPurpose in every corner of my life, being in "love magic" and "love synergy" with my significant other, giving love to my family, friends, and loved ones, ensuring that my time is spent productively and on purpose with the stuff of my TruthLoveMeaningPurpose, and making sure all my stuff and spaces reflects my TruthLoveMeaningPurpose!

The key to picking a career that suits you is to be truthful with yourself on this journey, to be ruthless with yourself when looking into the mirror, to confront what is truly important.

So if you are already living in your passion and love what you're doing, keep on finding things about it that bring you more joy, passion, and challenges. If you are not living in your passion, find the things about your job that are challenging and joyful, and see pushing your limits of what is possible as your challenge and joy. And if you are not feeling any energy at all with this current job, is it time for a change? If you have done everything you can to suck the life lessons out of this job, you have taken it as far as you could, and you feel stuck, not growing and evolving, then perhaps it is time to move on.

Only you know if you have given it 5000 percent. Only you know if you feel lifeless when you walk into the office. Only you know if you are mustering up as much energy as possible to get to work, pretending to make it work and to love it and be happy. Only you know if the job is draining you. Only you know if you are not giving it your all, if you don't want to admit the truth that you took the job just for the money, if this job is simply lackluster.

In the end, money is only the currency of the Universe, and all the money in the world will not bring you happiness if you are not in touch with the essences that will make you happy in a job. You can be making all the money in the world, but you can still be unhappy, unfulfilled, and unchallenged. Only you know what will truly fulfill you and bring you satisfaction and joy. It's unique and different for each person.

That is why, even with jobs and career choices, you must honor your TruthLoveMeaningPurpose.

You know.

.

exercise. *one day in the life of you.*

Are you in a job that is fulfilling? Are you in a job where you leap out of bed, excited to start the new day? Do you have a pep in your step as you leave your front door to go to work?

If you answered yes, that's terrific! You have found your passion, you're playing every single day, and your passion and joy have paved a clear pathway for infinite riches to flow in!

If you answered no, that's okay. Perhaps you already knew this. Perhaps you were not willing to confront the truth until now.

Start journaling about what you would really love to be doing that would sing to your heart. Start journaling about what you want your life to look and feel like.

Write at the top of your page: One Day in the Life of [your name]. Now, write down your ideal day, starting from the time you wake up in the morning to the time you go to sleep at night. Getting in touch with your vision is important, because it is only when you get clear about what you truly want that you can start taking action on those things that don't bring you joy, and/or that you don't truly want in your life. When you become aware of what your joy is—your TruthLoveMeaningPurpose—then you can start taking action regarding what is not.

The point is to exercise your "dream muscles," to activate the dreams and goals that have been hiding behind the clutter of fears and "I can't!" Let's declutter your heart and mind, and get to the truth of what you were truly born to be and do on this earth in this lifetime.

exercise. *three action steps to manifest your dreams.*

Now that you know more about your dream, write down at least three concrete action steps you can take in the next week that signal to yourself that you are moving forward with your new knowledge of this dream, which has been brought forth into the light. These action steps can be calling a friend to share your dream, doing Internet research, or even reading a book on your passion. Whatever you pick is perfect. Remember, you are already perfect as you are. We just need to get the clutter out of the way to see your full beauty and magnificence.

tolerance for yourself and others.
compassion and gratitude is the way.

Wouldn't you rather walk into a space where the air and stuff we breathe is forgiving, allowing, hopeful, and full of grace and compassion? Where the air space is clear?

Whether a space is clean or polluted has to do with the stuff we bring into that space. Wherever you are, you are responsible for the energy you bring to that space with the thoughts you are thinking, feelings you are feeling, and stuff you are carrying.

Remember: No one is polluting your space but you! If you truly believe that somebody else is causing pollution in your space, you have a choice to leave the space. Or express the truth of your heart and mind to that person, place, or thing. You can do something about it. You have a choice. Take responsibility for your stuff, and have compassion for other people's stuff.

I myself prefer being in a space that is clear: clear with my intentions and desires, and clear with gratitude and love. Even public spaces such as a café can be filled with positive mojo and clear intentions. Every single person is there to enjoy the space, whether they're visiting with their kids and enjoying a pastry, writing their book, and/or meeting a client. Every employee is clear about their intention of serving the customer and making the café the best place to visit.

We pollute our spaces with our anger, resentment, unforgiveness, hatred, and judgment. Have you ever felt somebody's energy being thrust your way with a look? It's almost as if they are broadcasting how they feel or what they think without saying a word. A frown can broadcast disgust, judgment, anger. However, a smile can broadcast acceptance, nonjudgment, tolerance.

Just imagine the stuff talking: "Don't be this way! Don't think this way! What are you saying? What you are thinking? What are you wearing?" Do you think all this judgment is the right environment to foster growth, new ideas, creativity, and innovation?

What if your stuff smiled at you and gave you a huge hug every time you walked into the room? What if your stuff lit up just at the sight of seeing you? Stop taking it out on your stuff. Have grace and compassion towards you and your stuff.

So let's go back to your stuff.
All you have to be concerned with is your stuff.
Your stuff.
Not anyone else's stuff.

If you have your stuff in order, and you are clear about your stuff, and you don't allow your stuff to get in your way, then you can help another with their stuff—but *only* with tolerance, compassion, and nonjudgment.

Don't shift the attention from you to someone else.

Many people choose to focus on others' stuff, because they don't want to deal with their own stuff. They have solutions for others' stuff, but they can't or won't face their own stuff.

It's so easy to judge other's stuff, and be self-righteous and justified about our own stuff, but if you have not cleared all *your* pathways, don't point the finger at someone else to clear up their stuff.

If you do the work of clearing your stuff, I guarantee that you will have less judgment and more tolerance of others' differences, more compassion for their journeys with their stuff.

Most importantly, you will have grace and compassion for yourself, and be less judging of yourself and your stuff. You will accept yourself and all of your brilliance. You will love what you judge to be the good, the bad, and the ugly. You will love all of yourself. You will love all your stuff.

And you will be grateful for all your stuff.

And guess what? The vortex of energy opens up for you to get even more of the stuff your heart desires.

Receive.

When we do, there will be a greater and deeper understanding of our differences. We will want to honor our own stuff and take care of our own stuff. We will love to hear about others' stuff, which is uniquely different from our own stuff.

Set yourself free. Stop judging yourself and others. Stop thinking that the "hot spot" is where everybody else is. You are the "hot spot," and where it is happening. You are happening.

Fall in love with your stuff, your life, and journey.

•

exercise. *let go of blaming others about your stuff.*

Is there somebody you blame for your mess and clutter? Who and what is it? Write about it, and keep on writing. Hash it out. Get it all out, without holding back.

Now shift gears. Believe you are a powerful creator. Stop playing the victim. You created the mess/person/issue to teach you something. Why? Why did you create this mess? To protect yourself? To shield yourself? Write about this, and keep digging until you get to the truth.

Forgive yourself. Forgive others. Forgive the stuff. Write about this, and the feelings that arise.

Now, is there an action step you can take in your own life that is connected to this issue? Is there a space in your own life you can clear up or clean up that is the source of your frustration in another space or another's life? Write about this, and how it is connected to your desire to clear up and clean up something in your own life. Write about how taking action in your life will inspire others to clear up and clean up their stuff.

After taking action on your stuff, write about that issue again. Does it seem to have the same "edge" or "hardness" it did prior to your taking action in your own life?

exercise. *let go of judgments about others' stuff.*

Write about your judgments, criticisms, and feelings about others and their stuff. What is it centered on? Write on this issue.

Now look within, and write about how these feelings are somehow connected to you and your life. Write about how you can take action in your own life to release the criticisms and judgments in others' lives.

Vow to stop spending needless energy gossiping, criticizing, writing, thinking, speaking, or reading about judgments on others and their stuff.

Notice whether this exercise shifts something within that makes you feel more compassion for others' journeys and others' stuff. Notice whether you become less combative, defensive, or critical. Notice whether your heart softens, and whether you start tolerating differences.

exercise. *practice nonjudgment and tolerance.*

For one week, if something unexpected happens to you, refrain from making any judgments and practice more tolerance and compassion. For instance, if your favorite barista is in a bad mood, shower that person with love. If the homeless man asks you for money at the freeway exit (again), this time, smile and give him your lunch. If your husband forgets to put the lid on that jar (again), forgive him. If your wife forgets her keys (again), forgive her. If your child forgets to bring his homework to school (again), let it go without saying a thing.

Sometimes not saying anything and silently showering that person with love is more powerful than saying something out loud, because that person can actually feel that outpouring of love or compassion.

MOVE FORWARD.
THE BEST JOURNEY.

the best journey is here and now. *be here now.*

think about how excited you get when you are going away. You take out your suitcase and your toiletries bags. You buy Frommer's guides and research on the Internet the best places to eat, see, or stay. You get this thrilling feeling inside, and you can't wait to go on this trip. You are bubbling over inside with excitement so that you can't contain yourself. Even when you are at work, it's as though you have this secret inside of you that makes you feel giddy! You fantasize about relaxing on the white sand beaches. You fantasize about the wine you'll be sipping and the buzzed feeling you'll get. You fantasize about the people you'll meet when you go dancing. You fantasize about the beautiful coral reefs and exotic fish you'll see when you scuba dive. Thinking about hiking in the lush rainy forest brings you a sense of peace. Or you might be anxious, thinking about what you must complete before leaving on this trip.

The journey of decluttering, simplifying, organizing, and curating your stuff is a lot like traveling. In fact, if you shift your perspective, it can be the best trip you will ever take, because you'll see beautiful sights along the way you can now appreciate. There's the fine china you got for your wedding, which you're not using because you think it's too nice to use, and that you have to save it for special company. Aren't you special? Isn't every day a special occasion? Bring this souvenir home right now and start using it!

You might see interesting historical landmarks, reminding you of the past, and honoring that past and the lessons learned. They give you pause to reflect, give thanks, and let go.

I must let go of that special lingerie from that last extremely dysfunctional relationship that caused me so much pain. Those workout clothes remind me of when I used to wake up at

4 a.m. to run, and I was starting to get into shape—I don't think I want to muster up the energy to do that again. Bye!

I remember when I moved in to this house and bought that special vase to go on the dining table, and I loved it so much. My tastes have changed so drastically in two years, and I can now let go of it. That vase reminds me of an empty container that needed to get filled up with my newfound identity after my divorce, and now that I am filled to the brim with happiness, I don't need that empty vase to remind me where I used to be.

I asked my mother to custom-make a pink comforter for me that would go perfectly against my racer hot pink wall, and this combined energy brought me back to my sensuality, sexuality, and femininity. The comforter reminds me of the countless hours we spent searching for just the right shade of light pink Dupioni silk. What will she think when I let it go? I am soooo grateful for all the time, love, and energy she spent helping me get grounded and decorating my home after my divorce.

So the journey of going through your stuff can be the best trip you will ever take in your lifetime. Your stuff can be landmarks for your journey, historical points to remember, and beautiful sights and views that inform your current perspective about life and the journey itself. Chronicle your journey, noting the different people you meet along the way—these people being all the parts of yourself that have lived with the stuff you have accumulated over your lifetime. Appreciate each part of you, in each chapter of your life, as unique, and have compassion for the choices you made in those chapters. Appreciate the lessons and blessings in each chapter. Do you want to go on that trip again—physically or mentally? If not, just remember the beautiful sights along the way and the beautiful lessons that you learned, and thank the people on your path who were messengers in the playground of your life.

So the choices you have with this journey span the universe. How do you choose to go on this journey of life with your stuff? Joyfully? Seeing every single sight, souvenir, and person as markers, messengers, and miracles on your journey? Or lamenting? What good does lamenting do for you? It keeps you stuck in your present situation, not moving forward, and living in the past. Do you keep going on that journey, over and over? Well, no wonder you keep recreating the same "trip" over and over again, with the same sights, players, and pain.

This time, create another trip—one where you are joyful to be on the journey. Take this trip and make it the best trip ever—one of gratitude, thanking every single scar, memory, person, and souvenir acquired.

.

exercise. *museum for your past? or sanctuary for your present?*

Is your space crowded with stuff from the past? Are you living in a museum glorifying your past? Do you want to make it a sanctuary to the authentic you of today? Then pick three items that represent that distant past and let go of this "baggage" from the past.. Thank these items for being in your life and loving you. Thank these items for teaching you important lessons. Then let go. Feel your feelings. Write about the feelings. Write about how difficult or easy it was to let go of these items. Notice what comes up.

Let the experience sit with you and become a part of the newly emerging ideal you, who is letting go of the past with love, and continue picking three more items and letting them go until you feel a shift in your space. Once the space feels differently to you, take a break and enjoy the energy of the new space with the old stuff gone. Take a tour of your space, and ask yourself, what story is your stuff telling now?

exercise. *best sightseeing tour ever.*

Pretend that you have paid a lot of money for the best sightseeing tour of your life. Close your eyes and use all of your senses to visualize yourself on this tour. Get excited about all the new sights, the new smells, and the new foods you will partake in.

Now imagine you are a tourist visiting the Land of [your name] in your world and your Universe. What do you see and experience? Write about this "tour."

What would you ideally love to see, experience, taste, smell, and feel? Write about it.

This exercise will get you back in touch with your highest vision of your ideal life.

live your life with no regrets. *today is the only day.*

What would you do if you were given only seven days to live?
When I asked my clients this question, they responded with: "I'd go to India on a spiritual adventure." "I'd climb Mount Everest." "I would tell everyone in my life that I love them." "I would thank everybody in my life who has helped me to become the person I am today." "I would not work and spend all my time with my family." "I'd spend all day in bed making love to my girlfriend and kissing every part of her body." "I'd play with the dolphins and go to the beach every day." "I'd watch the sunset every day."

The truth is you don't have to wait until you have only seven days left to live to do these things. Do these things today, and don't wait until tomorrow.

Write down everything you can think of that you want to do, so you will have no regrets, and then start doing those things and crossing them off your list.

This is the part where I tell you to f*** the rules of life, write down those things that have been on your heart forever, and do the things you have always imagined yourself doing. When you do, you will feel a renewed appreciation of life, and you will feel like you are living your life on the edge. As someone once said, "If you are not living your life on the edge, you're taking up too much space."

The truth is that I've told myself all my life, "I never want to have any regrets." And this adage kept me from staying safe and sorry inasmuch as possible.

I told myself to say the things I needed to say, to speak my truth to those I felt I must, to do the things that came up in my consciousness—like telling my boyfriend I'd love to be married to him forever, bungee jumping from a crane, telling myself I'm going for it in all of life, and eating a jumping shrimp in my soup bowl just to experience what it was like to taste a living creature jumping in my mouth. (Sorry, shrimp—I was curious, and I'm sorry if I hurt you, but it satisfied my curiosity, and I will never eat another live shrimp. Oh right, I'm allergic to shrimp now, and I'd get hives on my body . . . that's probably karmic . . .)

Back to here and now.

Today is all you have; tomorrow may never come. The truth is that I have been a witness to clients with many regrets, who said "I wish I coulda shoulda," and it was too late. I believe that these experiences and realizations were brought to me to strengthen my conviction and passion for doing things today, and not putting off anything until tomorrow.

I witnessed a client saying she wanted to visit an old friend, and then, while I was there, we happened to watch a television news show that reported her death. She had been planning to visit her in a few months in the spring, when things were just right in her life. I witnessed a client reading an old letter from a friend, and it triggered something inside to contact that old friend—but not knowing what to say, she waited, and when she finally wrote a letter to the friend, her sister called to let her know that the friend had passed away one month ago.

What if, in both of these instances, my clients had acted on their intuition and visited or called, and said the things they had been meaning to say? What if they said what they needed to say: "I love you still. I miss you. I wish we were still together. I'm so grateful for the time we had together."

You would have thought that I definitely would have gotten this message loud and clear, but two recent events highlight the point that I'm trying to make.

One of my best friends, Pam, gave me a red LIVE YOUR PASSION shirt for Christmas. I e-mailed her to thank her for the shirt, but I hadn't talked to her for months, playing phone tag. I kept on thinking, *I want to write a letter telling her how grateful I still am for our friendship, and although we have not connected, I am here for you and think of you often.* I finally decided to wear the red shirt on Tuesday, and eerily, that following day, I received a phone call from a mutual friend of ours letting me know that Pam had passed away the day before on that Tuesday. The call from the Universe asking me to think of her and wear the shirt was the message for me to take action, but strangely enough, I didn't. They later told me she was in a coma since the prior Friday, so I wouldn't have been able to speak to her. But had I called her even a month before that, just to connect with her—who knows? The "what ifs" are haunting; the "I wish I coulda shouldas" are heartbreaking.

This past April, I thought, I haven't probably given thanks to my former in-laws and their family for all the times we shared, all the gifts I received, and just for their love during my marriage. I had respected my ex-husband's desire not to communicate with them while we were separated, and then finally divorced, so it was as if there was just this cut off of communications—no good-bye, and no closing ceremony.

I believe that closure can happen and be complete when there is gratitude in our hearts for the lessons learned, the gifts received, and the love we had been given.

So, I thought, it has been nearly three and a half years, and I will finally write the thank-you letters to each family member, and especially to his parents, on Easter. Easter was a special holiday for them, and we always celebrated, getting all dressed up with a bang, with a scrumptious get-together brunch at a posh hotel. So I thought this would be the perfect time to say, "I remember our good times and thank you for everything!"

The week before Easter, I received a call from my brother, telling me my ex-father-in-law had passed away in his sleep. Wow! I was shocked! I couldn't believe that I had not taken the time to write the thank you before, and he passed away without knowing how much he had meant to me and how grateful I was for all he had done for me! Of course, I only went to the wake, as to not upset the balance with my ex-husband's new woman in his life, and not coincidentally, I saw every single one of his family members. We laughed, we cried, we mourned together—and I finally ended up writing those letters the following week, addressed to "Dear Dad & Mom," which I happily called them. For some reason, I knew that his dad was probably reading the letter from Heaven, but I used it as a wake-up call to not put stuff off until tomorrow that I could do today.

My message thereafter to every client I visited was to take care of your unfinished business today! Don't wait until tomorrow. It could be your last day. It could be somebody else's last day. It doesn't matter. What matters is that if you're thinking about doing it today, it's for a reason—so you can deal with it.

Otherwise, why would you think this thought all of a sudden? Why would you think of this person all of a sudden? Why would you be reminded of this memory?

Your work is to figure out why, suddenly, you are reading a letter from an old friend, or why you are thinking of somebody from your past, or why you have touched something that triggers you into thinking about someone or something.

Don't just shove the feeling under a rug. Don't push the task aside. Don't try to erase that memory from your mind. Feel your heart. If there is even an inkling of a thought or feeling to call, do it now. If you don't know why you're supposed to take action, do it anyway. If it keeps haunting you, do it today. If you don't know what to say, that's okay. Just say, "I called because I was just thinking of you."

So, you see, all you have is today. The time you use to deal with your stuff will trigger other stuff for you to deal with. That's why this stuff goes deep. The stuff reminds you of how you were betrayed, and reminds you to forgive. The stuff reminds you of the pain of that old relationship and reminds you to let go of the pain and create space for joy. The stuff reminds you of a longing for good times, and reminds you to honor those times and trust that the good times will come once again. The stuff reminds you of how lucky you are and how grateful you are for that person, encounter, and experience.

Yes, indeed, the greatest tragedy is dying without living. Are you living life to its fullest today? Are you fulfilling your greatest potential today? Are you utilizing your most precious commodity, time, and using each of those 86,400 seconds? Are you living your legacy today?

You don't need a lifetime to realize that life is for living!

When people are at the end, they're trying to cram everything in the short time they have left. Suddenly they realize how precious time is and how they want to spend it. Death is nothing to fear if we remember that each moment is precious, each moment has a life of its own, each moment is full of infinite possibilities, and each moment can be full of joy and light and happiness—if we choose to decide it is.

The truth is you don't have to wait until the last seven days of your life to do those things you have always wanted to do or kept putting off.

Do it today.

■

exercise. *bucket list.*

Write down every single thing you want to do in this lifetime. This could be your bucket list!

Pick one thing you want to do from this list, and decide to do it this year.

Put it into your schedule.

Don't worry about the other stuff.

Doing this one thing will activate in you the desire to get the other things done.

The point of this exercise is to get you off your butt (and "buts") to lead the life you want, actively doing what you can do today, and not worrying about everything else.

exercise. *take action on just one call or letter.*

Right now, call or write a letter to somebody you have been thinking of, and express whatever you need to express right now.

After taking this action, continue adding to your master list every single person you want to call and write.

The point of this exercise is to take action on one thing only. After that one, you'll be triggered to act on the others. Think about a river being dammed up with one giant log, where removing that one log creates a flow of water that runs through free and clear. Today, you are removing that one giant log by taking just one action you have been meaning to do for so long but have been putting off.

happiness. *not with our stuff, but in our hearts.*

n o matter what age you are, no matter where you are in the world, no matter what you do for a living, no matter what your gender, race, or religion is, we all strive for the same common denominator.

Happiness.

I read in a newspaper article that the number-one thing parents want for their kids is happiness. The Dalai Lama wrote a book called *The Art of Happiness*. There's another bestselling book called *The Happiness Project*. Tony Hsieh, founder of Zappos.com, wrote *Delivering Happiness*.

Is happiness that elusive? Why is happiness so important? How do you know if you are happy? What makes you happy?

Being able to discern the feeling of happiness within is of the utmost importance. If you don't know what makes you happy, and you are not even connected to your insides that know when you are happy, won't you keep chasing that "happiness" without even knowing what you are seeking? You might think that success at work will make you happy. You get promoted, and it does make you happy for a while, but then you realize that this wasn't really it, and you start striving for more: another promotion, an increase in salary. You might think that making more money will make you happy, but then you start making more money, and you buy stuff, experiences, and a lifestyle with the money, but it isn't quite what you had imagined.

I remember when in my twenties, after graduating from college, I had just begun searching for what brought me true bliss. What was my passion? In pursuit of my happiness and passion, I bounced from job to job, and then I ended up in a position where I was making double what I was making before, but that didn't matter. Now I felt my skills were not being utilized to their maximum capacity. I didn't feel appreciated as a peer or colleague for my business savvy or ambition in a company with a male chauvinistic viewpoint. Then, when a wonderful man saw my skills and started mentoring me, I still wasn't satisfied with having a beautiful office in a high-rise, overseeing downtown Los Angeles, lunching weekly at a private posh club, taking classes, making positive progression with my career, and learning every day. I was not learning and growing in my passion, so that did not bring me happiness.

Success at work? Being in love? Family? Friends? Career and work? A beautiful home? Vacations? Spiritual enlightenment? A new outfit?

What I've found, though, is that some people have it all turned around. They think that by having stuff, they will be happier and do the stuff they love in life. They think that by acquiring more stuff, they will somehow feel happy inside.

Shopping can be an addiction, where you look for stuff outside of you to make you happy. You think that the new stuff you buy will make you feel brand new. But it only works for a moment, because that brand-new feeling will need to be replaced with something new the minute you wear it; it quickly becomes old. Then you need another fix of something new on the outside to trigger the feeling inside of you that this is a brand new day.

Why not shift your perspective about your stuff, and instead start wearing new thoughts of happiness and thinking new thoughts about what makes you happy? How about appreciating the air we breathe and seeing that as a miracle, and letting that put a smile on your face? How about looking at the car you drive in a different light and being grateful that it gets you from point a to point b, remembering that without it, you would not be able to enjoy the sights along the way? How about appreciating the fact that you have a roof over your head, knowing that some people are homeless, and letting that make you happy? How about being grateful that you have a job, when many are unemployed? And, if you are homeless, how about having hope that one day you will have a roof over your head, letting that hope keep you alive and happy? How about being happy that you are searching for the next job, thinking about the new opportunities before you?

So, which came first, the chicken or the egg?

Does the person who has the stuff get more stuff and become happy? Or did that person just radiate a happy attitude, feel good inside, and attract the stuff that made him or her happy?

Instead of wishing you could have more stuff and better stuff, today choose to appreciate the stuff you do have, and the happiness will come from your heart that appreciates what is working and what you do have!

If the stuff you have does not make you happy, let go of it. Don't complain and say you wish you had more money to replace the unhappy stuff. The stuff you are unhappy with is permeating your space and clouding your life. It is bringing a giant rain cloud into the space you inhabit. Your unhappiness with the stuff is polluting the air and polluting the space itself. You cannot even see the happy stuff amidst the stuff that makes you unhappy, because all you see are the unhappy faces of your stuff frowning at you.

Drinking matcha green tea out of the mug made by my nieces, inscribed with the words TruthLoveMeaningPurpose, makes me happy. Calling my mother, and knowing she is happy and healthy, makes me happy. Writing a letter to my brothers telling them how much I care makes me happy. The beautiful orchid in the gorgeous white container given to me by my best friend makes me happy. Sipping the Bulletproof coffee every morning made by my significant other makes me happy. Listening to the song "Happy" by Pharrell Williams makes me happy. Wearing the custom-made infinity scarf made by my sister-in-law makes me happy. Connecting with my cousin in New York makes me happy. Masterminding with my best friend and knowing all her heart's desires are coming true makes me happy. Teaching my clients new ways of being and doing that transforms their lives makes me happy. Watching inspiring movies that make me cry makes me happy. Meditating makes me happy. Writing makes me happy. Learning something new makes me happy. Sharing my deepest truths and stories with you makes me happy.

Is this making sense to you?

Use your feelings as a powerful key to lead you to your next steps. Your effusive joy and unbridled energy oozing from your being within are all you need to know for your next best divine steps. If you realize that you are addicted to the high of acquiring new stuff and going shopping, put yourself on a fast, and see what happens when you say "no" to shopping and getting new stuff. Start shopping in your own home. Start fully using the stuff you have. If you find yourself walking by your stuff and you feel no energy every single time, you must let it go. Apply this approach to every single item in your space, and then see how you feel. See if you feel the inclination to go shopping again. Even if you were left with only four items in your space that made you wildly happy, these four items will be vibrating at such a high energy level that you won't be able to keep from smiling. Be happy with the here and now. If you can't be happy with it, let it go, so someone else can be happy with it. You have a choice.

∎

exercise. *get in touch with what makes you truly happy.*

Think about something in your life that you thought would make you happy, but the happiness did not truly last. Write about why you were so excited to have this thing or experience, or attain this goal. Write about how happy you were thinking about it. Now write about the attainment of this goal or item, and write about how it felt when you first got it and how you felt later. What did you learn about happiness and how fleeting it could be? Write your feelings about it. What is the deeper message to you about happiness that was triggered by doing this exercise?

exercise. *happy list.*

Write "My Happy List" at the top of a new page. Start listing everything that makes you happy and brings a smile to your face. Keep writing until you can't think of anything else. Include anything and everything, including people, stuff, experiences, sensations, music, books, and travel.

Now read over your list and put a check next to those items that you don't nurture or cultivate regularly, or have neglected or forgotten about.

Now pick one item to include in your task list for today whether it's taking action on it, thinking about it, thanking this item for being in your life, or just remembering in your heart what makes you happy.

exercise. *happiness is . . .*

Write "Happiness is . . ." at the top of a new page. Write your definition of happiness. Then keep listing all the things happiness means to you.

Look over your list and circle the top three definitions.

exercise. *lessons regarding happiness.*

Write "What I Learned about Happiness" at the top of a new page.

What did you learn from doing these two exercises? Are there any definitions that surprised you?

Is your happiness based on stuff you have, experiences, or people?

Is there an action step you can take to signal to yourself that you are taking new actions based on these new realizations about what makes you happy?

wake up. *world peace is within you.*

are you acutely aware of your feelings and what triggers the feelings you have within yourself? Day to day, moment to moment, are you an open and clear vessel for new stuff to come into your life?

How do you feel when you wake up in the morning? Do you wake up, spring out of bed, and rejoice, shouting, "Good morning, world! I'm sooooo excited to start the day! I can't wait for what will happen today! I can't wait for the miracles!"

Or do you think, "I dread going to work. I dread being here. Just another day—same ol,' same ol'."

What is your permanent default energy level/attitude/spirit?

Do you take charge from the moment you wake up, or do you let your moods be dictated by your circumstances?

As a child growing up, how did you wake up?

The night before the first day of school of whatever grade I was starting, I would be so excited that I wouldn't be able go to sleep. I would be excited to wear my new outfit, but also excited about the newness of a new class, new books to read, new stuff to learn, and new people to meet.

I still feel that way about every single day. I wake up and confess to myself an affirmation from one of my favorite authors, Florence Scovel Shinn: "My seemingly impossible good is now coming to pass. The unexpected now happens!" And this seems to set off a giant vibration into the Universe, where it does seem that my life is now filled with these amazing miracles coming to pass, every single day!

Today make the decision that you are now going to think differently and act differently, starting with the way you wake up in the morning. Get up on the "right" side of the bed—your side! Tune into your radio station. What kind of music do you want to be playing all day in your head and life? What words are you saying out loud to yourself, or whispering to yourself in quiet moments, that make you feel the way you feel? Turn on the best television station for your life. What kind of images do you want to fill up your head and heart with?

What day do you want to create today?

Stop being a victim of how you grew up.
Stop being a victim of your circumstances, where you live, and who you live with.

What life do you want to create and live?

Start living that life now.

Start making choices with the words you speak to yourself.

Are your moods and feelings dictated by the people around you?

Do you get easily affected by other's energies?

Decide that no matter what is happening around you, you will choose to remain grounded in your energy and life-force field, and you will continue to honor your TruthLoveMeaningPurpose in every space and every moment.

Imagine you are on a train ride, and you have decided that you want to be on the Miracle Ride of your life. If you have accidentally let others jump on your train, then it is no longer the Miracle Ride anymore. Get off that train and catch another. Jump off now! Sometimes we go on others' rides and allow their thoughts and feelings to interfere with our own ride. Switch trains immediately when this happens, realizing it is not the train ride you purchased for the day. Sometimes it is fun to go on another's ride to feel and see their perspective, but if we do it long enough, we get confused, and that other's ride becomes intertwined with our ride, so that we don't know whether we're coming or going, or even if we're on the ride anymore.

Once I decided to monitor my moods and feelings for a week. Every moment, from the moment I woke up each day, I checked in with how I was feeling, to be sure nothing was keeping me from moving forward, free and clear. Of course, if I was in a stressful situation, my mornings began with my worry about that situation. But immediately upon awakening, I made a conscious shift inside by saying to myself, "Everything is going to be okay. I am praying for the best positive outcome," and letting the rest of worry, doubts, and fears go. What good will that fear do anyway? What part does it play in my life, other than fueling more fear and stuff I cannot control?

Over time, as I continued this practice and shared my journey with others, sometimes my sharing would trigger others to share about their own fears about marriage, divorce, and death. I would acknowledge and listen, but then politely, inside my own consciousness, let go of their fears as well. When I shared about going through my divorce, I had to let go of their difficulty with their own divorce and their confusion about their marriage. When I shared about how my father was in the hospital, I had to let go of their suffering when dealing with an ill relative and their guilt about their own father. Instead, I had to be at one with how I feel about my own life. I had to get off the train ride of other's perceptions, feelings, and judgments, and go on my own ride of trusting that everything was going to be okay.

So check in with how you are feeling moment to moment. If the feeling or energy field you are generating is not to your liking, you can immediately shift it. Decide you are now going into the gear that honors you.

When you turn on the television and there is grim news on, does that affect you? When you wake up and your partner is moody, does that affect your mood?

When you monitor your moods and attitudes, you discover what you choose to let into your mind and heart and consciousness. What made your mood change from Great to Good in two hours? The traffic on the way to work? Getting your kids off to school? A co-worker's stupid remark? Forgetting your cell phone at home?

Understanding the triggers that set you up for a certain mood or attitude is paramount if you want to stay clutter free in your heart, mind, and consciousness as you go about your day. Checking in and getting to the root cause of the source of the triggers is of the utmost importance.

Once you figure out the cause, and it involves another person, express the truth of your heart to whomever you think is causing you this grief, pain, aggravation, or disturbance within you. Try not to gossip or talk to others about it, unless you are merely processing or figuring out the best resolution of the issue. Don't commiserate or complain to another co-worker or colleague, as this kind of "kvetching" just fuels the fire for more pain, keeps you stuck in this energy field, and makes you a victim.

Expressing your feelings does not mean you are accusing the other for making you feel a certain way; it means taking full responsibility for your stuff. All you can say is, "When you say or do this, it makes me feel . . ." Remember that no one is doing anything to you. You are allowing that person, place, or thing to cause you to feel a certain way. Remember too that you chose to feel this way and have allowed this experience into your life—perhaps to serve you, teach you and help you grow. Understand that the reason these feelings have arisen is to help you let go of what is clogging up your relationship.

Whether the incident is big or small, whether you are strangers or in an intimate relationship, I believe strongly that keeping our feelings inside breeds toxicity. The toxic stuff people manifest on the outside usually results from toxicity on the inside, because they cannot tell the truth about their own feelings or how someone "makes" them feel. Holding in your feelings is toxic. Period. And you are only hurting yourself.

Oftentimes, when we express the truth out loud to somebody, this "out loud" expression is exactly what is needed to heal everybody. Perhaps we were planted in their path to bring awareness to a situation. Just like the little child in the famous fable, who cried out, "The emperor is not wearing any clothes!" sometimes it might be our job to express the truth out loud to help everybody let go of the false stuff and the bad stuff that isn't truly them at all.

Once, at the grocery store, I noticed that the cashier was carelessly throwing the Fuji apples that I had carefully selected into the bag. Her actions triggered a reaction inside of me, and I started telling myself not to say anything. But knowing that even the smallest unexpressed stuff can be toxic, I exclaimed, "Are you okay? Sorry, but I have to ask you . . . can you not bruise my apples?" Blurting out my truthful feelings aloud not only released my frustrations, but also brought her back into the moment, when she realized that she was taking out her bad day on my apples.

This also happened most recently at my gym. Every time I went to work out, I would run into this same gym member who always seemed to be in a bad mood. It felt to me that he would huff and puff wherever I was in the gym. I finally said to him, "Is there something wrong? Am I bothering you? I honestly think I'm pretty cool, and I am giving you your space to do what you need to do. But when you huff and puff when I'm getting close to you, it feels to me like you're saying and acting as if you own the gym. I don't think you realize how you're coming across to me and to others." After I expressed my feelings to him, he expressed his frustration at how he felt he had to clean up after everybody at the gym and nobody respected the space. I empathized with him, smiled, and told him I understood. After that, he seemed to be more relaxed and happier when working out perhaps because he was able to release his truth to somebody else. We even exchanged smiles in the elevator the other day, and he didn't seem as grumpy.

In the end, there may not be a simple resolution to your feelings. But the greatest place to be is knowing you are doing the best you can to remain clutter free in your mind, heart, and consciousness. When you seek to have a greater understanding of others' feelings and perspectives, you will have greater compassion and tolerance for all humanity (including yourself) and more readily accept and love everyone just as they are, which cultivates an environment of harmony, tolerance, and respect.

You are contributing to world peace by cultivating peace in your own world and within yourself.

•

exercise. *your default energy level.*

For one week, keep a journal next to your bed, and write about the feelings you have when you wake up. How do you feel immediately when you awake? Great? Good? Okay? Get in touch with your "waking state" or "default state," absent of any stimuli, objects, stuff, or people.

If your default state is a feeling of elation every morning, then continue cultivating the activities and stuff that contribute to that upward feeling, and only fill up your life, space, mind, and heart with the stuff that makes you feel more and more elated.

If you notice that you are feeling down when you wake up in the morning, journal about your feelings each morning, and see what is unearthed. Ask your consciousness to reveal what is causing the "grumpiness" or "lack of energy" or "downward energy." Write what comes up.

exercise. *get in touch with energy shifts. create peace in your world.*

Now, go about your day and notice when your energy shifts to a different mode, whether it's with the space you are in, the stuff you are confronted with, or the people you encounter.

Write about every change that occurs within your being.

Notice your energy set point when you wake up, and change it if you are not happy with it. Go to sleep earlier if you are feeling tired. Turn off the television and feed yourself powerfully positive images before going to sleep. Declutter your brain of tasks before you go to sleep. Declutter yourself of worries, and write down your problems and ask for them to be resolved in your sleep travels.

Become acutely aware of what activates the shifts in your being and realize how often we let other's stuff get in our way of feeling and living a certain way. When do you allow yourself to be brought down by a seemingly negative encounter or comment? When do you allow yourself to feel uplifted and energized by another being?

Write about how powerfully affected you are by everything in your experience and your space, and vow to maintain your peace wherever you go, feeling peace within yourself and creating your own world of "peace" wherever you are, whomever you're with, or whatever you're surrounded with.

Cultivating this "world peace within" is the most important thing you can do for the planet and to advance world peace!

no more excuses. *enjoy the journey.*

here are no more excuses.

Only feelings. Only thoughts.

I know what I'm to do on this earth.
There's no more clutter in my way, deterring me from seeing the clear pathways to my
heart and soul.
It's so simple.
Live. Feel. Love.
Get out of my own way.
I feel so much.
My heart aches for things that I desire.
My heart knows that it's only a matter of time before it comes flowing to me.

Don't be scared.
You can handle it.
You can.
Don't worry.
Just let the feelings be wherever they are.
Don't judge.
Don't analyze.
Celebrate your existence.

You have no more excuses when you have no clutter standing in your way. No more clutter in your heart from feeling so much and not expressing it. No more clutter in your mind preventing you from moving forward.

The greatest place to be is here and now, clutter free. Your future is glorious. No more excuses. Pass Go now! You have everything it takes to move forward now! Don't stop now. Don't make up more excuses. Don't create more clutter. Don't create drama. Stop now and appreciate everything you have. Appreciate your appreciation of the present. Appreciate the dreams you know you will achieve.

Enjoy you. Enjoy your life.

Enjoy this journey.

.

exercise. *declutter the excuses.*

Write down all the excuses you have been using to prevent yourself from moving forward, from a cluttered house, to unhappiness in your job situation, to unfulfillment in your present relationship, to lack of finances. Write about how you have blamed these things for not living the life you want.

Vow now not to make up any more excuses. Give up complaining, blaming, and being a victim.

Start telling a new story that you will create in your life.

Start believing this time things will change, because you are doing things differently and thinking differently about your stuff.

exercise. *replace your excuse with taking one action step today.*

What excuses do you make when it comes to moving forward?

If your excuse is time, spend fifteen minutes every day to take action to move forward.

If your excuse is talent and skills, read a book and learn that skill now.

If your excuse is space, clear that space now.

If your excuse is other people, proceed without them, and/or find new people.

If your excuse is health, take care of your health now.

No more excuses about moving forward. You are fully equipped with all the tools you need to move yourself forward in the most positive way.

exercise. *enjoy today, no matter what happens.*

Vow today to not make up any excuses for why you are not having a great day.

Vow to have the best day ever–no matter what happens.

Journal about your best day ever and why it was–even though "stuff" happened.

Journal about how moving forward in this new way by seeing the seeming miracles in everything that happens is perhaps making you a powerful magnet for other 'miracles.'

moving forward. *a new world.*

You can continue living life as you have been, and not change a thing. You can read this entire book and not take a single action. That's okay. Perhaps something will trigger you to take action at a later date.

My hope, however, is that if you've come this far and have taken the time to read this book all the way through, that you are already beginning to think differently about your stuff and your life. My hope is that your relationship with your stuff has shifted significantly, and you have been radically altered inside forever. If you feel that something needs to change, that there must be a better way, just try going through your stuff. You have nothing to lose. If you are feeling overwhelmed, out of control, unhappy, or dead inside, try going through your stuff, and only keeping stuff that makes you feel alive!

The process outlined in this book is for anyone who wants to wake up to a whole new world. You can change the way you live and exist in this world. You can change the way you see yourself and your stuff. You can create a life where you love your spaces, the people in your life, and the stuff in your spaces. Change your stuff, and everything around you will change.

Use this process any time you feel stuck. Use it as a vehicle and a self-therapy tool to move, grow, change, learn about yourself, change your thoughts, shift your perspective, change your life, achieve your goals, and make your dreams come true!

Shift your stuff and spaces to accelerate where you are going here and now. You will be amazed at the difference even the slightest movement can make!

.

exercise. *move forward with just one page, one step, one moment at a time.*

Flip through this book innocently, without looking at the pages, while asking yourself, "What's the next best thing I can do to move forward?" Then stop flipping, and see what page you land on. I guarantee that there are no accidents, and you will land exactly on the page you are "supposed to read" to move you forward in the best way possible for your unique journey.

CONCLUSION.

the journey continues...

You don't need all this stuff.
You have everything you need within yourself.
Don't let the stuff make you feel complete or whole, or define you.
You are enough and all that you were born to be without your stuff.
The stuff should just be an extension of you.
This stuff is connected to you, your dreams, your potential.
Piece together the puzzle of your life and stuff.
Devise a simple system for your stuff.
Let go, once and for all, of the stuff that doesn't belong.
Be at peace with your stuff, and
Create space for miracles to flow in, and
You will soar in life!
Go on the ride of your life with your stuff!
Look at your stuff in a whole new light.
Discover what lies beneath your stuff, and
Get to the truth of who you are so
You can lead an authentic life.

Congratulations on going on the journey with me, courageously welcoming change, and immersing yourself in a different perspective. Thank you for sharing this space and time with me.

I hope you have radically transformed for the highest good, that you are feeling closer and closer to your true self, that you are appreciating more and more of your true self, that you are feeling more and more of your heart, and that you are inspired more than ever to lead a simpler, authentic life that honors the truth of you. I hope that TruthLoveMeaningPurpose has resonated deeply within your consciousness, transformed you on a deep level, and inspired and moved you deeply, so you can move forward in your life with faith, hope, insight, wisdom, and most importantly, with your own TruthLoveMeaningPurpose as your guide.

My heart's desire is that you and every single person on this planet—no matter where you are, regardless of age, gender, sex, or sexual preference—can say out loud and proudly confess, "I love my life!"

My heart's desire is also that every person on this planet can make this confession without fear of judgment, condemnation, or imprisonment, and know that a life honoring each person's TruthLoveMeaningPurpose will lead to world peace, compassion, forgiveness, and tolerance. The only world to strive for is a world where we coexist side by side with our hopes, dreams, passions, and loves being fulfilled. If every person experienced peace of heart and peace of mind, there would be no desire to encroach on somebody else's territory, to steal from somebody else, to envy somebody else's life or stuff, or to be jealous of somebody else, because there would be no comparison. We would truly believe on a deep level that we were already living our best lives, authentically honoring our own TruthLoveMeaningPurpose. We would no longer compare ourselves to our friends, neighbors, and celebrities, because we would feel so grounded and happy with our own lives we were creating and living that moment. Our hearts would be cracked wide open, not fearing anything or anyone. We would trust that we will be okay, and that we will always have the tools, resources, and stuff to deal with anything that comes up. That we will always have the love we need in our lives to live fully. That we already have everything we need or will ever need within the beautiful selves we were born into.

Our stuff would then become a gift to ourselves, an outward extension of our inner beauty and truth. The stuff contains the soul of who we are. The stuff extends beyond ourselves, and radiates in all directions. And all the stuff that resonates with the truth of who we are inside will create an explosive vortex of energy that will perpetually move us forward.

Let go of whatever is no longer serving you and create space now for miracles!
Let Go!
Now!

So the journey continues.

I love where I am.
I love my stuff.
I can sleep at night, knowing I have taken care of my stuff.

thank you.

First, to all my fabulous and brave clients: thank you for sharing your journeys with me. Thank you for letting me into your homes, offices, and minds and sharing the truth of what's going on with your stuff so we could make it better, and for not running away from my constant questioning, "What is that?" Thank you for gifting me with a "playground" where I can share my gifts with you!

Matthew, thank you for going on the ride with me, with your heart cracked wide open, leaving all your stuff and comfort zone behind. Thank you for inspiring me to keep expressing my heart, and for being inspired enough by my life's work to encourage me to share it all with the world.

Steven, thank you for always believing in my greatness as my "big brother," and for investing countless hours in negotiating, and wheeling and dealing all my stuff for me! Thank you for inspiring me by being a rock star in your own life, and always achieving all the goals you set for yourself!

John, thank you for loving me and supporting me unconditionally for twenty years, believing that I could do whatever I wanted because of the stuff I was made of, and for gifting me with the space for me to "grow up" and find out what I really wanted to be and do.

Emma, thank you so much for being the best mastermind partner and soul sister. You were not only the first to read the book, but you read it over and over throughout its many incarnations. Thank you for encouraging me to be brave on my journey and share my gifts with the world, even as you bravely faced your own seemingly insurmountable obstacles.

Ken, thank you for inspiring me to never stay in boredom by fearlessly changing jobs if they did not thrill you—all while creating a great life for you, Sadako, Staci, and Lisa.

Sandy Meisner, thank you for teaching me that "acting is living truthfully under imaginary circumstances," which led me to live more truthfully in my real life.

Pam, thank you for playing with me, noticing my bravery when expressing my truth, and for believing in me on the red carpet. Christine, thank you for always asking about my book and never giving up on me and my dream of becoming a published author. Hiromi, thank you for telling me my true self is enough, wonderful, and unique. Alexia, thank you for spreading the word regarding my teachings, believing that God is working through me in a huge way to heal people's lives. Karsha, thank you for being the best cheerleader/PR consultant all these years! Debra, thank you for getting what TruthLoveMeaningPurpose is about on all levels, and believing that the world needs to hear my message. Cindy, thank you for being an ardent supporter of my life's work, and believing in my Promised Land.

My friends and colleagues in every arena of my life, from when I was little until now (especially Edie, Fay, Karen, and Becky)—thank you for loving me and for being there for me when I needed you, and for allowing me to just be me. Every single person who has ever taken the time to challenge me, encourage me, or support me—you made a difference because you were a powerful messenger to me, helping me to stay grounded in my TruthLoveMeaningPurpose and encouraging me that my words and speaking do make a difference, and to keep going.

My faithful and loyal team member, Christine, thank you so much for giving your heart to be of service to me and my life's work, so I can be a servant to the world.

Thank you to the awesome team who helped me share this message with the world: Michael Ebeling, thank you for recognizing the treasure in my writing, and being an undeniable link in birthing it. Amanda Rooker, thank you so much for being my fearless editor and for bravely going on the "ride" with the TruthLoveMeaningPurpose of this book, so its true essence, soul, and heart could be all that it was born to be! I especially loved your heart-based intuitive edits, and how you fully immersed yourself in the "June" world so you could maintain the integrity of my June-isms, voice, and message. Thank you to proofreaders Patricia Faust and Lori Paximadis, who tweaked the book to Pollyanna-esque perfection. And thank you to everybody at Morgan James who made my book possible: David Hancock, Rick Frishman, David and Cindy Sauer, Jim Howard, Bethany Marshall, Tiffany Gibson, Lyza Poulin, Rachel Lopez, and Bonnie Bushman.

Lastly, thank you, God/Infinite Intelligence/Universe/Source Energy/Divine Mind. Without you and your unfailing inexhaustible supply, divine guidance, and wisdom, I would not be able to do what I am doing and have done. I am eternally grateful to you for listening to my prayers and giving me everything I needed in your divine order and timing. Thank you for choosing me to channel the teachings of TruthLoveMeaningPurpose to share with the world. Thank you for giving me tremendous faith and hope to continue spreading the word about you, that you live inside of each of us, and you are the true key to freedom and happiness in life!

a special gift.

Thank you so much for purchasing my first book and going on this journey with me!

To express my gratitude, I have a special gift for you.

To claim your gift, simply go to www.junesaruwatari.com/gift.

about june.

June Saruwatari is a lifestyle, business, & relationship coach, productivity & organizing consultant, inspirational speaker, and founder of The Organizing Maniac™. For nearly twenty years, her transformational approach of TruthLoveMeaningPurpose™ has helped hundreds of people declutter their minds, hearts, spaces, and stuff to create lives and businesses they love! The co-host of TLC's first season of *Home Made Simple*, June has appeared on *The Nate Berkus Show* and has contributed to publications such as *Woman's Day, 31 Words to Create an Organized Life*, and *Practically Posh*.

Continue your journey with June at www.junesaruwatari.com.

CPSIA information can be obtained at www.ICGtesting.com
Printed in the USA
BVOW02*1435080515

399592BV00012B/209/P